Be A Better READER

EIGHTH EDITION

NILA BANTON SMITH

PEARSON

Pronunciation Key

Symbol	Key Word	Respelling	Symbol	Key Word	Respelling
a	act	(akt)	u	book	(buk)
ah	star	(stahr)		put	(put)
ai	dare	(dair)	uh	cup	(kuhp)
aw	also	(AWL soh)	ə	a *as in*	
ay	flavor	(FLAY vər)		along	(ə LAWNG)
				e *as in*	
e	end	(end)		moment	(MOH mənt)
ee	eat	(eet)		i *as in*	
er	learn	(lern)		modify	(MAHD ə fy)
	sir	(ser)		o *as in*	
	fur	(fer)		protect	(prə TEKT)
				u *as in*	
i	hit	(hit)		circus	(SER kəs)
eye	idea	(eye DEE ə)	ch	chill	(chil)
y	like	(lyk)	g	go	(goh)
ir	deer	(dir)	j	joke	(johk)
	fear	(fir)		bridge	(brij)
			k	kite	(kyt)
oh	open	(OH pen)		cart	(kahrt)
oi	foil	(foil)	ng	bring	(bring)
	boy	(boi)	s	sum	(suhm)
or	horn	(horn)		cent	(sent)
ou	out	(out)	sh	sharp	(shahrp)
	flower	(FLOU ər)	th	thin	(thin)
oo	hoot	(hoot)	*th*	then	(*then*)
	rule	(rool)	z	zebra	(ZEE brə)
yoo	few	(fyoo)		pose	(pohz)
	use	(yooz)	zh	treasure	(TREZH ər)

Acknowledgments: Grateful acknowledgment is made to the following for copyrighted material: **ASPCA:** *"ASPCA Online Store"* from ASPCA Online Store. Copyright © 2007 by ASPCA. Reprinted by permission. **Elizabeth Fuller:** "The Thing at Exeter" by John Fuller from *Incident At Exeter.* Reprinted by permission of Elizabeth Fuller. **John Wiley & Sons, Inc.:** "Pliers, Plight, Plight, Plimsoll Mark, Plink, Plinth, Pliny, Plot, Plover, Plow, Plowboy, Plowman, Plowshare, Ploy, Plum, Plumage, Plumate" from *Webster's New World Dictionary, Basic School Edition.* Copyright © 1989 by John Wiley & Sons, Inc. Reprinted by permission of John Wiley & Sons, Inc. Note: Every effort has been made to locate the copyright owner of material reproduced in this component. Omissions brought to our attention will be corrected in subsequent editions.

Photo Credits: Cover images, clockwise from top left: © Slavoljub Pantelic/Shutterstock, © Art Explosion, © Getty Images, Charmaine Whitman/Pearson, © JuiceDrops, © Steve Estvanik/Shutterstock, © Getty Images, © Getty Images, © Getty Images, © Brand X Pictures; Cover background: © JuiceDrops; Lesson and unit opener: © Stockbyte; p. 7: © Aaron McCoy/Nonstock/Jupiter Images; p. 12: © SGM/Stock Connection/Jupiter Images; p. 13: © Dennis Cox /Alamy; p. 14: © Vladimir Korostyshevskiy/Shutterstock; p. 18: © Brand X Pictures; p. 19: © NASA; p. 40: © Dmytro Korolov/Shutterstock; p. 42: © Carla Signorini/Images of Africa Photobank/Alamy; p. 46: Colin Keates © Dorling Kindersley, Courtesy of the Natural History Museum, London; p. 47 (right): © Sinclair Stammers/Photo Researchers, Inc.; p. 58 (left): © Steve Bloom Images/Workbook Stock/Jupiter Images; p. 58 (right): © Willie Sator/Alamy; p. 63: © Rusty Kennedy/AP Images; p. 77: © iofoto/Shutterstock; p. 86 (top): © Tony Bee/photolibrary/Jupiter Images; p. 86 (bottom): © Oliver Gerhard/imagebroker/Alamy; p. 100: © Adrian Lindley/Shutterstock; p. 104 (bottom): © Mike Hill/Alamy; p. 105 (top): © EcoPrint/Shutterstock; p. 105 (bottom left): © Vishal Shah/Shutterstock; p. 105 (bottom right): © Doxa/Shutterstock; p. 115: © Lili Iravani/UPI Photo Service/Newscom; p. 150: © Reggie Casagrande/Graphistock/Jupiter Images.

Staff Credits: Joshua Adams, Melania Benzinger, Karen Blonigen, Laura Chadwick, Andreea Cimoca, Katie Colón, Nancy Condon, Barbara Drewlo, Kerry Dunn, Marti Erding, Sara Freund, Daren Hastings, Ruby Hogen-Chin, Mariann Johanneck, Julie Johnston, Mary Kaye Kuzma, Mary Lukkonen, Carol Nelson, Carrie O'Connor, Marie Schaefle, Julie Theisen, Chris Tures, Mike Vineski, Charmaine Whitman, Sue Will

ISBN-13: 978-0-7854-6659-8

ISBN-10: 0-7854-6659-2

1-800-992-0244

www.pearsonschool.com

7 8 9 10 V069 16 15

Contents

Contents
continued

How to Use *Be a Better Reader*

For more than thirty years, **Be A Better Reader** has helped students improve their reading skills. **Be A Better Reader** teaches the comprehension and study skills that you need to read and enjoy all types of materials—from library books to the different textbooks that you will encounter in school.

To get the most from **Be A Better Reader**, you should know how the lessons are organized. As you read the following explanations, it will be helpful to look at some of the lessons.

In each of the first four lessons of a unit, you will apply an important skill to a reading selection in literature, social studies, science, or mathematics. Each of these lessons includes the following nine sections.

▶ BACKGROUND INFORMATION
This section gives you interesting information about the selection you are about to read. It will help you understand the ideas that you need in order to learn new skills.

▶ SKILL FOCUS
This section teaches you a specific skill. You should read the Skill Focus carefully, paying special attention to words that are printed in boldface type. The Skill Focus tells you about a skill that you will use when you read the selection.

▶ CONTEXT CLUES OR WORD CLUES
This section teaches you how to recognize and use different types of context and word clues. These clues will help you with the meanings of the underlined words in the selection.

▶ STRATEGY TIP
This section gives you suggestions about what to look for as you read. The suggestions will help you understand the selection.

▶ SELECTIONS
There are four kinds of selections in **Be A Better Reader**. A selection in a literature lesson is similar to a selection in a literature anthology, library book, newspaper, or magazine. A social studies selection is like a chapter in a social studies textbook or an encyclopedia. It often includes maps or tables. A science selection, like a science textbook, includes special words and sometimes diagrams. A mathematics selection will help you acquire skill in reading mathematics textbooks.

▶ COMPREHENSION QUESTIONS
Answers to the questions in this section can be found in the selection itself. You will sometimes have to reread parts of the selection to complete this activity.

▶ CRITICAL THINKING ACTIVITY
The critical thinking activity includes questions whose answers are not directly stated in the selection. For these questions, you must combine the information in the selection with what you already know in order to infer the answers.

▶ SKILL FOCUS ACTIVITY
In this activity, you will use the skill that you learned in the Skill Focus section at the beginning of the lesson to answer questions about the selection. If you have difficulty completing this activity, reread the Skill Focus section.

▶ READING-WRITING CONNECTION
In this writing activity, you will have a chance to use the information in the selection you read about, by writing about it. Here is your chance to share your ideas about the selection.

Additional Lessons
The remaining lessons in each unit give you practice with such skills as using a dictionary, an encyclopedia, and other reference materials; using phonics and syllabication in recognizing new words; locating and organizing information; and adjusting your reading rate. Other reading skills that are necessary in everyday life, such as reading a bus schedule, are also covered.

Each time you learn a new skill in **Be A Better Reader**, look for opportunities to use the skill in your other reading at school and at home. Your reading ability will improve the more you practice reading!

Outer Space

LESSON 1

Skill: Point of View

BACKGROUND INFORMATION

"The Thing at Exeter" is a true story. It is based on a news report about the sighting of a UFO (unidentified flying object) in Exeter, New Hampshire, in 1965. People have observed UFOs, for hundreds of years. After World War II, however, sightings became more common. Some people claim that UFOs are spaceships from other planets. Others think that UFOs have natural causes.

SKILL FOCUS: Point of View

Point of view means the eyes through which a story is written. Some stories are told from the **first-person point of view**. Others are told from the **third-person point of view**. In the first-person point of view, a story character tells the story. This character uses the pronouns *I*, *me*, *my*, and *we* to describe events. A first-person narrator tells his or her own experiences and thoughts about story events. This type of narrator cannot enter the minds of other characters, though, or describe events that he or she has not seen.

In the **third-person point of view**, the narrator is someone outside the story. The narrator uses the pronouns *he*, *she*, and *they* to tell what the characters think and do. A third-person narrator can tell what different characters are thinking and doing.

▶ Read the following section from a story. On the chart in the next column, write the narrator's point of view and how you determined it.

Walking home, Mr. Perez heard a loud roar. Looking up, he saw a circle of light race across the night sky and then suddenly disappear. Perez's first instinct was to keep silent, to pretend it hadn't happened. After all, he thought, what could the police do? What might people think of him if he claimed he had seen a flying saucer?

Point of View	
Narrator's Point of View	How You Determined It

CONTEXT CLUES: Synonyms

Synonyms are words with similar meanings. Sometimes you can use a synonym in the same sentence or a nearby sentence to figure out the meaning of a new word.

Read the sentences below. Look for a synonym for the underlined word.

*Officer Toland listened suspiciously to Muscarello's story. Afterward, the officer admitted that he had reacted **skeptically**.*

If you don't know the meaning of *skeptically*, the synonym *suspiciously* can help you figure it out. *Suspiciously* and *skeptically* have similar meanings.

▶ In the sentence below, circle the synonym that suggests the meaning of the underlined word.

*However, Air Force officials insisted that Operation Big Blast had ended by the time of the sightings. None of the aircraft from the exercise, they **asserted**, were in the area after 1:35 A.M.*

As you read, look for synonyms to help you figure out the meanings of the underlined words *extraordinary*, *crystalline*, and *hovering*.

Strategy Tip

As you read "The Thing at Exeter," think about the point of view the narrator uses to tell the story.

THE THING AT EXETER

Are there visitors from outer space? Nobody has proved anything one way or the other. However, people around Exeter, New Hampshire, haven't stopped talking about the "thing" that appeared the night of September 3, 1965.

That night, 18-year-old Norman Muscarello arrived at the Exeter police station. He was pale and trembling. Officer Reginald Toland, who was on desk duty, got Muscarello to calm down a bit. Then Muscarello told him an incredible story.

Muscarello said he had been hitchhiking home along Route 150, just outside Exeter. Suddenly, in the moonless night sky, a huge, silent, glowing object glided toward him across an open field.

Muscarello leaped from the road into a shallow ditch and watched. He later admitted that he was terror-stricken. The object drifted and circled over a nearby house. Muscarello estimated that the dome-shaped, saucerlike object was about 80 feet wide. He noticed that it had flashing red lights and made no noise. When it seemed to back away, Muscarello jumped up and ran to another house. He banged with his fists on the door, but the people inside would not open it. He then ran to the road and waved down a car. A middle-aged couple drove him to the police station.

Officer Toland listened suspiciously to Muscarello's story. Afterward, the officer admitted that he had reacted skeptically. He didn't think that Muscarello had seen anything <u>extraordinary</u>. Rejecting the claim of an unusual sighting, Officer Toland thought that Muscarello had probably spotted a low-flying plane or helicopter. However, when Muscarello insisted that he had seen something very strange, Toland called in another officer from patrol.

On arriving at the police station, Officer Eugene Bertrand reported an odd coincidence. He had stopped on a bypass of Route 101 to check a parked car. The driver told him that even after she had taken the detour from the main road, a silent object with flashing red lights continued to follow her. It glided above her for about 9 miles and, at times, came within a few feet of her car.

When he heard this report, Toland turned to Muscarello and said, "Does this sound like the 'thing' you saw?" Muscarello said it did.

Officer Toland asked Bertrand to escort Muscarello back to the open field where he had sighted the strange object. At 3:00 A.M., Officer Bertrand and Norman Muscarello got out of the car at the field along Route 150.

The sky was clear. It was <u>crystalline</u>. Visibility was unlimited and there was no wind. The stars were like bright pinpoints against the dark.

The two walked down the sloping field. Bertrand took out his flashlight and shined it on the shrubs and distant trees. About a hundred yards from the roadside was the barn in which Carl Dining kept his horses. Bertrand and Muscarello reached the fence and still saw nothing.

The "thing" at Exeter was first seen as a "huge, silent, glowing object" against the night sky.

Bertrand told Muscarello that he must have seen a helicopter. The youth insisted that, because he was familiar with all types of aircraft, he would have recognized a helicopter.

Muscarello walked away into the field. Bertrand turned his back to the barn and shined his light toward the trees. Suddenly, the horses in the barn began to kick and whinny. The dogs penned up nearby began to whimper and howl.

Muscarello shouted, "I see it! I see it!" Bertrand wheeled around and looked at the trees beyond the barn. He reported that a bright, round object rose slowly into the air from behind two tall pine trees. Making no sound, it moved toward them in a seesawing motion, like a leaf fluttering in the air. The entire area was bathed in brilliant red light. The white sides of Carl Dining's house looked blood red.

Officer Bertrand reached for his .38, hesitated, and then shoved the gun back into its holster. Looking again at the red light, he shouted at Muscarello, "It might be radioactive! Run for cover!" He grabbed Muscarello and yanked him toward the cruiser. Bertrand called Toland, back at the station, on his car radio. "I see the thing myself!" he screamed.

Just then, another officer, David Hunt, sped up to the farm in his police car. He had heard Bertrand and Toland talking on the radio and rushed to see what was going on.

As he jumped out of his patrol car, he could see the "thing." It was hovering about a hundred feet in the air. Suspended noiselessly, it slowly started to move east. The three men stared in surprise at the UFO. If it was a plane or a helicopter, it was like no other they had ever seen. It didn't move like an airplane or a helicopter. It could speed away, stop in a second, and then hover. It could change its direction instantly. Lights along its bottom rim flashed in a left-to-right and then right-to-left pattern. The two officers and Muscarello said that it didn't seem like anything of this world.

After the "thing" disappeared over the horizon, the three men headed back to town and filled out a police report. Although Officer Hunt filled out a long report about the sighting, he no longer discusses the case.

Officer Bertrand later said that his fellow officers didn't make fun of him for reporting having seen a UFO. "We saw something out in that field," he said. "I think there is probably some explanation. I don't say it was from outer space. But I know there was some sort of flying craft. I was in the Air Force, and I know aircraft make noise. This one didn't. It was silent; no hum…. Just moving through the air silently. And the light, so bright it lighted up the whole field. There was something there. We weren't all seeing something that wasn't there!"

During the 1960s, the U.S. Air Force was in charge of looking into UFO sightings. What was the Air Force's opinion of the "thing" at Exeter? The Air Force said that the Eighth Air Force was carrying out an operation known as Big Blast in New England that night. Air Force officials stressed that the "general description of flashing lights is somewhat like reports of aircraft during refueling or when taking low-level pictures."

However, Air Force officials insisted that Operation Big Blast had ended by the time of the sightings. None of the aircraft from the exercise, they asserted, were in the area after 1:35 A.M. The Air Force report simply stated that "since no aircraft can be placed in the area at 2:00 A.M., the case is listed as unidentified."

COMPREHENSION

1. Which four people saw the mysterious "thing"?

_____

_____

_____

2. When and where did the story take place?

_____

_____

_____

3. Describe the "thing."

_____

_____

_____

_____

4. Explain why Norman Muscarello rushed to the police station.

_____

_____

_____

5. Describe how Officers Bertrand and Hunt reacted when they saw the "thing."

_____

_____

_____

6. Describe how the Air Force listed this case in its final report.

_____

_____

_____

7. Draw a line to match each word with its correct meaning.

extraordinary   **a.** clear

crystalline   **b.** suspended

hovering   **c.** unusual

CRITICAL THINKING

1. Why do you think Officer Bertrand stopped to check on the car parked on the bypass?

_____

_____

2. Explain why Carl Dining's farm animals became upset and agitated as the UFO came near.

_____

_____

3. Contrast the UFO with an airplane or helicopter.

_____

_____

4. Give a reason why Officer Hunt might have decided not to talk about the sighting.

_____

_____

5. Explain why the Air Force listed the sighting as unidentified.

_____

_____

6. Draw your own conclusion about what the "thing" was. Support your conclusion with details from the story.

_____

_____

1. **a.** Is the narrator of "The Thing at Exeter" a participant in the event or an outsider?

   _____

   _____

   b. Reread the opening paragraphs of the story. Does the narrator use first-person pronouns or third-person pronouns to describe the events?

   _____

   _____

   c. Whose thoughts and feelings does the reader learn about in the story?

   _____

   _____

   d. From what point of view is the story told?

   _____

   _____

2. Explain how the story might have been different if it had been told by a participant in the events, such as Norman Muscarello or Officer Toland.

   _____

   _____

   _____

   _____

3. Tell whether you would rather read a first-person account of a UFO sighting or a third-person account. Give reasons for your answer.

   _____

   _____

   _____

Reading-Writing Connection

Suppose a UFO was sighted in your community. Write the first paragraph of a newspaper article that a reporter might write about the sighting. Use third-person point of view.

Skill: Distinguishing Fact From Opinion

BACKGROUND INFORMATION

"Ancient Visitors?" describes three ancient mysteries—the huge patterns scratched in the desert soil of Peru, the gigantic statues of Easter Island, and the amazing pyramids of ancient Egypt. Archaeologists have long wondered how the people of ancient times could have created these and other huge monuments. To find out, some scientists have attempted to recreate the ancient wonders. Using primitive tools and methods, these scientists have drawn some fascinating conclusions about the mysterious builders of ancient times.

SKILL FOCUS: Distinguishing Fact From Opinion

Many social studies articles include statements of fact and statements of opinion. A **fact** is a statement that can be checked or proven. The following statement is a fact.

Some of the statues weigh as much as 30 tons and stand 12 feet high.

You could check this fact in books. You could even go to Easter Island and measure the statues yourself.

An **opinion** is a belief, feeling, or judgment that cannot be proven or checked. The following statement is an opinion.

These people believe that more advanced beings from outer space told the Egyptians how to build the pyramid.

So far, there is no way to prove this statement. The existence of life on distant planets cannot be proved or disproved. There is no way of proving that beings from other planets once visited Earth. Different people have different beliefs or opinions about this subject.

When you read, try to distinguish facts from opinions. Then think about the conclusions the author draws. Ask yourself if the conclusions are based on facts or on opinions. A conclusion that is based on facts is stronger than one that is based on opinions.

▶ Fill in the chart below with these statements.

Few places on Earth are more mysterious than Easter Island.

There are no trees on Easter Island today.

Fact	Opinion

CONTEXT CLUES: Appositive Phrases

An **appositive phrase** is a group of words that explains the meaning of a word that comes just before or just after it. Usually, an appositive phrase is set off with commas or dashes. It often starts with the word *or*.

In the sentence below, look for the appositive phrase that explains the meaning of the underlined word.

In addition, people who are not scientists have come up with some startling __theories__, or possible explanations, of their own.

If you don't know the meaning of the word *theories*, the appositive phrase, *or possible explanations*, can help you figure it out.

▶ In the sentence below, circle the appositive phrase that explains the meaning of *crater*.

These statues were carved from the volcanic rock of a __crater__—a bowl-shaped hole at the opening of a volcano—on the island.

In the selection, use appositive phrases to help you figure out the meanings of the underlined words *extraterrestrials*, *unravel*, and *mortar*.

Strategy Tip

As you read "Ancient Visitors?" look for statements of fact and statements of opinion. Remember that conclusions based on facts are more valid than conclusions based on opinions.

ANCIENT VISITORS?

The earliest civilizations on Earth stretch far back in time toward the unknown past. Yet we do have knowledge about the way these groups of people lived. People have always left their marks on the Earth. Their marks, or remains, include buildings, tools, weapons, and drawings on cave walls. All of these remains help us to create a picture of the past.

Some ancient peoples, however, left remains that are mysterious to us. Several of these remains have become famous. In the Nazca (NAHZ kah) Desert in Peru, there are huge patterns scratched into the Earth that can be seen only from the sky. Easter Island in the Pacific Ocean has giant statues of strange-looking people. In Egypt, pyramids loom over an empty desert.

Although there are many different opinions about these ancient remains, so far no one explanation is complete. Scientists, using observable facts and evidence, have attempted to explain the ancient remains in many ways. In addition, people who are not scientists have come up with some startling theories, or possible explanations, of their own. Some theories suggest that these mysterious remains prove that <u>extraterrestrials</u>—beings from other planets—came to Earth long ago.

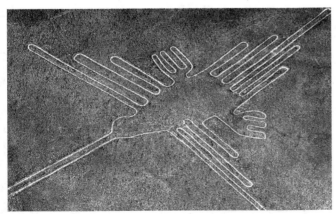

These patterns scratched into the Earth in the Nazca Desert can be seen only from the air.

The Nazca Desert Patterns

The Nazca Desert is on a high plateau. On this plateau, huge figures and patterns are scratched into the ground. These patterns are clear only when seen from the sky.

In 1939, when planes began to fly over the desert plain of southern Peru, pilots recognized huge figures in these patterns on the ground. These figures included giant birds, fish, lizards, and other animals. One eight-legged spider measures over 150 feet (45 meters) in length.

Other patterns are geometric shapes. There are angles, triangles, and lines. Some straight lines in the patterns run for 5 miles (8 kilometers). They were laid out straighter than if they had been measured with modern air-survey techniques.

The patterns were made by scratching away a thin top layer of dark stones. The light-colored soil underneath the stones formed the patterns. Although the Nazca patterns are more than 1,000 years old, they have not been affected by time, because the climate of the area creates little soil erosion. Scientists know how the patterns were made, but there is little information about who made them and why.

Many scientists believe that the patterns were made by the Nazca Indians. The Nazcas lived in this area of Peru long ago, but little else is known about them. Some people think the Nazcas were able to make the patterns by doing them first on a small scale and then on a large scale on the desert surface. The perfectly straight lines were probably the most difficult to create. Logs may have been erected as sighting posts to help the Nazcas lay the lines straight.

Why were the patterns made? Some scientists think that the Nazcas studied a kind of **astronomy** (ə STRAHN ə mee). The patterns may have shown the positions of the stars and the Sun. Other people believe the patterns were part of the Nazca's religion. Perhaps they were messages to the sky gods who could see them from above.

Another explanation for the strange patterns connects them with extraterrestrial visitors. A man named Erich von Daniken suggested that the patterns served as landing strips for ancient astronauts. Because the patterns can be seen only from the air, he claimed that they must have been made by beings who were capable of flight. Von Daniken believed that visitors from outer space used their more advanced **technology** (tek NAHL ə jee) to create the Nazca patterns. Technology refers to practical methods for doing work based on an understanding of scientific principles.

The Easter Island Giants

Easter Island, or Rapa Nui, a remote island in the South Pacific Ocean, is famous for the giant statues that have stood on its soil for centuries. These statues were carved from the volcanic rock of a crater—a bowl-shaped hole at the opening of a volcano—on the island. First more than 300 statues were discovered in various places on the island. Later about 400 more were found inside the crater. Many of the statues in this second group were unfinished.

✘ The Easter Island statues are large, heavy, and strange-looking. Some of the statues weigh as much as 30 tons and stand 12 feet (4 meters) high. One giant statue found inside the crater weighed 50 tons. The appearance of the statues is unusual. They look like human beings, but they have long earlobes and squared-off heads.

Many mysteries surrounded the statues after their discovery. Who carved them? How were they moved out of the crater? How were they raised into an upright position? What was their purpose? Who were the ancient people of Easter Island?

Many researchers have visited Easter Island to try to <u>unravel</u>, or figure out, the secrets of its mysterious past. Thor Heyerdahl (HY ər dahl), a famous writer and explorer, visited the island in 1956. With the help of the native people, he tried to recreate how the statues may have been carved and moved. Using stone tools, the workers carved out the general shape of one statue in three days. Then with ropes tied around the statue, 150 people dragged it a short distance.

Since Heyerdahl's experiments, many other researchers have investigated how the huge statues could have been moved. Searching for evidence, they found stone posts that had been used to secure

Much about the gigantic statues on Easter Island remains a mystery.

ropes. They also found wear marks on the statues from ropes that had been wrapped around them. Researchers also found that the bases of some statues were chipped, indicating that the stone had rubbed against something. In addition, some statues that were found along the transport route lie broken into separate pieces—something that would happen only if they had fallen from an upright position. Based on this evidence and their own experiments, researchers concluded that the statues were moved while standing upright on wooden platforms and that the platforms were dragged over rollers cut from tree trunks.

There are no trees on Easter Island today. However, scientists have found evidence that at least some parts of the island were once covered with thick forests of palm trees. The evidence for these forests includes ancient palm nuts, fossilized roots of palm trees, and thick layers of palm pollen in the mud at the bottom of a lake.

Heyerdahl believed that the original settlers of Easter Island had sailed there from South America to the east. However, recent studies of skeletal remains found on the island show that the islanders' ancestors came from the Polynesian Islands to the west. Many of the words in the Rapa Nui language spoken by some people on Easter Island today are the same as words in languages spoken in the Polynesian Islands.

Erich von Daniken and others believed that the Easter Island statues are further proof of ancient visitors from outer space. Von Daniken argued that the statues are too large and heavy to have been moved by ordinary people. He believed that the statues were erected by ancient astronauts visiting Earth from distant planets. He also believed that these extraterrestrials carved the statues in their own likeness.

The Great Pyramid of Egypt

The Great Pyramid of Egypt has long been one of the wonders of the world. Built more than 5,000 years ago, it is the largest and most impressive of the many pyramids that dot the Egyptian desert.

✔ The Great Pyramid covers 13 acres of land. It stands almost 500 feet (150 meters) high, as tall as a 42-story building. The pyramid is made of more than 2 million stones, each weighing about 2.5 tons.

The pyramid is not only very large but also precisely made. Its corners are almost perfect right angles. The four sides face exactly north, south, east, and west. The stones are so perfectly shaped that they fit together without <u>mortar</u>, a mixture of cement, water, and sand often used to hold stones together. Not even a knife blade can be put between them.

How were the ancient Egyptians able to move and raise such huge stones? How did they acquire their knowledge of geometry and architecture? Most experts believe that the Egyptians knew enough about geometry and astronomy to build and position the Great Pyramid. History books claim that thousands of laborers worked more than 600 years to construct the pyramid. Historians believe that these laborers of ancient Egypt pulled the stones over the desert with ropes or on wooden rollers. They may have used ramps to pull the stones to the top of the pyramid.

Some people, however, doubt that the Egyptians could have built the Great Pyramid on their own. These people believe that more advanced beings from outer space told the Egyptians how to build the pyramid. They think that these visitors to Earth gave the Egyptians a special power source or special machines to raise the heavy stones. In the opinion of these people, the Great Pyramid is more evidence that extraterrestrial visitors once came to Earth.

There is no proof that extraterrestrials have ever visited Earth. Many people would like to believe that the theory is true. Yet, until it is proven, it is simply one fascinating theory about the mysteries of Earth's past.

This photograph gives you an idea of the relative size of the Egyptian pyramids.

COMPREHENSION

1. Match the details listed below with the ancient remains that they describe. Write the correct letter on the line.

   a. Nazca Desert patterns

   b. Easter Island statues

   c. Great Pyramid of Egypt

   _____ as tall as a 42-story building

   _____ portray figures of animals

   _____ some found in a crater

2. Write the cause for the effect below.

   Cause: _____

   _____

   Effect: The patterns scratched into the Nazca Desert have not been affected by time.

3. Reread the paragraph with an ✗ next to it. Then underline the sentence that best states its main idea.

4. Fill in the circle next to the word that correctly completes each sentence.

   a. Some people believe that there are

   _____ living on other planets.

   ○ Nazcas   ○ craters

   ○ extraterrestrials

   b. The detective tried to _____ the mystery of the disappearing cats.

   ○ recognize   ○ unravel   ○ scratch

   c. Many builders work with stone, brick,

   and _____.

   ○ mortar   ○ lava   ○ extraterrestrials

CRITICAL THINKING

1. Write the effect for the cause below.

   Cause: The Nazca patterns are clear only when seen from the air.

   Effect: _____

   _____

2. Look at the photograph on page 12 of the patterns scratched on the surface of the Nazca Desert. What does the figure resemble?

   _____

   _____

3. What could help solve the mystery of why the Easter Island statues were erected?

   _____

   _____

   _____

   _____

4. List the different theories given to explain the purpose of the Nazca figures and shapes.

   _____

   _____

   _____

   _____

5. Reread the paragraph in the selection with a ✔ next to it. Write a sentence that states its main idea.

   _____

   _____

   _____

   _____

1. List two facts about the Nazca Desert patterns.

   a. _____

   b. _____

2. List two opinions about why the patterns were made.

   a. _____

   b. _____

3. List two facts about the Easter Island statues.

   a. _____

   b. _____

4. List two opinions about the statues.

   a. _____

   b. _____

5. List two facts about the Great Pyramid of Egypt.

   a. _____

   b. _____

6. List two opinions about how the Great Pyramid was constructed.

   a. _____

   b. _____

7. Choose one of the mysterious objects described in the selection. Draw a conclusion that explains how you think it came to be. Explain what facts you based your conclusion on.

   _____

   _____

8. What conclusions can you draw about the extraterrestrial visitor theory that some people use to explain these mysteries?

   _____

   _____

Reading-Writing Connection

On a separate sheet of paper, write a paragraph explaining which of the three ancient remains you think is the most mysterious. Give facts to support your opinion.

BACKGROUND INFORMATION

"The Origin of the Moon" explains different ideas scientists have proposed about how the Moon was formed. Ever since people first looked up at the night sky, they have wondered about the Moon. In 1969, American astronauts finally walked on the Moon. In later Moon flights, astronauts explored the Moon's craters. They gathered Moon rocks and performed experiments, too. The information they collected has helped scientists reach new conclusions about the Moon's origin.

SKILL FOCUS: Making Inferences

Sometimes you have to **make inferences**, or figure out information that is not stated in a text. To make an inference, combine the details in a selection with what you already know.

Read the following sentences. As you read, make an inference about the Fission hypothesis. You can use a graphic organizer like the one below to record the inference.

According to the Fission hypothesis, the Moon was once a chunk of the Earth. If this hypothesis were true, the two bodies would be made of very similar materials.

Inference About the Fission Hypothesis:

Details in Text		What I Already Know		Inference
If the Fission hypothesis were true, the Earth and Moon would be made of similar materials.	+	The Moon is covered with dust; it has no water; Moon rocks are not like rocks on Earth.	=	The Fission hypothesis is not true because the Earth and Moon are made of very different materials.

▶ Read the sentences below. Then make an inference about the Earth's temperature when it was formed. Use details in the text and what you already know.

Picture in your mind the newly formed Earth, still a ball of molten, or liquid, stone. As it spun rapidly in orbit, this soupy mass of matter began to bulge out at its center.

_____

_____

CONTEXT CLUES: Definitions

Some reading selections include the **definitions** of new words. A definition is usually given in the next sentence.

Read the following sentences. Look for the definition of the underlined word.

Tremendous heat from the crash turns much of Earth's <u>mantle</u> *to vapor. The mantle is the layer of Earth that lies between its crust and its core.*

If you don't know the meaning of *mantle*, the second sentence gives you the word's definition.

▶ Read the following sentences. Circle the definition that tells you the meaning of the underlined word.

By the 1880s, scientists had devised their first <u>hypothesis</u> *about the Moon's origin. A hypothesis is a possible explanation that can be tested.*

In the selection, use definitions to learn the meanings of the underlined words *coalesced*, *bombardment*, and *simulations*.

Strategy Tip

As you read "The Origin of the Moon," combine the facts and the hypotheses presented in the text with your previous knowledge to infer information that is not stated directly.

The Origin of the Moon

For hundreds of years, scientists have asked questions about the Moon. How old is it? How did it form? In what ways is it similar to and different from Earth? By the 1880s, scientists had devised their first **hypothesis** (hy PAHTH ə səs) about the Moon's origin. A hypothesis is a possible explanation that can be tested. If scientists are able to collect enough evidence to support a hypothesis and become convinced that it is a likely explanation, the hypothesis is then called a **theory**.

The Fission Hypothesis

Picture in your mind the newly formed Earth, still a ball of molten, or liquid, stone. As it spun rapidly in orbit, this soupy mass of matter began to bulge out at its center. At the same time, the top of the Earth got narrower, until the whole planet looked something like a bowling pin. Eventually the tip of this "bowling pin" snapped off. Flying into space, it went into orbit around the Earth.

That startling image of the Moon's birth is called the **Fission** (FISH ən) **hypothesis**. *Fission* means "splitting." To understand this hypothesis better, visualize a merry-go-round spinning faster and faster, out of control. At a certain speed, a rider on the merry-go-round would be flung off.

According to the Fission hypothesis, the Moon was once a chunk of the Earth. If this hypothesis were true, the two bodies would be made of very similar materials. In the early 1900s, scientists did not know what we know today about the differences between the Earth and the Moon. Nevertheless, they soon rejected the Fission hypothesis. For the Moon to have broken off the Earth, our planet would have to have been spinning four times faster than it is today. The Fission hypothesis had no explanation for why the Earth would have spun so fast. A sound hypothesis must be a likely one. It has to fit with known laws of mathematics and physics. The Fission hypothesis did not.

For centuries, people have wondered about the origin of the Moon.

The Sister Hypothesis

Scientists next thought that the Moon and the Earth formed separately, but in a similar way. According to this hypothesis, a huge field of loose rocks and dust orbited the Sun billions of years ago. Gradually this matter <u>coalesced</u> to form planets. *Coalesced* means "came together." Earth, the other planets, and the Moon were all thought to have formed this way. Eventually, this hypothesis said, the Moon began to revolve around the Earth.

This hypothesis suggested that the Moon and Earth are similar, like two sisters. As scientists learned more about the Moon, though, the "family resemblance" became less obvious. The Earth is a watery planet with seas covering much of its surface. The Moon has no water. The Earth also has a huge iron core. The Moon, by contrast, has little iron and not much of a core at all. Scientists decided that the Earth and the Moon could not be so different if they were formed from the same matter in the same way.

The Capture Hypothesis

Could the Moon have formed somewhere else in space and then cruised into our solar system? Could Earth's gravity then have "captured" the passing

Moon, sending it into its present orbit? At first, this Capture hypothesis seemed reasonable.

However, scientists soon decided that this hypothesis was not very likely. To have gone into orbit around the Earth, the Moon would have to have been in precisely the right spot and traveling at precisely the right speed. Otherwise it would have crashed into the Earth or shot past it and back into space. The chances of the Earth capturing the Moon are about a trillion to one or less. A good theory cannot be based on such an unlikely event.

A New Hypothesis

By the early 1970s, scientists had rejected the Fission hypothesis, the Sister hypothesis, and the Capture hypothesis. However, they finally found some hard evidence to help them. *Apollo* astronauts had taken photographs and left measuring devices on the Moon. They had also brought back 840 pounds of moon rocks. This evidence helped scientists devise a new theory of the Moon's origin.

Geologists, or scientists who study the origin, history, and structure of the Earth, noted that all the moon rocks had one specific chemical element—an isotope of oxygen. **Isotopes** (EYE sə tohps) are different forms of the same element with different properties. Rocks on the Earth contained the same isotope of oxygen that was found in the Moon rocks. This evidence suggested that the Earth and the Moon did have a common origin, even if they were not "sisters." The Moon had almost certainly not cruised in from distant space, as the Capture hypothesis claimed.

The Moon rocks also had molecules of iron in them. The presence of iron molecules was hard to explain. Iron is common on Earth, especially in the Earth's core, its innermost layer. The Moon, however, has almost no iron on its surface. Scientists also had evidence that the inner layers of the Moon were very similar to its surface. Scientists knew there was not enough iron on the Moon to explain the presence of iron molecules in the Moon rocks.

Rocks from some parts of the Moon also had a lot of a very light mineral called feldspar. Scientists wondered what had happened while the Moon was forming to concentrate this light mineral in the outer layers of the moon rocks. The answer came as they studied the craters of the Moon.

Evidence from astronauts' Moon missions suggested that the craters had been caused by meteors crashing into the Moon. The gray areas of the Moon are highlands of rock and dust. Scientists speculated that these rocks had been tossed up as countless asteroids and meteorites blasted craters in the Moon's crust.

Scientists have named this period of high asteroid activity "the Heavy Bombardment." Bombardment means "a heavy bombing or attack." Scientists say that this event ended about 4 billion years ago and that it occurred throughout the solar system. The Earth apparently grew to its present size by absorbing meteorites that struck it.

The Giant Impact Hypothesis

As scientists carefully studied the Moon rocks and evidence of the Heavy Bombardment, a new hypothesis about the Moon's origin emerged. This is what scientists now think really happened.

About 4.5 billion years ago, a newly formed Earth stood in the direct path of a gigantic meteor from space. This was no ordinary meteor. It was as big as Mars, or even bigger. Roaring in, the planet-sized monster knocked Earth off course with a terrible blow. Tremendous heat from the crash turned much of Earth's **mantle** to vapor. The mantle is the layer of Earth that lies between its crust and its core. Earth absorbed most of this invading planet. The rest—mixed with Earth's

Moon rocks brought by *Apollo* astronauts provided evidence for a new hypothesis of the Moon's origin.

flaming mantle—was flung high into space. There it coalesced into the Moon.

Although it sounds like science fiction, this Giant Impact hypothesis explains many facts. By absorbing this giant meteor, scientists say, Earth got its heavy iron core. The Moon has no such core, but traces of iron that were flung up during the blast can still be found in rocks on the Moon's surface. Rocks on the Moon and on Earth contain the same isotope of oxygen for a simple reason: Moon rocks originally came from Earth!

The Giant Impact hypothesis also explains the lack of water on the Moon's surface. According to this hypothesis, the Moon's water boiled away during its fiery birth. Furthermore, scientists say, the hypothesis explains the presence of feldspar on the surface of Moon rocks. For some time after it formed, the Moon was an ocean of magma, or liquid rock. In this bubbling stone soup, lighter elements, such as feldspar, floated to the surface and hardened there as the temperature cooled.

The timing is also right. Tests on the Moon rocks suggest that the Moon was formed only 60 million years after the solar system itself began. According to scientists' calculations, that was about the same time that "the Heavy Bombardment" occurred.

Using what they know, scientists have made computer <u>simulations</u> of the Giant Impact. A simulation is an experiment that attempts to recreate certain conditions. The results of these simulations support the Giant Impact hypothesis. They suggest that the Moon would have coalesced about a year after the crash. The simulations also show that at first the Moon would have been only 14,000 miles (22,530 kilometers) away from Earth. Now it is 239,000 miles (384,615 kilometers) away. Powerful gravitational forces then pushed the Moon outward, rapidly at first. Today the Moon is still receding, or moving farther away, but at a snail's pace—about 1.5 inches (3.8 centimeters) a year.

The giant collision may also have helped to create the Earth as we know it today. For one thing, the Earth-shaking crash may have given our world its 23-degree tilt. The newly formed Moon may then have stabilized the Earth in its current position. Without the Moon, the Earth would probably wobble, tugged by the gravity of different planets. Without the tilt of its axis, the Earth would have no changing seasons. One hemisphere would be plunged into a constant unbearable winter while the other would face a constant intolerable heat.

Because it seems to explain so many facts, the Giant Impact hypothesis has now become a popular theory of how the Moon was formed. As new information becomes available, the theory may change or even be abandoned. For now, however, it is the best explanation we have for how the Moon came to be.

COMPREHENSION

1. What is the difference between a hypothesis and a theory?

   _____

   _____

   _____

2. Why did scientists reject the Fission hypothesis of how the Moon was formed?

   _____

   _____

   _____

3. Why did scientists reject the Sister hypothesis?

   _____

   _____

4. Complete each sentence with the correct word.

   coalesced   bombardment   simulations

   a. The _____ of the Moon by meteors was intense, forming many craters.

   b. Materials from a giant meteor crashing into the Earth may have _____ to form the Moon.

   c. Today scientists use computer _____ to test new hypotheses.

CRITICAL THINKING

1. Compare the Giant Impact hypothesis and the Fission hypothesis.

   _____

   _____

2. Contrast the Sister hypothesis with the Capture hypothesis.

   _____

   _____

3. Write a statement that explains what factors scientists consider when deciding whether to accept or reject a hypothesis.

   _____

   _____

SKILL FOCUS: MAKING INFERENCES

Read each passage below. Then make an inference based on the passage.

1. *By the early 1970s, scientists had rejected the Fission hypothesis, the Sister hypothesis, and the Capture hypothesis. However, they finally found some hard evidence to help them.*

   What inference can you make about why scientists changed their hypotheses?

   _____

2. *Scientists have named this period of high asteroid activity "the Heavy Bombardment." Scientists say that this event ended about 4 billion years ago and that it occurred throughout the solar system. The Earth apparently grew to its present size by absorbing the meteorites that struck it.*

   What inference can you make about the size of the planets when they were first formed, compared to their size today?

   _____

3. *Without the Moon, the Earth would probably wobble, tugged by the gravity of different planets. Without the tilt of its axis, the Earth would have no changing seasons. One hemisphere of Earth would be plunged into unbearable winter while the other would face intolerable heat.*

   What inference can you make about life on Earth if there were no Moon?

   _____

Reading-Writing Connection

On a separate sheet of paper, write a hypothesis for an occurrence in nature, such as a rainbow or lightning. Compare your hypothesis with facts about the occurrence.

Skill: Understanding Exponential Notation

BACKGROUND INFORMATION

"Writing Very Large Numbers" is about exponential notation, a system used by scientists and mathematicians to write very large numbers. The number system that we use today is based on place values measured in groups of 10, 100, 1,000, and so on. When scientists have to write very large numbers, they need a shorthand way to express numbers with many place values. Chemists, for example, know that 22.4 liters of any gas contains six hundred two billion trillion particles. Writing the number six hundred two billion trillion in numerals takes a lot of space and a lot of zeroes. Here is how the number would look:

602,000,000,000,000,000,000,000.

To save time and space when working with numbers this large, scientists developed a shorthand system called exponential notation. In this selection, you will read about the base 10 number system and exponential notation.

SKILL FOCUS: Understanding Exponential Notation

Exponential notation is a special method for writing very large numbers in an abbreviated form. Exponential notation is useful in many fields, such as mathematics, astronomy, and chemistry, where extremely large numbers are frequently used.

An **exponent** is a small numeral written above and to the right of a number. The number below the exponent is called the **base number**. The exponent shows the number of times that the base number should be multiplied by itself.

In the following mathematical expression, 10 is the base number and 2 is the exponent.

$$10^2$$

Exponential notation uses the base number 10 with different exponents to express very large numbers. The exponent tells how many times the base number 10 should be multiplied by itself. Following are some examples:

$$10^2 = 10 \times 10 = 100$$
$$10^3 = 10 \times 10 \times 10 = 1,000$$

▶ Write each number below as a base number with an exponent.

$$10,000 = \underline{\hspace{1cm}}$$
$$100,000 = \underline{\hspace{1cm}}$$

WORD CLUES

When reading the selection, look for these three important math words: *exponential notation, exponent,* and *base number.* They will help you understand more about exponential notation.

▶ Use what you have just learned in the Skill Focus to complete the following sentences.

1. The _____ is the small number written above and to the right of a number.

2. The _____ is the number below an exponent.

3. The special method for writing very large numbers in an abbreviated form is

   _____.

Strategy Tip

"Writing Very Large Numbers" explains how to read and write numbers with exponents. Read the explanations carefully. Reread any sections that you have difficulty understanding.

Writing Very Large Numbers

The number 10^2 is an example of **exponential notation** (EK spoh NEN chal noh TAY shan). In the number 10^2, the numeral 2 is the **exponent** (ek SPOH nant). It is written above and to the right of the **base number**, which is 10. The exponent tells how many times the base number is used as a **factor**. Factors are numbers that form a product when multiplied together. Thus, the mathematical expression 10^2 means that 10 is used as a factor twice, or 10×10. The expression 10^2 is read *ten to the second power*, or *ten squared*.

$$10^2 = 10 \times 10 = 100$$

Look at the following powers of 10. The dots between the tens stand for multiplication, just as the symbol $\times$ does.

$10^3 = 10 \cdot 10 \cdot 10$	$= 1,000$
$10^4 = 10 \cdot 10 \cdot 10 \cdot 10$	$= 10,000$
$10^5 = 10 \cdot 10 \cdot 10 \cdot 10 \cdot 10$	$= 100,000$
$10^6 = 10 \cdot 10 \cdot 10 \cdot 10 \cdot 10 \cdot 10$	$= 1,000,000$

The mathematical expressions 10^3, 10^4, 10^5, and 10^6 are read *ten to the third power*, or *ten cubed, ten to the fourth power, ten to the fifth power*, and *ten to the sixth power*, respectively.

For each of these examples, look at the exponent and then count the number of zeros in the product. What do you notice? In each case, the exponent and the number of zeros in the product are the same. The exponent shows how many zeros

are in the product. Ten to the seventh power, or 10^7, has a product with 7 zeros, which is 10,000,000, or 10 million. Ten to the twelfth power, or 10^{12}, has a product with 12 zeros, which is 1,000,000,000,000, or 1 trillion.

The number 10 is represented as 10^1.

The number 1 is represented as 10^0.

Any number can be written using exponential notation. However, exponential notation is most useful with extremely large or extremely small numbers. It is easier and quicker to write a very large number using exponential notation than it is to write the number with all its zeros. For this reason, scientists find exponential notation useful in their work. For example, instead of writing 60 billion as 60,000,000,000, they write $6 \cdot 10^{10}$. This expression is read as *six times ten to the tenth power*, which is $6 \cdot (10 \cdot 10 \cdot 10 \cdot 10 \cdot 10 \cdot 10 \cdot 10 \cdot 10 \cdot 10 \cdot 10)$. The parentheses indicate that the mathematical process inside them must be completed before the result can be used in another mathematical process. Therefore, the tens must be multiplied before their product can be multiplied by the number 6.

Eight hundred thousand, 800,000, is written $8 \cdot 10^5$, or *eight times ten to the fifth power*.

Three hundred trillion, 300,000,000,000,000, is written $3 \cdot 10^{14}$, or *three times ten to the fourteenth power*.

Look at the diagram below. You can see that the average distance of Mars from the Sun is

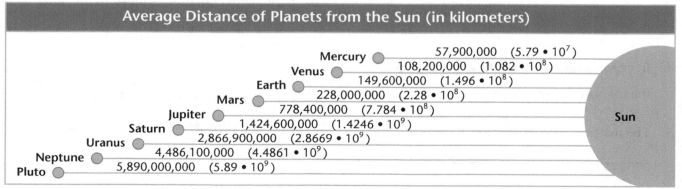

Average Distance of Planets from the Sun (in kilometers)

Mercury — 57,900,000 $(5.79 \cdot 10^7)$
Venus — 108,200,000 $(1.082 \cdot 10^8)$
Earth — 149,600,000 $(1.496 \cdot 10^8)$
Mars — 228,000,000 $(2.28 \cdot 10^8)$
Jupiter — 778,400,000 $(7.784 \cdot 10^8)$
Saturn — 1,424,600,000 $(1.4246 \cdot 10^9)$
Uranus — 2,866,900,000 $(2.8669 \cdot 10^9)$
Neptune — 4,486,100,000 $(4.4861 \cdot 10^9)$
Pluto — 5,890,000,000 $(5.89 \cdot 10^9)$

Sun

Exponential notation allows scientists to express very large numbers as small numbers multiplied by powers of ten.

MATHEMATICS

228,000,000 kilometers. The number of kilometers can be written as $228 \cdot 1{,}000{,}000$, or $228 \cdot 10^6$. Scientists prefer to express the number before the multiplication sign as a value between 1 and 10. Instead of writing $228 \cdot 10^6$, they express the number as $2.28 \cdot 10^8$. The whole number 228 is changed to the decimal 2.28 by moving the decimal point two places to the left. To make up for the two decimal places, the exponent is increased by 2, from 6 to 8. Both $228 \cdot 10^6$ and $2.28 \cdot 10^8$ equal 228,000,000.

It is not necessarily easier and quicker to write moderately large numbers using exponential notation. For numbers other than 10, each digit of the number is written in terms of its place value. In the number 245, for example, the 2 is in the hundreds place and can be written as $2 \cdot 100$. The 4 is in the tens place and can be written as $4 \cdot 10$. The 5, in the ones place, is simply written as 5.

$$245 = (2 \cdot 100) + (4 \cdot 10) + 5$$

This can be further simplified using exponents.

$$245 = 2 \cdot (10^2) + (4 \cdot 10) + 5$$

Following are two more examples of writing numbers using exponential notation.

$$
\begin{aligned}
92{,}476 &= (9 \cdot 10{,}000) + (2 \cdot 1{,}000) + (4 \cdot 100) + (7 \cdot 10) + 6 \\
&= 9 \cdot (10^4) + 2 \cdot (10^3) + 4 \cdot (10^2) + (7 \cdot 10) + 6
\end{aligned}
$$

$$
\begin{aligned}
236{,}512 &= (2 \cdot 100{,}000) + (3 \cdot 10{,}000) + (6 \cdot 1{,}000) + (5 \cdot 100) + (1 \cdot 10) + 2 \\
&= 2 \cdot (10^5) + 3 \cdot (10^4) + 6 \cdot (10^3) + 5 \cdot (10^2) + (1 \cdot 10) + 2
\end{aligned}
$$

COMPREHENSION

Fill in the correct word or words to complete each sentence.

1. In the mathematical expression 10^8, 8 is the _____.

2. In the mathematical expression 10^4, 10 is the _____.

3. In exponential notation, the _____ tells how many times the _____ is used as a _____.

4. In exponential notation, the exponent equals the number of zeros in the _____.

5. The mathematical expression 10^2 is read _____, or ten _____.

6. The mathematical expression 10^3 is read _____, or ten _____.

7. The mathematical expression 10^6 has _____ zeros in the product.

8. Exponential notation is most useful with _____ numbers.

9. In exponential notation, scientists prefer to express the number before the multiplication sign as a value between _____.

Circle the letter of the best answer to each of the following questions.

1. If $10^4 = 10 \cdot 10 \cdot 10 \cdot 10$, what does 6^4 equal?

   a. $6 \cdot 6 \cdot 6 \cdot 6$

   b. $10 \cdot 10 \cdot 10 \cdot 10 \cdot 10 \cdot 10$

   c. $4 \cdot 4 \cdot 4 \cdot 4 \cdot 4 \cdot 4$

   d. $6 \cdot 4 \cdot 6 \cdot 4$

2. In which situation below would exponential notation be most useful?

   a. to show the distance from here to the Moon

   b. to show the height of a person

   c. to show the speed of a moving car

   d. to show the distance between your home and your school

3. What effect does lowering the value of the exponent have on the product?

   a. It increases.

   b. It decreases.

   c. It equals zero.

   d. It stays the same.

4. What effect does raising the value of the exponent have on the product?

   a. It increases.

   b. It decreases.

   c. It equals zero.

   d. It stays the same.

SKILL FOCUS: UNDERSTANDING EXPONENTIAL NOTATION

A. Write the standard numerals for the following mathematical expressions.

   1. $10^5 =$ _____

   2. $10^0 =$ _____

   3. $10^9 =$ _____

   4. 10^1 $=$ _____

   5. 10^{11} $=$ _____

   6. $8 \cdot (10^3) =$ _____

   7. $3 \cdot (10^2) + (2 \cdot 10) + 3$

      $=$ _____ $+$ _____ $+$ _____ $=$ _____

   8. $7 \cdot (10^4) + 6 \cdot (10^3) + 9 \cdot (10^2) + (1 \cdot 10) + 6$

      $=$ _____ $+$ _____ $+$ _____ $+$ _____ $+$ $=$ _____

B. Write the following numbers using exponential notation. The first one is done for you.

   1. 40   _____$4 \cdot (10^1)$_____

   2. 600 _____

   3. 16,200,000 _____

   4. 8,000   _____

C. Write the following numbers using exponential notation.

   1. $3,764 =$ _____

      $=$ _____

   2. $84,652 =$ _____

      $=$ _____

Reading-Writing Connection

Find out the population of your state. On a separate sheet of paper, write a paragraph about your findings, including some numbers in exponential notation.

Skill: Syllables

To help you pronounce long words, divide the words into **syllables**. Then pronounce each syllable until you can say the whole word. There are several different ways of deciding how a word should be divided.

RULE 1: Compound Words

One of the easiest rules to use in dividing words is the one for a compound word. Because a compound is made up of two words, it must have at least two syllables. Always divide a compound word into syllables by separating it between the two smaller words first. If one or both of the smaller words in a compound word have more than one syllable, it may be necessary to use another rule. However, you can pronounce most compound words if you divide them into two words.

sailboat   sail boat

A. Read each of the following compound words. Divide the word into two syllables, writing each of the two smaller words separately on the line next to the compound word.

1.	windstorm _____	11.	moonlight _____
2.	driveway _____	12.	bookcase _____
3.	northwest _____	13.	earthworm _____
4.	goldfinch _____	14.	sandpile _____
5.	drugstore _____	15.	footstep _____
6.	textbook _____	16.	landlord _____
7.	limestone _____	17.	cardboard _____
8.	seashore _____	18.	campground _____
9.	campfire _____	19.	spaceship _____
10.	sunlight _____	20.	drawbridge _____

RULE 2: Words With Double Consonants

Another rule that you may use is for words with double consonants. Divide the word into two syllables between the two consonants and read each syllable.

ribbon   rib bon

B. Divide each of the following two-syllable words into syllables. Write each syllable separately on the line next to the word.

1.	dinner _____	5.	muffin _____
2.	account _____	6.	message _____
3.	swimmer _____	7.	narrow _____
4.	bottom _____	8.	scrimmage _____

9. summon _____
10. mammal _____
11. blossom _____
12. passage _____
13. blizzard _____
14. correct _____

15. allow _____
16. raccoon _____
17. plummet _____
18. effort _____
19. ballad _____
20. command _____

RULE 3: Words With a Prefix or Suffix

A prefix or a suffix always has at least one sounded vowel. Therefore, a prefix or a suffix always contains at least one syllable. You can divide a word that has a prefix or a suffix between the prefix or suffix and the base word.

restring   re string
pitcher   pitch er

C. Divide each of the words below into two syllables between the prefix or suffix and the base word. Write each syllable separately on the line next to the word.

1. harmless _____
2. useful _____
3. westward _____
4. breakage _____
5. singer _____
6. nonsense _____
7. refill _____
8. swiftly _____
9. mistreat _____
10. untie _____

11. subway _____
12. kindness _____
13. react _____
14. weaken _____
15. prejudge _____
16. actor _____
17. insight _____
18. foolish _____
19. dislike _____
20. healthy _____

D. Divide each of the words below into syllables. Write the syllables separately on the line next to the word. Then, on the line to the left of the word, write the number of the rule or rules that you used to divide the word. Some words have three syllables. The first one is done for you.

1. __3, 2__ rearrange ___re ar range___
2. _____ careful _____
3. _____ Tennessee _____
4. _____ quarrelsome _____
5. _____ homemade _____
6. _____ transplant _____
7. _____ doorway _____

8. _____ gossip _____
9. _____ postwar _____
10. _____ unhappy _____
11. _____ roadside _____
12. _____ cunning _____
13. _____ buttermilk _____
14. _____ reappear _____

Skill: Main Idea—Stated or Unstated

When you read a chapter in a textbook, the **main idea** of each paragraph will often be stated in a sentence. The sentences in the rest of the paragraph will contain supporting details that give additional information about the main idea.

Sometimes the main idea of a paragraph is unstated. Then you need to use information in the paragraph to **infer**, or figure out, the main idea. To do this, you need to ask yourself what the paragraph is about. Then think of a sentence that summarizes this idea.

Read the following selection. Is the main idea of each paragraph stated or unstated?

The War of the Worlds

1. On October 30, 1938, the Earth was invaded by creatures from Mars! At least that's what thousands of radio listeners in the United States believed. Actually, on that evening a man named Orson Welles directed and starred in a radio broadcast entitled *The War of the Worlds*. The radio play was based on a book of the same title by H. G. Wells, an English writer. The performance described a fictional attack on New Jersey by invaders from Mars. The broadcast was not about a real event. However, it seemed so real that it caused a national panic.

2. In the 1930s, radio had a great influence on life in the United States. Television sets were not yet available for home use, so there were no live TV broadcasts to show people events as they happened. It was, therefore, not totally surprising that so many radio listeners believed what they heard on *The War of the Worlds*.

3. The story of the Martians' invasion, only a small part of the original story of *The War of the Worlds*, was used for the radio program. Playwright Howard Koch, who rewrote the story for radio, had picked up a map at a New Jersey gas station to find a location in the United States for the Martians' landing. He opened the map, closed his eyes, and pointed his pencil. The pencil landed on the town of Grovers Mill, New Jersey.

4. The radio play was presented like a regular radio broadcast—with music, a weather report, and then a series of special news bulletins. An introduction before the show began identified it as fiction. However, many listeners missed or did not listen to the introduction of the program: "The Columbia Broadcasting System and its affiliated stations present Orson Welles and the Mercury Theatre of the Air in *The War of the Worlds* by H. G. Wells." The newspaper listing for the show also identified the title of the program. In addition, three announcements during the program stated that the broadcast was fiction.

5. The first "news bulletins" and "eyewitness accounts" during the broadcast described a meteor that was supposed to have landed near Princeton, New Jersey. Later "reports" changed the meteor to a metal cylinder containing creatures from Mars armed with death rays. The creatures finally burst into flames, and the whole field where they had landed caught fire, spreading destruction.

6. Because radio listeners were used to interruptions in broadcasts during the recent threats of war in Europe, the program seemed real and caused fright and panic. Some families grabbed their personal belongings and fled into the streets. Traffic came to a standstill. Outraged citizens flooded radio stations, newspapers, and police headquarters with telephone calls. For days afterward, the broadcast was the topic of newspaper headlines.

7. Following the broadcast, a Grovers Mill farmer collected a 50-cent parking charge from each of the hundreds of carloads of people who wanted to see where the invaders had attacked. Even 30 years later, land in Grovers Mill was being sold at high prices because it was advertised as the site of the Martians' landing. The choice of Grovers Mill, New Jersey, as the town where the Martians landed helped to create new business opportunities there.

8. One New Jersey woman summed up many people's feelings when she said, "I thought it was all up with us. I grabbed my boy and just sat and cried." Believing that the entire human race faced death, many a person reached for someone nearby, for few people wanted to die alone. Others merely accepted their fate. A woman who had some leftover chicken in her icebox said to her nephew, "We may as well eat this chicken—we won't be here in the morning." Her remark was an attempt to make life go on as usual.

9. One woman said, "My only thought was delight that if the Martians came, I wouldn't have to pay the butcher's bill." A man who enjoyed spreading news said, "It was the most exciting thing that ever happened to me. I ran all through my apartment building telling everybody the Martians were here."

10. Close to one-quarter of the estimated 6 million listeners believed that the broadcast was fact. Surprisingly, many listeners failed to change to another station to check whether the broadcast was true. Why were so many people ready to believe this outrageous fantasy, and why did they react in panic? As one person remarked, "Being in a troublesome world, anything is liable to happen. . . . So many things we hear are unbelievable." If we can learn anything from the public reaction to the broadcast of *The War of the Worlds*, it is that we should not be too quick to believe everything that we hear and see over the airwaves and read in print.

A. **For each paragraph in the selection, if the main idea is stated, write *stated* on the line. If the main idea of a paragraph is unstated, choose a main idea from the sentences below and write the letter on the line.**

a. Many people believed that they were going to die.

b. The broadcast described how the Martians landed and caused destruction.

c. People thought that a radio program about invaders from Mars was real.

d. Listeners reacted to the broadcast with mixed feelings.

e. The producers of the broadcast took several measures to ensure that people would know that the show was not about a real event.

f. The broadcast appeared in the newspapers the next day.

g. The original English story needed to be rewritten with a location in the United States.

h. Some listeners reacted to the broadcast with delight.

i. The inhabitants of Grovers Mill were thrilled that their dull lives were changing.

j. Music and comedy helped people forget about the Great Depression.

Paragraph 1 _____   **Paragraph 6** _____

Paragraph 2 _____   **Paragraph 7** _____

Paragraph 3 _____   **Paragraph 8** _____

Paragraph 4 _____   **Paragraph 9** _____

Paragraph 5 _____   **Paragraph 10** _____

B. **Now go back to each paragraph that has a stated main idea, and underline the sentence that expresses the main idea.**

Skill: Using a Table of Contents

The **table of contents** at the beginning of a book gives a quick overview of the topics covered in the book. It lists the titles of the chapters and the page on which each chapter begins. Sometimes it also lists the most important topics included in each chapter. It may also give the page on which each topic begins.

To use a table of contents, glance through the chapter titles and topics until you find the subject you want to read about. Then turn to the page number given next to the chapter title or topic. Skim this section until you find the information that you need on your subject.

Below is a table of contents from a book on transportation. Use it to answer the questions on page 31.

CONTENTS

1. You need to find information about road travel used by the colonists.

   a. Under which chapter title would you look?

   _____

   b. Under which topic would you look?

   _____

   c. On which page would you start to read?

   _____

2. You need to find information about the first transcontinental railroad.

   a. Under which chapter title would you look?

   _____

   b. Under which topic would you look?

   _____

   c. On which page would you start to read?

   _____

3. You need to find information about space travel.

   a. Under which chapter title would you look?

   _____

   b. Under which topic would you look?

   _____

   c. On which page would you start to read?

   _____

4. You need to find information about the use of trucks.

   a. Under which chapter title would you look?

   _____

   b. Under which topic would you look?

   _____

   c. On which page would you start to read?

   _____

5. You need to find information about how early explorers used the compass.

   a. Under which chapter title would you look?

   _____

   b. Under which topic would you look?

   _____

   c. On which page would you start to read?

   _____

6. You need to find information about the first balloon flight.

   a. Under which chapter title would you look?

   _____

   b. Under which topic would you look?

   _____

   c. On which page would you start to read?

   _____

7. You need to find information about Peter Cooper's "Teakettle on Wheels."

   a. Under which chapter title would you look?

   _____

   b. Under which topic would you look?

   _____

   c. On which page would you start to read?

   _____

8. You need to find information about the effects that the automobile had on family life.

   a. Under which chapter title would you look?

   _____

   b. Under which topic would you look?

   _____

   c. On which page would you start to read?

   _____

Skill: Reading a Paycheck Stub

An employee, or worker, earns a fixed amount of money per hour or per year. Yet the money that is taken home is usually not the whole amount the worker earned during a pay period. Money is deducted, or taken out, from most **paychecks** for taxes and other things. **Gross pay** is the amount of money earned before any money is deducted. **Net pay** is the amount of take-home pay after deductions.

Most paychecks have two parts. One part, the actual check, can be cashed for the amount of take-home pay. The other part, the stub, contains a statement of earnings and deductions for the person's records. Information on the stub tells how much of a person's gross pay has been deducted. If all the deductions are added together and then subtracted from the gross pay, the amount left equals the net pay.

The paycheck stub below shows how much money has been deducted from Linda Wong's paycheck. The federal, state, and local taxes that she pays are used for defense, education, highways, parks, welfare, and other services and programs. Employers also may deduct money from the gross pay of each employee for retirement funds, health insurance, and any professional or union dues.

The deduction for the Federal Income Contribution Act, or FICA tax, goes to the federal government for Social Security payments. When an employee either retires or becomes unable to work due to injury, he or she receives money from Social Security. The amount of FICA tax on the earnings statement is half the total amount that is due. The employer pays the other half.

Read the paycheck stub below to answer the questions on page 33.

ACE SPACECRAFT MECHANICS
Wong, Linda

CHECK # **616545**

AMT. OF CHECK ▶ 1,173.00

PAY DATE	PAY PERIOD	SOCIAL SECURITY NO.
1/31/08	1/16/08–1/31/08	555-55-5555

	GROSS PAY	TAXES	DEDUCTIONS	NET PAY
THIS CHECK	1,800 00	567 00	60 00	1,173 00
YEAR TO DATE	3,600 00	1,134 00	120 00	2,346 00

DEDUCTIONS	THIS CHECK	YEAR TO DATE
FEDERAL TAX	306 00	612 00
FICA TAX	135 00	270 00
STATE TAXES	90 00	180 00
LOCAL TAXES	36 00	72 00
HEALTH INSURANCE	52 00	104 00
UNION DUES	8 00	16 00

OTHER EARNINGS — AMOUNT

STATEMENT OF EARNINGS AND DEDUCTIONS • DETACH AND RETAIN FOR YOUR RECORDS

A. Fill in the circle next to the correct answer to each question.

1. How much money did Linda Wong earn before deductions in this pay period?
   ○ $1,173.00   ○ $1,800.00   ○ $567.00   ○ $3,600.00

2. Which is the largest deduction?
   ○ FICA tax   ○ state tax   ○ federal tax   ○ health insurance

3. Which is the smallest deduction?
   ○ local tax   ○ union dues   ○ health insurance   ○ FICA tax

4. What is the total amount deducted for health insurance and union dues each pay period?
   ○ $6.00   ○ $52.00   ○ $92.00   ○ $60.00

5. How much money does Linda Wong's hometown receive directly from this paycheck?
   ○ $135.00   ○ $306.00   ○ $90.00   ○ $36.00

6. What is the total amount deducted from this paycheck?
   ○ $627.00   ○ $567.00   ○ $60.00   ○ $612.00

7. How much money has been deducted from Linda Wong's paycheck for the year to date?
   ○ $567.00   ○ $1,134.00   ○ $1,254.00   ○ $913.00

8. Which of the following statements about Linda Wong's deductions is true?
   ○ The deduction for FICA tax is less than the deduction for state taxes.
   ○ The combined deductions for health insurance and union dues are less than the deduction for local taxes.
   ○ The federal tax deduction is greater than the other deductions combined.
   ○ The federal tax deduction is greater than the state and local taxes combined.

9. How long is the pay period for each of Linda Wong's paychecks?
   ○ 1 day   ○ 1 month   ○ 1 week   ○ half a month

10. What do the numbers on the second line below the words "GROSS PAY," "TAXES," "DEDUCTIONS," and "NET PAY" stand for?
    ○ amount of money for the year to date
    ○ amount of money employee will receive for the next paycheck
    ○ amount of money employee has earned so far at current job
    ○ amount of money employee will earn next year at current job

B. Complete each sentence using information from the paycheck stub.

1. The amount of money that Linda Wong took home from this paycheck was _____.

2. The date that Linda received this paycheck was _____.

3. Linda Wong's Social Security number is _____.

4. Linda Wong's employer is _____.

Animals Through the Ages

LESSON 9

Skill: Plot

BACKGROUND INFORMATION

"The Gift of Betrayal" is a story based on events from the Trojan War, a conflict between ancient Greece and the city of Troy. The war probably took place in the mid-1200s B.C. We know about this war mainly from the Greek poet Homer. He wrote two epic poems—the *Iliad* and the *Odyssey*—that describe events during and after the fighting. Though they are based on historical facts, these poems also describe actions of gods and fictionalized heroes.

SKILL FOCUS: Plot

A story's **plot** is the series of events that happen in the story. Most plots follow a five-part pattern.

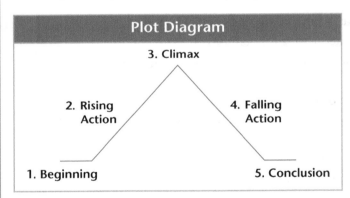

Plot Diagram

3. Climax

2. Rising Action

4. Falling Action

1. Beginning

5. Conclusion

1. **Beginning:** The beginning of the plot introduces the main characters and the setting.

2. **Rising Action:** The plot begins to build as a conflict develops. The main characters struggle to achieve a goal or to solve a problem.

3. **Climax:** The plot events build to a climax, or high point. This is the most exciting part of the story and marks a turning point.

4. **Falling Action:** The events after the climax show how the characters resolve, or deal with, the conflict in the story. This part of the plot is also called the resolution.

5. **Conclusion:** A final event ends the story.

▷ Choose a novel you have read or a film you have seen. Think about the parts of its plot. Then make a large copy of the plot diagram on a separate sheet of paper. Fill in events from the plot of the book or movie under the appropriate labels on the diagram.

CONTEXT CLUES: Footnotes

Footnotes are explanations of names, places, and other special words in a selection. Words with footnotes have a small raised number next to them. The footnotes themselves usually appear at the bottom of the page on which the word appears.

Read the sentence below. Look at the underlined word.

*The siege of **Troy**[1] is not going well, thought Odysseus.[2]*

The raised number 1 after the underlined word *Troy* is a signal to look at the bottom of the page for a footnote with the same number. A footnote gives a brief definition or explanation of the word or phrase.

[1] Troy (TROY): an ancient city in what is now northwestern Turkey; scene of the Trojan War.

[2] Odysseus (oh DIS ee əs): King of Ithaca; one of the Greek leaders in the Trojan War.

▷ Read the sample sentence again. Circle the details in the footnote that explain the meaning of the second footnoted word.

As you read, use footnotes to learn about *Helen*, *Sparta*, and the *Aegean Sea*.

Strategy Tip

As you read "The Gift of Betrayal," use the plot diagram in the Skill Focus to help you understand the story's plot.

THE GIFT OF BETRAYAL

The siege of Troy[1] is not going well, thought Odysseus.[2] The kings and princes of Greece had been at war with the Trojans for ten long years. Unfortunately, there had been a decade of bloody battles outside the walls of the strong city and of waiting for a stroke of luck to help conquer Troy.

Many valiant warriors on both sides had been slain. Odysseus wondered if the terrible death toll was too high for the rescue of one person. Yet, he told himself, the person in question was <u>Helen</u>,[3] the beautiful wife of Menelaus, King of <u>Sparta</u>.[4] She had been kidnapped ten years before by Paris, son of the King of Troy. Her kidnapping had enraged the kings of the Greek cities. With a huge fleet, they had set sail across the <u>Aegean Sea</u>[5] to rescue Helen and destroy the Trojans. Yet the Trojans had defended themselves well in their walled city.

There must be a way to bring the wearying, terrible war to an end, thought Odysseus. Perhaps if they made a special offering to the gods, the gods might look kindly on their gift and reward them with the city of Troy. Odysseus thought hard. Suddenly, he was struck by an idea—a gift! A gift! They would win Troy with a gift!

Odysseus gathered the kings and princes of Greece together and presented his plan. They would build a glorious, huge, wonderful wooden horse. While the horse would seem magical and beautiful, its large belly would be hollow. Inside the horse, a group of Greek warriors would hide. At the same time, the rest of the Greek warriors would appear to set sail for home in defeat. However, they would sail only to a small neighboring island, just out of sight

of the shore, where they would wait until the moment for attack.

The leaders of Greece accepted Odysseus's plan and set to work. They built their horse within sight of the walls of Troy. Its mane curved gracefully down a strong neck, its head was held high, and its legs were strong.

Finally the horse was finished. Under cover of darkness, the small group of chosen warriors hid inside. The next day, the rest of the Greek warriors pretended they were leaving sadly, as if in defeat. They boarded their ships and quietly sailed out of the bay.

---

[1] Troy (TROY): an ancient city in what is now northwestern Turkey; scene of the Trojan War.

[2] Odysseus (oh DIS ee əs): King of Ithaca; one of the Greek leaders in the Trojan War.

[3] Helen: wife of Menelaus, taken to Troy by Paris; known as the most beautiful woman in the world.

[4] Sparta (SPAR tə): an ancient, powerful military city in southern Greece.

[5] Aegean (i JEE ən) Sea: the arm of the Mediterranean Sea between Greece and Turkey.

The Trojans were elated! With shouts of triumph, they swarmed out of their city onto the plain near the shore. They had been imprisoned inside the city for years and now the land was theirs again!

Yet what was this horse? Certainly, it was a thing of beauty, but why had the Greeks built it? Even more mysteriously, why had they left it behind? Was it a curse or a blessing? The horse did not answer, as it towered silently and woodenly over the Trojans. Its steady gaze was directed toward the sea, but the Trojans did not notice.

A Trojan priest named Laocoön (lay AHK ə wahn) approached the horse. He walked around the huge steed. He admired it, inspected it, struck it with his staff. A hollow sound rang out! The priest did not know why, but this sound bothered him. "I do not like this horse!" he cried. "We must burn it! It should be destroyed or else, I fear, it will destroy us! I fear the Greeks even when they bear gifts."

The people of Troy believed their priest. They began to move threateningly toward the horse, which could not move or defend itself. The men inside feared that their lives were at an end.

Then the gods interfered by sending two huge sea serpents from out of the ocean onto the shore. The serpents twined their poisonous coils around the young sons of Laocoön. When the priest tried to save his sons, he too was trapped and slain. The serpents' appearance frightened the people of Troy, who saw their arrival as a sign that the gods were not pleased with the priest or his predictions.

Still, the giant horse stood unmoving on the plains outside the city. The mystified Trojans wondered what it could be for.

Then some Trojan warriors rushed up to the people with a captured Greek slave. The slave told the Trojans that the Greeks had made the horse as a peace offering to the gods. The enemy had finally given up in defeat and sailed for home.

With songs of joy and triumph, the Trojans took the horse as their own, pulling it through the gates of their city. For them, the horse was a symbol of a hard-won victory.

For hours after they dragged the horse into the center of the city, the people of Troy celebrated their victory. They made offerings to the gods, feasted, sang, and danced. Finally exhausted, they found their way home and went to bed.

As the city of Troy grew dark and silent, the horse appeared to gaze solemnly over it. A watching Trojan might have imagined the horse was standing guard—but it was not. Even as it stood in quiet majesty, the horse was betraying the city and its people.

Suddenly, the belly of the animal opened, and the Greek warriors silently crept out. They sneaked up to the gates of the city and, just before dawn, opened the gates wide. Outside stood the Greek armies, who had sailed back to the shores of Troy in the dark of night.

The Greeks swept into the city, killing all who challenged them. As the Trojans rallied to defend their city, the fighting grew fierce. Warriors, priests, women, children, princes, and kings were all swept up in the jaws of battle.

Through it all, the horse stood motionless and quiet above the battle. Guard or betrayer, it had no further part to play in the fight for the proud city.

Although the Trojans fought bravely, in the end the Greeks took the victory. The Trojans who survived were banished from their city, and Helen was rescued and returned to her husband, Menelaus. Most of the Greeks immediately set sail for their native land.

Before the Greeks left, however, they set fire to Troy. As it burned, flames flickered and licked at the wooden feet of the horse. The scarlet, orange, and black colors of the fire cast an eerie glow on the steed. The treacherous horse of Troy caught fire, but still it did not move.

As the horse flared into full flame and burst into a shower of sparks and burning timber, Odysseus stood outside the walled city, deep in thought. He was tired because the war had gone on too long, and too many friends had died in the fighting. Now he wanted to be in Ithaca, his home in Greece.

1. Why were the Trojans puzzled by the wooden horse?

_____

_____

_____

2. What fact about the wooden horse disturbed Laocoön?

_____

_____

_____

3. The captured Greek slave told the Trojans that the Greeks had made the horse as a peace offering to the gods. What effect did this information have on the Trojans?

_____

_____

_____

4. Complete each sentence with the correct word or words.

   Helen   Aegean Sea   Sparta

   a. The abduction of _____ by Paris started the Trojan War.

   b. _____, a city in ancient Greece, was home to Menelaus and Helen.

   c. The _____ lies between Greece on the west and Turkey on the east.

1. Explain why the Greek warriors in the horse were able to open the gates of Troy without getting caught.

_____

_____

2. Explain how the wooden horse was a "gift of betrayal."

_____

_____

3. a. The Trojans wondered whether the horse was a blessing or a curse. For whom was it a blessing? Explain.

_____

_____

   b. For whom was the wooden horse a curse? Explain.

_____

_____

Listed below are some events in the story "The Gift of Betrayal." The events are not in the correct order. On the lines provided in the plot diagram, write the letters of the events that belong in each part of the plot. First decide which event is the climax.

a. Odysseus watches the fall of Troy and yearns to go home.

b. The Greek kings and princes accept Odysseus's plan to conquer Troy.

c. Laocoön's warning to the Trojans to destroy the wooden horse is ignored.

d. The Greeks build a wooden horse large enough to contain a group of armed warriors.

e. The Greek warriors creep out of the belly of the wooden horse and open the gates of the city.

f. The Trojans bring the wooden horse through the gates into their city.

g. Before sailing out of the bay, the Greeks leave the wooden horse outside the gates of Troy.

h. Under cover of darkness, the Greeks sail back to Troy.

i. The Greeks storm the city of Troy and rescue Helen.

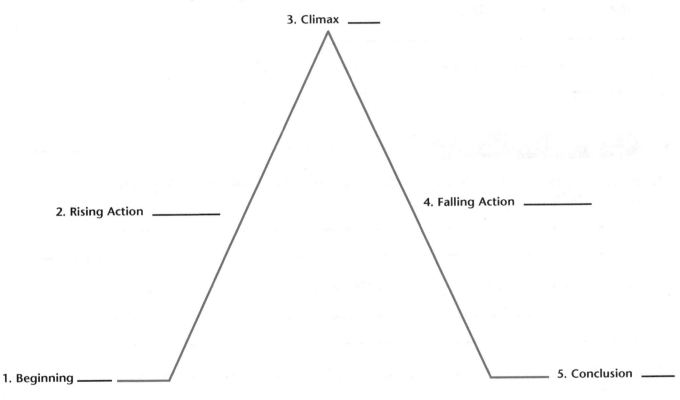

3. Climax _____

2. Rising Action _____

4. Falling Action _____

1. Beginning _____

5. Conclusion _____

Reading-Writing Connection

How might the story have ended differently if the Trojans had followed Laocoön's advice? On a separate sheet of paper, write a paragraph describing events that might have occurred in the climax, falling action, and conclusion as a result of this decision.

Skill: Cause and Effect

BACKGROUND INFORMATION

"The Bedouin and the Masai: Herders of Animals" tells about the Bedouin people of the Middle East and the Masai people of Africa. Both groups are nomads, people who move from place to place in order to survive. The earliest humans were probably nomadic, moving from place to place to hunt and gather food. Today, the Bedouin and Masai peoples continue this nomadic lifestyle, herding their animals across the countryside in search of water and pasture land.

SKILL FOCUS: Cause and Effect

When one event causes another event to happen, the process is called cause and effect. A **cause** is an event that makes something happen. An **effect** is what happens as a result of the cause.

Sometimes two or more causes bring about one effect, as in this example.

Cause 1	Cause 2
Camels can survive in the desert for prolonged periods without water.	Camels can travel long distances in the desert without stopping.

Effect

Camels are important animals to desert dwellers.

A single cause can also bring about two or more effects, as in this example.

Cause

The Bedouin are desert herders who must move often to find new grazing land for their animals.

Effect 1	Effect 2
The Bedouin possess few material goods.	The Bedouin live in easily moved tents.

▶ Read the following sentences. Circle the cause. Underline two effects.

Because cars and trucks are now used as transportation in the desert, camels are no longer as valuable as they once were. Raising sheep is becoming more profitable than herding camels.

CONTEXT CLUES: Definitions

Some reading selections include the **definitions** of important new words. Look for these definitions to help you understand the new words and ideas.

Read the following sentence. Look for the definition of the underlined word.

Because these wells are shared in common and used equally by all, they are called __communal__ wells.

If you don't know what *communal* means, the first part of the sentence gives you its definition. *Communal* means "shared in common."

▶ Read the following sentences. Circle the definition that tells you the meaning of the underlined word.

In the past, the Bedouin herded only __dromedaries__. These single-humped camels were not only the most important animals in the desert, but also the chief means of transportation for desert people.

In the selection, use definitions to learn the meanings of the underlined words *yogurt*, *savannas*, and *bomas*.

> ### Strategy Tip
>
> As you read "The Bedouin and the Masai: Herders of Animals," look for cause-and-effect relationships. Recognizing causes and effects will help you understand the ideas you read about.

The Bedouin and the Masai: Herders of Animals

In some remote areas of the world, there are groups of people whose lives are closely intertwined with the lives of their animals. These people, called **herders**, still live much as their ancestors did centuries ago.

Animals are important in every aspect of the herder's life. The wealth of a herder is measured by the size of the herd. Everyday life revolves around the care of the animals. Many customs and rituals have been influenced by the animals that enable the herder to survive. From their animals, herders get most of what they need to survive. The animals supply them not only with food, drink, and clothing, but also with shelter and fuel. In return, the herders care for the animals. They take them to fresh pastures, care for the sick ones, and protect them from predators.

Unlike farmers, herders do not keep their animals in one place. Because the animals need more than one small area can provide, the people and their herds move frequently from one grazing place to another.

Constant movement is a major feature of the lives of herders. They do not have permanent homes. As a result, their easily built dwellings can be carried with them or left behind. Herders possess few material belongings. They own only as much as they can carry with them.

Of all the herders still existing in various parts of the world, two groups are especially interesting. One group is the Bedouin (BED ə wən) of the Middle East, and the other is the Masai (mah SEYE) of eastern Africa.

The Bedouin

In the dry, vast deserts of the Middle East, herders of camels, sheep, and goats live an ancient, **nomadic** (noh MAD ik) life. They are the Bedouin, the Arab inhabitants of the desert. With little grass

Camels are as important to modern Bedouins as they were in the past.

in the harsh desert, the Bedouin move often to find new pastures for their animals.

A Bedouin camp is both beautiful and practical. Long, low, black tents, adapted to the needs of Bedouin life, are pitched together on the white sand. Each tent is made from long strands of goat, camel, and sheep hair. When wet, these fibers expand, making the tent waterproof. During the hot days, the sides of the tent are rolled up to provide shade and to let cool breezes through. At night, they are rolled down to keep out the cold wind. When the Bedouin decide to move their herds to new grazing land, they can lower their tents and pack their belongings within a few hours.

In the fall, winter, and spring, the Bedouin live and travel together in family groups of two to twenty tents. They move their herds across the desert, often following rain clouds. In the summer, the Bedouin gather together at wells, the only sources of water in the dry summer. Because these wells are shared in common and used equally by all, they are called communal (kə MYOO nəl) wells. Hundreds of tents are pitched together near the communal well and remain there for three or four months.

✗✗ The Bedouin rely on their animals for most of their diet. Camel milk is the most important part of many meals. Sometimes it is drunk fresh, and other times it is made into <u>yogurt</u>. Yogurt is a semisolid food made from milk that is fermented by a bacterium. Because the camels are so valuable, they are seldom killed to be eaten. On special occasions, however, the Bedouin enjoy camel meat as a festive treat. The Bedouin also make a kind of butter and a hard, white cheese from their sheep's milk.

✗ The Bedouin cherish and respect the camel. Various Bedouin groups prize camels of a particular color—white, black, brown. The Arabic word for camel (*jamal*) comes from the same root as the Arabic word for beautiful (*jamil*). Many Arabic words describe the various ages and kinds of camels.

In the past, the Bedouin herded only dromedaries (DRAHM ə dair eez). These single-humped camels were not only the most important animals in the desert, but also the chief means of transportation for desert people. A camel can survive for long periods of time without water and can also tolerate extreme heat. In addition, the camel has great endurance and courage.

Until modern times, the wealth of a Bedouin family was measured only by the number of camels it owned. An average herd consisted of 40 to 50 camels. Today, sheep are becoming more and more important to the Bedouin economy. Because cars and trucks are now used as transportation in the desert, camels are no longer as valuable as they once were. Raising sheep is becoming more profitable than herding camels.

Much of Bedouin life, however, remains unchanged. The people still travel the desert, following their herds and keeping up old traditions.

The Masai

The high, rolling, treeless plains in the countries of Kenya and Tanzania are unique to eastern Africa. They are called <u>savannas</u>. On these plains live the Masai. Although the Masai are herders of cattle, sheep, and goats, they value their cattle most. To them, no other possession is of equal worth. This attitude is the result of the important role cattle play in every aspect of Masai life.

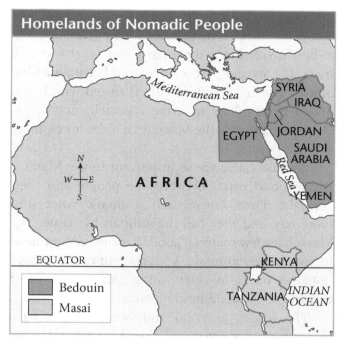

Homelands of Nomadic People

AFRICA

- Bedouin
- Masai

The Bedouin live in the deserts of the Middle East. The Masai live in the savannas of eastern Africa.

A Masai village consists of a group of <u>bomas</u>. Built by the Masai women, bomas are dwellings made from a framework of twigs and covered by grass and leaves. To keep the structure warm and waterproof, it is plastered with a layer of cattle dung. Fences are put up around the boma village to protect the animals at night.

✗ Everyday life in the village revolves around the care of the cattle and other animals. Masai women and girls milk the cattle and prepare food using the milk. The men inspect the cattle for disease and treat any sick ones. During the day, the young boys take the cattle out to pasture and guard them from predators. When necessary, the boys help a pregnant animal give birth to a kid or calf.

When their cattle need new grazing land, the Masai move, leaving their bomas behind. If they come to a grazing place on the savanna where they have been before, the Masai patch up their old bomas. The women can do this task in half a day. If the grazing place is new, the women and girls build new bomas. When staying in a place for just a short while, the Masai live in simpler dwellings made of mud and animal hides.

✔ From their cattle, the Masai get meat, milk, and blood for nourishment. After a cow is milked, the milk is divided into three parts. One part is drunk fresh. The second part is stored and becomes a kind of sour cheese. The third part is mixed with blood drawn from a cow to make a protein-rich drink. Cattle also provide the Masai with hides for clothing and bed covers.

Because cattle are so important to the Masai, a strong bond exists between the people and their animals. They know each animal's voice and markings, and they call the animals by name. The Masai have few material goods because all they need to own is their animals. A Masai man cannot marry until he owns his own cattle. An average herd consists of about 75 head of cattle.

The Masai, a proud and noble people, have always been respected and feared by other African people. To become a warrior, a young man must prove himself by killing a lion with a spear. In the past, the Masai raided neighboring camps for cattle to make their own herds larger. According to Masai belief, all the cattle were given to the Masai at the beginning of the world. No one else had a right to possess any.

In recent years, the Masai have come to lead more peaceful lives. Still, modern civilization has not greatly affected them. The young people have the chance to go to the cities, but most Masai remain herders of cattle. They are close to their families and friends, and their love for their animals remains constant. They are proud to be Masai.

Masai women and children in traditional dress sit in front of a boma.

Herders live a life that is unique in today's world. Living in close contact with nature, they have no need for luxury or conveniences. They remain in family groups, and they take pride in caring for the animals that ensure their survival.

COMPREHENSION

1. How are Bedouin homes different from those of the Masai?

   _____

   _____

   _____

2. Reread the paragraph that has an ✗✗ next to it. Underline the sentence that states its main idea. Circle at least three sentences in the paragraph that give details in support of the main idea.

3. Reread the two paragraphs that have ✗s next to them. Underline the sentence in each paragraph that states the paragraph's main idea.

4. Decide if each statement is true or false. Write *true* or *false* on the lines provided.

   _____ a. Along with milk and butter, <u>yogurt</u> is found in the dairy section of a supermarket.

   _____ b. The <u>savannas</u> of East Africa are suited to the raising of cattle, sheep, and goats.

   _____ c. The Bedouin fences, found in the deserts of the Middle East, are called <u>bomas</u>.

CRITICAL THINKING

1. List two ways in which the life of a farmer is different from the life of a herder.

_____

2. Explain how the Bedouin and the Masai feel about the animals they herd.

_____

_____

3. Identify the following statements by writing *fact* or *opinion* on the lines provided.

_____ **a.** Of all herders, the Bedouin and the Masai are the most interesting.

_____ **b.** The Bedouin move often to find new pastures for their herds.

_____ **c.** A Bedouin camp is both beautiful and practical.

_____ **d.** The Masai have few material goods because their main goal is to own cattle.

_____ **e.** The Masai are a proud and noble people who will never change their ways.

4. Reread the paragraph with a ✔ next to it. Circle the letter next to the sentence that states the paragraph's main idea.

   a. The Masai get milk from their cattle.

   b. The Masai's cattle provide them with food, drink, and clothing.

   c. The Masai kill cattle for their blood.

   d. After a cow is milked, the milk is divided into three parts.

5. How do you think the lives of the Bedouin and Masai herders may change in the coming years?

_____

_____

SKILL FOCUS: CAUSE AND EFFECT

1. Give two effects for each cause listed below.

   a. Cause: In the dry summer, a communal well is the Bedouin's only source of water.

   Effect: _____

   Effect: _____

   b. Cause: Trucks and cars have begun to replace the camel as a means of transportation in the desert.

   Effect: _____

   Effect: _____

2. Give two causes for each effect listed below.

    a. Cause: _____

      Cause: _____

      Effect: In the past, the Masai raided neighboring camps for cattle.

    b. Cause: _____

      Cause: _____

      Effect: Most Masai young people stay with their own people rather than move to cities.

3. Complete each of the following sentences by explaining one effect for the cause stated.

    a. Because animals influence how and where herders live, how they dress, and

      what they eat and drink, _____

      _____

    b. Because the camel can survive for long periods of time without water, _____

      _____

    c. When their cattle need new grazing land, the Masai _____

      _____

    d. When cars and trucks came into use in the desert, _____

      _____

4. Sometimes effects have to be inferred, or figured out, because they are not directly stated in a selection. Answer each of the following questions by inferring a possible effect.

    a. What will happen to the Bedouin way of life as sheep begin to replace camels?

      _____

      _____

    b. What will happen to the Masai way of life if more and more young people go to the cities?

      _____

      _____

Reading-Writing Connection

On a separate sheet of paper, write a paragraph describing one part of the Bedouin or Masai way of life that appeals to you. Give reasons to support your choice.

Skill: Classifying

BACKGROUND INFORMATION

"The Dinosaur-Bird Connection" is about recent discoveries that show how birds are related to dinosaurs. To understand dinosaurs, scientists depend mainly on fossils, ancient bones that have turned to stone. Fossils show that dinosaurs first appeared 230 million years ago. As the Earth's geography and climate changed, the dinosaurs did, too. They were able to spread out all over the Earth, from the Arctic to the South Pole. After thriving for more than 150 million years, dinosaurs died out 65 million years ago. However, many scientists now believe that birds are the living relatives of one group of dinosaurs.

SKILL FOCUS: Classifying

Classifying is a way to organize information by grouping similar things together. You classify people and things every day. If you were describing a friend, for example, you might say he or she was an athlete, a good student, or a talented artist. *Athlete*, *Student*, and *Artist* are classifications. Members of each group share certain qualities or traits.

When scientists classify plants and animals, they break large groups into smaller ones. The members of each smaller group are similar in some way. The dinosaurs Tyrannosaurus rex (T. rex) and Velociraptor, for example, are classified together in the same group. These meat-eating dinosaurs are called *theropods*, which means "beast foot." One similarity that all theropods share is their three-toed, clawlike feet.

Brachiosaurus and Diplodocus are classified together in another group of dinosaurs. These plant eaters are in a group called *sauropods*, which means "lizard foot."

When reading about different groups of living things, ask yourself these questions.

- What do the things in the same group have in common?

- How are the things in one group different from those in another group?

▶ Complete the chart in the next column. Use the information you have read on this page to classify two types of dinosaurs.

Two Types of Dinosaurs		
Type	**Meaning of Name**	**What It Eats**
theropod		
sauropod		

CONTEXT CLUES: Definitions

Sometimes the sentences around a new word include the word's **definition**.

Read the paragraph below. What definition is given for the underlined word?

In the early 1920s, scientists dug up what they thought were the eggs of a __herbivorous__ dinosaur. On top of the eggs, they found the skeleton of a carnivorous dinosaur. Herbivorous means "plant-eating," and carnivorous means "meat-eating."

If you don't know the meaning of *herbivorous*, you will find its definition in the last sentence. *Herbivorous* means "plant-eating."

▶ Circle the definition of the underlined word in the following sentences.

Most __paleontologists__ now believe that the birds of today are the living cousins of dinosaurs. Paleontologists are scientists who study the remains of ancient animals.

In the selection, use definition clues to find the meanings of the underlined words *aerodynamic*, *camouflage*, and *metabolism*.

Strategy Tip

Before you read "The Dinosaur-Bird Connection," study the headings and the illustrations. As you read, think about the similarities and differences that scientists use to classify dinosaurs.

The Dinosaur-Bird Connection

Do you think all dinosaurs are extinct? Well, look out your window, and you might just see a living relative of one. Of course, you won't see a Tyrannosaurus (tə RAN ə SAUR əs) rex or a Diplodocus, (də PLAHD ə kəs), but you might spot a pigeon or a crow. If so, you might just be looking at a descendant of the dinosaurs. Most paleontologists (PAY lee ən TAHL ə jists) now believe that the birds of today are the living cousins of dinosaurs. Paleontologists are scientists who study the remains of ancient animals.

Ancient Wings

This possible connection between birds and dinosaurs is not really a new idea. In 1861, a beautiful **fossil** was dug up in a quarry in Germany. Fossils are the remains of ancient animals that have turned to stone. This crow-sized fossil showed the impression of an animal that had the wings and feathers of a bird but the teeth and tail of a reptile. Scientists called the animal Archaeopteryx (ahr kee AHP tə riks), which means "ancient wing." The fossil was 150 million years old and was the remains of the earliest known bird.

This fossil of Archaeopteryx shows its wings. It may have been capable of flight.

Over the years, more examples of Archaeopteryx turned up in the German quarry. The same layers of stone also yielded the fossil of a small chicken-sized dinosaur called Compsognathus

(KAHMP sahg NAY thəs). This animal apparently had no wings or feathers, but in other ways it looked like Archaeopteryx. This evidence led Thomas Huxley, a well-known English scientist, to suggest a startling hypothesis: Birds and dinosaurs existed at the same time and were close relatives.

For a long time, Huxley's hypothesis was not widely accepted. However, recently discovered fossil evidence now clearly shows the close relationship between birds and a type of dinosaurs classified as theropods (THAIR ə pahdz).

Geologic Time

To understand dinosaurs, it is important to know the names and dates of **geologic periods**. The Paleozoic (PAY lee ə ZOH ik), Mesozoic (MEZ ə ZOH ik), and

The Eras of Geologic Times		
Era	**Period**	**Approximate Number of Years in the Period**
Cenozoic	Quaternary	65 million
	Tertiary	
Mesozoic	Cretaceous	183 million
	Jurassic	
	Triassic	
Paleozoic	Permian	300 million
	Carboniferous	
	Devonian	
	Silurian	
	Ordovician	
	Cambrian	

Different kinds of dinosaurs appeared in different periods of the Mesozoic Era.

Cenozoic (SEN ə ZOH ik) eras cover the last 548 million years of Earth's history. Dinosaur fossils have been found only in rocks from the Mesozoic Era.

The Mesozoic Era is divided into three periods—the Triassic (try AS ik), Jurassic (jə RAS ik), and Cretaceous (krə TAY shəs) periods. The oldest dinosaur fossils scientists have found are from the late Triassic period (about 230 million years ago). The youngest dinosaur fossils found are from the end of the Cretaceous period (about 65 million years ago). Based on this fossil record, we believe that dinosaurs roamed the Earth for about 165 million years.

Theropods and Birds

Theropods, the cousins of today's birds, lived in the Jurassic period. *Theropod* is a Greek word meaning "beast foot." These meat-eating beasts had feet with three large toes and a smaller, thumblike "big toe" at the back of the ankle.

The foot structure of theropods was very similar to that of today's birds. In fact, fossilized footprints of theropods were once thought to be the footprints of prehistoric birds.

Theropods were fast and agile, or able to move easily and quickly. They walked on their two hind legs and used their shorter front limbs as hands to grab and tear apart prey. Their sharp teeth and strong jaws were well-adapted for eating animal flesh.

Two well-known dinosaurs—Tyrannosaurus rex and Allosaurus—were theropods. So were several smaller dinosaurs called raptors. Raptors all had long tails held high to control their balance. They also had toes with sharp talons, which they used for killing their prey. Raptor fossils show many similarities to bird skeletons.

Among the fastest of the raptors was the six-foot-long Velociraptor, whose name means "swift robber." Living 65 million years ago, Velociraptor used its speed and enormous claws to prey on other animals. One reason raptors could run so fast was that they had hollow, lightweight bones. These bones were much like the bones of modern birds.

Paleontologists who unearthed Velociraptor fossils in Mongolia found an interesting crescent-shaped bone in the dinosaur's wrist. Today this type of bone is found only in the arms of birds. Birds use it when flapping their wings or when folding them in before diving.

How did this bone help the raptors? When chasing prey, a raptor could have folded its arms against its body to be more <u>aerodynamic</u>. Aerodynamic means "sleek, or shaped in a way that cuts down on air resistance." This wrist bone also let the raptor's hand swivel to snatch prey. This motion was similar to a flap of a bird's wing.

✘ You are probably familiar with wishbones, the V-shaped breastbones you find in chickens and turkeys. All birds have wishbones. For many years, paleontologists thought that dinosaurs did not have wishbones. Recently unearthed Velociraptor skeletons, however, have proved otherwise. In these skeletons, the collarbones are joined together in a wishbone, just as in bird skeletons.

Another birdlike theropod was Oviraptor. The story of how scientists discovered the truth about

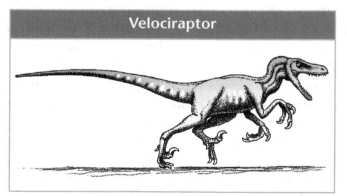

Velociraptor

A Velociraptor used its speed and enormous claws to prey on other animals.

Dinosaur eggs were fossilized in mud, ash, or silt along with other remains of the dinosaur.

this incorrectly named raptor reveals another similarity between theropods and birds.

In the early 1920s, scientists dug up what they thought were the eggs of a herbivorous dinosaur. On top of the eggs, they found the skeleton of a carnivorous dinosaur. Herbivorous means "plant-eating," and carnivorous means "meat-eating."

The scientists assumed that the carnivore was stealing the eggs of the herbivore. So they named the carnivore *Oviraptor*, or "egg-stealer." Sixty years later, however, other scientists examined the same fossil eggs with new tools. They discovered that the eggs actually contained baby Oviraptors. The Oviraptor had not been stealing eggs. It had been sitting on them like a mother hen!

✔ The Oviraptor eggs were in a huge dinosaur nesting ground. In such areas, hundreds of dinosaurs of the same species gathered to lay eggs. Today, certain species of birds, such as penguins, also form huge groups when laying eggs. By studying these modern birds, paleontologists hope to gain insight into how their dinosaur ancestors may have lived.

Recent Theropod Discoveries

A number of fossils found in the 1990s reveal even more similarities between theropods and birds. In 1996, the windswept plains of Patagonia, in southern Argentina, yielded the 90-million-year-old bones of a previously unknown theropod. This new specimen was eight feet long. Its front limbs were so winglike that it was named Unenlagia. This name means "half bird" in a native language of the region.

According to paleontologists, Unenlagia was able to fold its front limbs in the same way that birds fold their wings. It could also move its shoulder joints to raise its front limbs. This is the same movement that birds use to start each downward flight stroke.

Unenlagia could not fly. It could only move its arms up and down, like a person balancing on a tightrope. However, this motion is similar to wing flapping and is essential for flight.

The Feathered Theropods

Feathers are probably the most characteristic feature of birds. Any fossil that showed impressions of feathers would surely belong to a close relative of modern birds. However, it is difficult to find fossil evidence of feathers because they are so soft and delicate that they quickly decay in the ground. Only layers of very fine volcanic ash can preserve the outlines of feathers in a fossil.

Recently, scientists have been lucky enough to find such fossils. In the late Cretaceous period, about 125 million years ago, large lakes covered a region in northeastern China. Volcanoes erupted there often, burying creatures under layers of ash. Chinese fossil diggers have found many fossils of fish, turtles, and mammals there. In the late 1990s, a number of perfectly preserved theropod fossils also turned up. To everyone's amazement, these dinosaur fossils showed the outlines of feathers!

This was the first time that evidence of feathers had ever been found on any animal other than birds—living or extinct. Scientists could now add feathers to the list of the many other similarities between theropods and birds.

The first feathered theropod found in China was the Sinosauropteryx (SY noh sor AHP tər iks). Its name means "Chinese lizard feather." According to the fossil evidence, this creature was about three feet long. It did not have true feathers, only a dense coat of featherlike fibers. It also had no winglike structures and could not even flap its arms.

Scientists think that the Sinosauropteryx may have used its feathery coat to keep warm. Another possibility is that the feathers were <u>camouflage</u>. Camouflage is a body coloring or shape that lets an animal blend in with its surroundings.

The same lake bed also yielded fossils of another small theropod, which scientists named Caudipteryx (cahd IP tər iks), meaning "tail feather." Caudipteryx, too, was about three feet long. Its feathers, which lined its hands as well as its tail, look a lot like the feathers on today's birds. Still, the shape of these feathers and the dinosaur's bones show that Caudipteryx could not have flown.

Perhaps Caudipteryx used its feathers to ward off enemies. Another possibility is that it used its feathers the way a peacock does, to attract mates.

Another amazing theropod found in the Chinese fossil bed is Sinornithosaurus (syn ORN ə thə SOR əs), or "Chinese bird reptile." The skeleton of this creature is very similar in form to that of its cousin, the Velociraptor. The Chinese fossil, however, is much older. It belongs to a creature that lived 125 million years ago—60 million years before Velociraptor.

Like the other feathered theropods found at the site, Sinornithosaurus was about three feet long. Fossil evidence shows that it is the most birdlike of all the feathered dinosaurs. Its bones show that it could lift its arms well above its head and flap them. The big jaws of Sinornithosaurus, however, were filled with dagger-sharp teeth. Its mouth parts looked nothing like the beaks of birds today.

Warm-Blooded or Cold-Blooded?

The discovery of the feathered dinosaurs in China raises an old question about dinosaur metabolism (mə TAB ə liz əm). An animal's metabolism includes all the processes by which it breaks down food and uses energy from the food for heat and growth. Warm-blooded animals, like birds and mammals, maintain a constant body temperature. Cold-blooded animals, like reptiles, have a body temperature that changes as their surroundings change. Their blood is hotter in summer and during the daytime and cooler in winter and at night.

Since the feathered dinosaurs did not fly, of what use were their feathers? Perhaps the downy feathers were insulation to help maintain their body temperature. If so, these creatures may have been warm-blooded. A cold-blooded animal would not be able to maintain its body temperature, no matter what kind of skin covering it had.

The fossil evidence of an Oviraptor sitting on its nest of eggs is another clue. Why would a cold-blooded animal sit on its eggs? If it had the same body temperature as the air around it, it could not possibly keep the eggs warm. A cold-blooded reptile, like a turtle, usually lays its eggs and then walks away.

If scientists could study the internal organs of a dinosaur, they might be able to resolve this issue once and for all. Soft body parts, however, are never fossilized. For now, some scientists think that the small, fast-moving raptors were warm-blooded. Heavy plant eaters might have been cold-blooded.

Dinosaurs Live On?

The fossil evidence found so far does not give a neat, chronological picture of the history of birds and theropods. Different types of fossils from different times and places show early feathers and wings.

Paleontologists once thought that all dinosaurs died out 65 million years ago. The departure of the dinosaurs, scientists believed, left room for the mammals to take over. Today, scientists propose a different ending to the story of the dinosaurs. They now believe that one class of dinosaurs lives on in the form of birds. So the next time you go outside, take a new look at pigeons, robins, and crows. You might still be living in the Age of Dinosaurs.

SCIENCE

COMPREHENSION

1. Based on fossil evidence, what did Archaeopteryx look like?

   _____

   _____

2. During which three periods of the Mesozoic Era did dinosaurs live?

   _____

   _____

3. Reread the paragraph with a ✔ next to it. Then underline the sentence that states its main idea.

4. Complete each sentence with the correct word.

   aerodynamic   camouflage   metabolism

   a. A small, fast animal burns a lot of energy

      and has a high _____.

   b. Dull-colored feathers can serve as

      _____, while bright feathers call attention to birds.

   c. Holding her arms closer to her body gave

      the runner a more _____ shape.

1. Explain why the discovery of Archaeopteryx fossils and the fossil of Compsognathus led Thomas Huxley to believe that birds and dinosaurs lived at the same time.

_____

_____

2. Compare Velociraptor with today's birds.

_____

_____

3. Reread the paragraph in the selection with an ✘ next to it. On the lines below, write a sentence that states the paragraph's main idea.

_____

_____

4. Explain how paleontologists know that the feathered dinosaurs found in China could not fly.

_____

_____

SKILL FOCUS: CLASSIFYING

A. Complete the chart below by listing characteristics that make each type of theropod different from other types.

Types of Theropods			
Word	Size	How Old?	Bones/Covering
Velociraptor			
Unenlagia			
Caudipteryx			
Sinosauropteryx			
Sinornithosaurus			

Reading-Writing Connection
Which dinosaur in the selection did you find the most interesting? On a separate sheet of paper, write a paragraph that gives reasons for your choice.

Skill: Word Problems

BACKGROUND INFORMATION

"Reading Word Problems" will help you solve math word problems. A math word problem is any practical, situational problem that you can use addition, subtraction, multiplication, or division to solve. Some word problems require only one math operation. Others require two.

SKILL FOCUS: Word Problems

You can solve most math word problems with this simple five-step process.

1. **Read the problem.** Be sure that you are familiar with all the words in the problem, including labels such as *pounds*, *grams*, *miles*, and *kilometers*. All problems ask a question or ask for information that is not given. Picture in your mind the information that is given in relation to the information that you need to figure out. Reread the problem.

2. **Decide how to find the answer.** It usually helps to write a sentence about each fact that is given in the problem. After you determine the information needed to solve the problem, decide which mathematical operations to use. Do you need to carry out one operation or two? If the problem requires only one operation, write a mathematical sentence you can use to find the answer. If you need to use two operations, write two mathematical sentences. Be sure to look for key words in the problem to help you decide which operations to use.

3. **Estimate the answer.** Use rounded numbers to estimate the answer to each mathematical sentence you are using to solve the problem.

4. **Carry out the plan.** Solve each of the mathematical sentences you have written. If there are two mathematical sentences, you will usually need the answer from the first one to solve the second one.

5. **Reread the problem.** Does your answer to the problem make sense? How close is it to your estimate? If it is not close, rethink the problem. Look for any errors in writing the mathematical sentences or in carrying out the operations.

▷ Read the following math word problem. Then answer the questions below.

Toni cares for 5 circus elephants. All together, the elephants eat about 600 pounds of hay a day. Toni has 800 bales of hay, each of which weighs about 50 pounds. How long will this hay last?

1. What question does the problem ask?

   _____

2. How can you figure out how many pounds of hay Toni has in all? _____

3. How can you figure out how long the total amount of hay will last? _____

WORD CLUES

As you read word problems, look for key words that are clues to what operations you need to use. Key words such as *and*, *total*, *all together*, and *twice as much* tell you that the answer will be larger than the other numbers in the problem. You will have to add or multiply.

The key words *difference*, *less*, *each*, *per*, and *divided* usually tell you that the answer will be less than at least one of the numbers in the problem. Often you will either subtract or divide to find the answer.

The words *find the average* are a special clue. They signal that you need to add and then divide by the number of items you added.

▷ Circle the key words in the problem below that show that you need to divide.

Toni also cares for 5 circus lions. Each week, she orders 420 pounds of meat for them. If she divides the meat equally among them, how much meat does each lion eat per day?

> ### Strategy Tip
>
> As you read "Reading Word Problems," decide whether you need to use one or two operations to solve each word problem. Also look for key words that suggest which operations to use.

Reading Word Problems

In order to protect wildlife, scientists need to know important details about how different types of animals live. Much of the research about animal life involves using numbers to solve word problems.

Use the following five steps to solve word problems.

1. Read the problem.
2. Decide how to find the answer.
3. Estimate the answer.
4. Carry out the plan.
5. Reread the problem.

Read the Problem

In 1964, George Schaller studied the animals in Kanha National Park in India. One of the most common animals in the park was the axis deer. The largest herd Schaller saw in one month numbered 175 deer. The average herd that month numbered only 32.4 deer. What is the difference between the sizes of the largest herd and the average herd?

Read the problem again. Are there any words that you do not know? If so, look them up to find their meanings. Be aware that the proper nouns, or names, used in the problem usually cannot be found in a dictionary. The phrase *axis deer* is the name of a kind of deer.

Does this problem ask a question or tell you to do something? Often questions are asked or instructions given in the last sentence of the problem. The last sentence of this problem asks a question. *What is the difference between the sizes of the largest herd and the average herd?*

Decide How to Find the Answer

Of the three numbers mentioned in the problem, one is a date, and it is not used in solving the problem. The other two numbers are used in solving the problem. Write a short sentence about each number.

1. *The largest herd had 175 deer.*
2. *The average herd had 32.4 deer.*

Although the word *average* is used in the problem, you are not asked to find the average. It is given to you. The clue to what you are asked to find is in the phrase *what is the difference*. This phrase tells you that you need to subtract. The largest herd is greater than the average herd. Write a mathematical sentence, or equation, that shows the difference between the two herds. Let n be the unknown number that is the answer to the question.

$$175 - 32.4 = n$$

The solution to the equation will answer the question *What is the difference between the sizes of the largest herd and the average herd?* The letter n represents a number of deer. Because the average is a decimal, the number of deer in the answer will also be a decimal.

Estimate the Answer

In addition or subtraction, the most common way to estimate is to round each number to the highest place in the smaller number. In this problem, the highest place for the smaller number, 32.4, is the tens, so it is rounded to 30. The larger number, 175, is also rounded to the tens place, or 180. The following equation can be used for the estimate.

$$180 - 30 = n$$

Your estimate is 150.

Carry Out the Plan

$$\begin{array}{r} 175.0 \\ -\underline{32.4} \\ 142.6 \end{array}$$

Notice that it is helpful to rewrite 175 as 175.0 before subtracting.

Reread the Problem

The difference between the sizes of the largest herd and the average herd is 142.6 deer. In this case, the answer is close to the estimate. If your answer is not close to your estimate, you should figure out whether you made a mistake in writing the equation or in carrying out the operation.

Use the five steps to solve this problem.

Read: *Tony Sinclair estimated that in the Serengeti National Park in Africa, about 52,000 wildebeest, a large antelope, die or are killed every year. About 11,400 are killed by lions, while hyenas kill about 7,500. The others are victims of disease or old age. Find out how many wildebeest die as a result of old age or disease.*

The problem does not ask a question, but the last sentence tells you what to do. *Find out how many wildebeest die as a result of old age or disease.*

Decide: There are three numbers in the problem. Each stands for a fact about the wildebeest in the Serengeti Park. Write a sentence for each fact.

1. *About 52,000 die or are killed each year.*
2. *Lions kill about 11,400.*
3. *Hyenas kill about 7,500.*

The information you are to find is the *difference* between the total number that die or are killed and the *sum* of the wildebeest killed by lions and hyenas. Write equations that show how to solve the problem.

$$52,000 - s = d$$
$$11,400 + 7,500 = s$$

Which equation should you solve first? You must solve the equation that has one variable first. A variable is a letter that stands for a number.

Estimate: In addition and subtraction, you round to the highest place in the smaller number. In the equation $11,400 + 7,500 = s$, the smaller number is 7,500. The highest place in 7,500 is thousands, so round to thousands.

$$11,000 + 8,000 = s$$

A good estimate for s is 19,000.

Now round in the other equation. What is the smaller number? What is its highest place?

$$50,000 - 20,000 = d$$

A good estimate for the answer to the problem is 30,000 wildebeest.

Carry Out:

$$11,400 + 7,500 = 18,900$$
$$52,000 - 18,900 = 33,100$$

Reread: *As a result of disease or old age, 33,100 wildebeest die each year.* This is close to the estimate of 30,000 wildebeest.

COMPREHENSION

1. In which sentence of a problem are you most likely to find the question or the directions for what you need to do?

   _____

   _____

2. Which step do you complete after you have decided on a plan?

   _____

   _____

3. **a.** When you estimate in addition or subtraction, which number do you use to determine which place you should round to?

   _____

   b. In that number, which place do you round to?

   _____

4. When you are subtracting a decimal from a whole number, what should you do to the whole number?

   _____

   _____

5. Suppose that two equations are to be solved for a problem and that one equation contains one variable while the other equation contains two variables. Which equation do you solve first?

_____

_____

6. What is the last thing that you should do in solving a word problem?

_____

_____

CRITICAL THINKING

1. In the problems in the selection, the letters *n*, *d*, and *s* are used as variables. What might these letters stand for?

_____

_____

_____

2. Give a reason why estimating the answer is an important step in solving word problems.

_____

_____

_____

SKILL FOCUS: WORD PROBLEMS

Follow the steps to solve each word problem.

1. **Read:** In 1968, George Schaller timed a tiger that was walking at normal speed. It traveled at 4 kilometers per hour. How many kilometers can a tiger cover in 12 hours if it continues at that speed?

Decide: _____

Estimate: _____

Carry Out: _____

Reread: _____

2. **Read:** Robert Yerkes tried to find how many tries different animals would need to discover in which one of nine boxes he had hidden their food. For each animal, he hid the food in the same box every try. Yerkes found that the crow took 50 tries, the rat took 170 tries, the pig took 50 tries, and the monkey took 132 tries. Find the average number of tries needed for the animals listed.

Decide: _____

Estimate: _____

Carry Out: _____

Reread: _____

3. **Read:** One of the smallest animals at birth is the opossum, which averages only 2 grams in weight. If 13 opossums are born at one time, what is their total weight?

   Decide: _____

   Estimate: _____

   Carry Out: _____

   Reread: _____

   _____

4. **Read:** A giraffe weighs about 38.5 kilograms at birth. How many newborn opossums (Problem 3) would it take to weigh as much as one newborn giraffe? (Hint: 1 kilogram = 1,000 grams)

   Decide: _____

   Estimate: _____

   Carry Out: _____

   Reread: _____

   _____

5. **Read:** A hibernating woodchuck breathes only once every 5 minutes. If a woodchuck hibernates for 2 months (60 days), how many breaths does it take?

   Decide: _____

   Estimate: _____

   Carry Out: _____

   Reread: _____

   _____

6. **Read:** Cheetahs can weigh from 75 to 150 pounds. Bengal tigers can weigh from 396 to 583 pounds. How much more does the heaviest Bengal tiger weigh than the heaviest cheetah?

   Decide: _____

   Estimate: _____

   Carry Out: _____

   Reread: _____

   _____

Reading-Writing Connection

On a separate sheet of paper, write a word problem about animals that live in your area. Exchange papers with a partner, and solve each other's problems.

Skill: Syllables

You have already learned three rules for dividing words into syllables. Here are three more rules.

RULE 4: Words With Two Consonants Between Two Sounded Vowels

A word that has two consonants between two sounded vowels is usually divided into syllables between the two consonants.

cactus   cac tus

A. Divide each word below into two syllables by writing each syllable separately on the line next to the word.

1. public _____
2. carbon _____
3. limber _____
4. walnut _____
5. contain _____
6. bargain _____
7. margin _____
8. engine _____

9. border _____
10. mixture _____
11. fertile _____
12. garden _____
13. chapter _____
14. oblong _____
15. discuss _____
16. surface _____

RULE 5: Words With One Consonant Between Two Sounded Vowels

Rule 5a: A word that has one consonant between two sounded vowels, with the first vowel long, is usually divided into syllables before the consonant.

bacon   ba con

Rule 5b: A word that has one consonant between two sounded vowels, with the first vowel short, is usually divided into syllables after the consonant.

cabin   cab in

B. Say each of the words below to yourself. If the first vowel is long, use Rule 5a to divide the word into two syllables. If the first vowel is short, use Rule 5b. Write each syllable separately on the line next to the word.

1. tenant _____
2. hotel _____
3. camel _____
4. climate _____
5. modern _____
6. laser _____
7. topic _____
8. fever _____

9. minor _____
10. famine _____
11. limit _____
12. native _____
13. solid _____
14. canine _____
15. critic _____
16. moment _____

RULE 6: Words With Blends

The word *between* has two consonants between two sounded vowels. Because *tw* is a consonant blend, you do not divide between the two consonants. The letters *tw* should be treated as a single consonant.

be tween

In a word that has three consonants between two vowels, two of the consonants may be a blend or a digraph. You treat the blend or digraph as one consonant. For example, *athlete* has a *th* digraph. You divide the word between the digraph and the consonant.

ath lete

C. Circle the blend or digraph in each of the words below. Then divide the word into two syllables by writing each syllable separately on the line next to the word.

1. secret _____   5. concrete _____

2. marshal _____   6. complex _____

3. poultry _____   7. zebra _____

4. machine _____   8. surprise _____

When a word ends in *-le*, the *-le* and the consonant before it make up a syllable, as in *gen tle*.

D. Divide each word below into two syllables by writing each syllable separately on the line next to the word.

1. bugle _____   5. ladle _____

2. ankle _____   6. noble _____

3. tangle _____   7. uncle _____

4. staple _____   8. candle _____

E. Divide each word below into syllables. Write the syllables separately on the line to the right of the word. On the line to the left of the word, write the number of the rule you used to divide each word. Some words have three syllables. The first one is done for you.

1. __4, 5a__ consonant ___con so nant___   10. _____ phantom _____

2. _____ danger _____   11. _____ petal _____

3. _____ carpenter _____   12. _____ interest _____

4. _____ member _____   13. _____ patient _____

5. _____ fragrance _____   14. _____ particle _____

6. _____ absolute _____   15. _____ orthodox _____

7. _____ holster _____   16. _____ lemon _____

8. _____ Atlantic _____   17. _____ crumple _____

9. _____ legal _____   18. _____ embargo _____

Skill: Main Idea and Supporting Details

Paragraphs are packed with information. Knowing how to find a paragraph's main idea and important supporting details helps you understand what you read. The **main idea** expresses the subject of a paragraph. Many paragraphs have two kinds of supporting details: major details and minor details. A **major detail** is a supporting idea that is an important example or fact about the main idea. A paragraph usually contains more than one major detail.

The major details of a paragraph help develop or complete the thought expressed by the main idea. The main idea and major details work together as a unit. You could say that the main idea depends on major details.

Not all the details in a paragraph are major details. Paragraphs often contain details that are not as important to the main idea. They are called **minor details**. They explain or tell more about the major details. The minor details add interest to the main idea, but the main idea does not depend on them.

The paragraph in the next column is about the gaits, or movements, of two different animals. The diagram below the paragraph shows its main idea and major details.

Gaits, or the ways in which animals move their legs, differ in many ways. A moose trots when it is in a hurry. When trotting, the moose moves a front leg and the opposite hind leg at the same time. In this way, two diagonal legs are always in contact with the ground, giving the animal's body stable support. A camel, on the other hand, paces when it is in a hurry. In pacing, both legs on the same side of the body move together. This gait is useful only on flat land because it is not as stable as a trot.

In the diagram below, the sentences that explain how the legs move when trotting and pacing are not listed as major details. They are minor details that explain the major details.

Main Idea

> Gaits, or the way in which animals move their legs, differ in many ways.

Major Details

> A moose trots when it is in a hurry.

> A camel paces when it is in a hurry.

As you read the following paragraphs, look for each paragraph's main idea and major details.

1. Four-legged animals have many different gaits. The slowest of the gaits, the walk, can be performed by all four-legged animals except kangaroos, wallabies, and some monkeys. Animals with short legs cannot gallop, because at some point in the stride all four feet must be off the ground. Only long-legged animals can push themselves high enough to gallop. A much less common gait is the

The springbok is a gazelle that pronks.

The springbok can also run quickly.

pronk, in which all four of an animal's legs take off and land nearly together. Many deer and antelope use this gait.

2. How fast an animal is able to move depends on the length of its legs and on its body size and weight. Animals with long legs can take greater strides and move faster than shorter-legged animals. The deer, with its long legs and slimmer body, can move much faster than the pig. The pig, with its short legs and proportionally heavier body, cannot move as quickly. Massive animals with long legs, however, can often move very quickly despite their huge size. Such animals include bison and elephants.

3. The large front legs of the praying mantis enable it to catch prey, or living food. The mole uses its front legs to shovel through soil underground. It eats any earthworms it finds along the way. Many grasshoppers chirp by scraping together their third set of legs. The cassowary, a flightless bird, uses spurs on its legs to defend itself. Thus, animals use their legs for a variety of functions.

Complete the diagram below for each paragraph. In the box labeled *Main Idea*, write the sentence that states the main idea as it appears in the paragraph. Use your own words for filling in the boxes labeled *Major Details*.

Paragraph 1

Main Idea

Major Details

Paragraph 2

Main Idea

Major Details

Paragraph 3

Main Idea

Major Details

Skill: Shopping Online

Today there are many ways to shop. You can go to a store, purchase items over the phone, or use the **Internet**. Many of your favorite stores also offer **online** shopping on the Internet. These online stores let you shop anywhere you can access the **Web**.

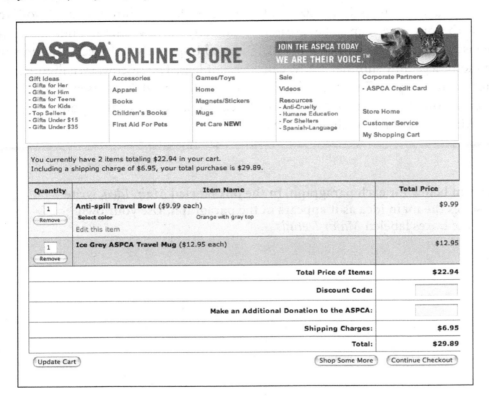

A. Study the online Shopping Cart page above. Use the information from the Web page to answer each question.

1. What is the name of this Internet store? _____

2. **a.** What products are in the Shopping Cart? _____

   _____

   b. What does each cost? _____

3. If the quantity changes, how can you find the new purchase total? _____

4. How could you continue shopping for a goldfish aquarium? _____

   _____

5. Why is the Total at the bottom of the page different from Total Price of Items? _____

   _____

Once you have found the item you want to buy, you are ready to check out. Steps for checking out at online stores may not all be exactly the same.

Most online stores require you to create a **username** and **password**. You create a username to identify yourself on the Internet. A password is a secret code you use to confirm your identity. Providing your username and password gives the store a record of your personal information. It also protects that information so others cannot use your account—and therefore your money—to order products.

B. Study the online Checkout page above. Use the information from the Web page to answer each question.

6. What is the name of the person shopping? _____

7. How could this person save his account information for future shopping? _____
   _____

8. Is it safe to give credit card information on this Web site? How can you tell? _____
   _____

9. **a.** What information is required in order to buy something from this Web site? _____
   _____

   b. How do you know which fields to fill in? _____

10. What could you do if you did not know what a Verification Code is? _____
    _____

LESSON 16
Skill: Character

BACKGROUND INFORMATION

"No Ordinary Baseball Player" is a biography of the legendary baseball player Roberto Clemente, the first Latino player in the Baseball Hall of Fame. Each year, a group of sports writers elects a few of the best baseball players to the Hall of Fame in Cooperstown, New York. Most players who receive this honor have been retired from baseball for many years. Roberto Clemente was so widely admired, however, that he was elected to the Hall of Fame less than a year after his death.

SKILL FOCUS: Character

Characters are the people in a story. Most stories have one **main character** who plays the major part in the story's action. Often the main character wants to achieve a goal or solve a problem.

In fiction, the characters are invented by the author. A biography, however, tells the story of a real person's life. As with fictional characters, we learn about the subjects of biographies from what they say and do. Through their words and actions, characters reveal their **character traits**, or personal qualities such as honesty, greed, determination, compassion, or laziness.

The following questions will help you understand the main character of a story or biography.

1. Who is the main character?

2. What goal or problem does the main character face?

3. What does the main character do to achieve the goal or to solve the problem?

4. What character traits does the main character reveal through his or her words and actions?

▶ Write the name of a person you admire in the center of the Idea Web. In the outer circles, describe the person's goals, actions, words, and traits.

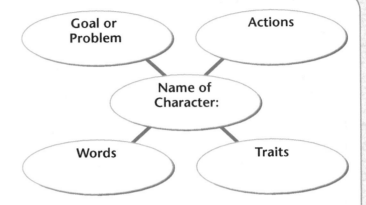

CONTEXT CLUES: Details

The **details** in a sentence can often help you figure out the meaning of a new word. In the sentences below, look for details that explain the meaning of the underlined word.

*A Central American country had been **devastated** by an earthquake. The tremors were violent enough to destroy buildings, reduce villages to ashes, and leave other property in ruin.*

If you don't know the meaning of *devastated*, the details about destroyed buildings and villages will help you figure it out. *Devastated* means "totally destroyed or ruined."

▶ Read the following sentences. Circle the details that explain the meaning of the underlined word.

*Clemente's father, Melchor Clemente, worked as a **foreman** at a sugar cane plantation, overseeing workers in the cane fields.*

In the selection, use details to figure out the meanings of *machetes*, *arduous*, and *exasperated*.

Strategy Tip

As you read "No Ordinary Baseball Player," think about how Roberto Clemente's character traits are revealed through words and actions.

No Ordinary Baseball Player

The cargo plane rumbled down the runway at an airport near San Juan, Puerto Rico. In the humid evening air was a salty tang from the Atlantic Ocean, lying just beyond the city. It was New Year's Eve, 1972. The plane was on a mission of mercy, carrying medical supplies to aid the people of Nicaragua, a Central American country that had been devastated by an earthquake. The tremors were violent enough to destroy buildings, reduce villages to ashes, and leave other property in ruin. Many Nicaraguans who had survived were seriously injured. Many were homeless.

Roberto Clemente won the batting championship four times.

As the plane took off, a bystander noticed flames licking at one of the engines. The plane began to wobble as it headed out to sea. The pilot radioed that the plane was turning back to the airport. Then, eyewitnesses said, the plane suddenly dove into the ocean and disappeared.

News of the crash flashed across the island— and throughout the Americas. Roberto Clemente, a professional baseball star and hero of Puerto Rico, was among those killed in the accident.

It was Clemente who had organized the shipment of supplies to Nicaragua and who had decided to go along on the flight. Part of the plane's cargo was a pair of artificial legs for a Nicaraguan boy who had lost his own. Clemente wanted to be there to make sure that the boy got his new legs.

Why had this baseball superstar organized a mercy mission? Friends said it was typical of him. He was no ordinary person. From his childhood, they noted, Roberto Clemente was someone special.

Clemente was born in 1934 in Carolina, a lovely old town on the island of Puerto Rico. He was the youngest of seven children in a family that did not have much money.

Clemente's father, Melchor Clemente, worked as a foreman at a sugar cane plantation, overseeing workers in the cane fields. From a distance, cane fields appear to be beautiful, with their soft green leaves topped by snowy white tassels. Up close, the cane fields give a very different impression. The cane grows in tall, woody stems that are as thick and as tough as a young tree. The cane workers use heavy, swordlike knives with broad blades to chop the stalks. Even with the aid of these <u>machetes</u> (mə SHET eez), chopping sugar cane is an <u>arduous</u> task.

Experience quickly teaches cane cutters how to work hard, and Clemente's father taught all his children not to fear hard work. He told them that there was dignity in pushing themselves to do their best. Hard work would teach them honor and self-respect—values that would be important to them throughout their lives.

Like many of his friends, Clemente grew up playing baseball. Baseball may be the national pastime in most of the United States, but it is the national rage in Puerto Rico. After all, it can be played year-round in the island's sunny, warm climate.

As a small boy, Clemente played so much ball, according to his mother, that he would forget to eat. His forgetfulness displeased his mother very much. One time, his mother grew so <u>exasperated</u> that she tried to burn his bat—but nothing could stop Roberto Clemente.

Clemente didn't have much money for equipment. He often played with a cheap rubber ball, which he threw against a wall for hours on end. Sometimes, when he didn't have a ball, he would hit tin cans for batting practice.

By the time Clemente was 18 years old, his long hours of practice and play were beginning to pay off. He was playing baseball for a professional team in Puerto Rico. He could throw a ball fast, he was a great fielder, and he could hit. Scouts from major-league teams began to look him over.

In 1954, Clemente had a chance to prove himself to a major-league team. The Brooklyn Dodgers, the same team that had hired his idol Jackie Robinson, hired Clemente. The Dodgers sent him to play with their "farm team" based in Montreal, Canada.

The following season, the Pittsburgh Pirates hired Clemente, and he got to play in the major leagues for the first time. He spent the rest of his career with the Pirates.

A friend of Clemente's once said that he played every game as if it were the World Series. Once, early in his career, Roberto made a spectacular catch by jumping up against a stadium fence. His belt got caught in the fence, and he hung there until his teammates got him down! To Clemente, making the catch meant everything.

Clemente gave so much of himself to every play that he was often injured. Fans may cheer when an outfielder makes a spectacular catch against the stadium wall or dives into the turf to snag a grounder. Yet few realize how hard the wall is or how fast the player is running when he hits it. After a few years, Clemente had so many breaks, tears, pulls, and aches in his body that he was sometimes unable to play.

Because his performance when he did play was so good, some fans and sportswriters became critical and accused him of being lazy. "He can't be that sick!" they would say. "He looked great on the field yesterday. If he could play so well yesterday, why is he on the disabled list today?" They didn't realize how hard Clemente fought the pain of his injuries every time he played. He made playing look easy, but it wasn't.

The fans also didn't realize that even though he was often injured, Clemente played more games than any other Pittsburgh Pirate. In 15 years, he never missed an opening game. The fans' attitude bothered Clemente's sense of dignity and self-respect. Hadn't his parents taught him to always work hard?

Clemente believed that he had a special responsibility. He was a Puerto Rican. He believed that he had to show the world how talented, hard-working, and caring the people of his island were. Clemente also wanted to prove himself by throwing farther, hitting harder, and running faster than other players.

He had little trouble proving himself. In 18 years, he led the National League in batting four times and he was elected Most Valuable Player once. He received the Gold Glove award for his fielding 12 times.

In the 1971 World Series, Clemente really showed his stuff. The Pirates were up against the Baltimore Orioles, a tough team to beat. The first two games went to the Orioles, and the losses scared some of the Pittsburgh players. Few teams that lose the first two games of a series go on to win it.

Clemente didn't let this fact bother him. He played his best, getting at least one hit in each game. His fielding was great. He encouraged the other players.

The seventh and last game of the series was very close. Three innings went by without a score on either side until Clemente suddenly hit a home run. Many of his teammates say that run helped them feel like winners. They played hard and kept the other team from scoring more than one run. In the eighth inning, the Pirates scored again. They won, two to one! Clemente was chosen the outstanding player of that World Series.

Yet the years of hard playing had taken their toll on Clemente. At one time, he had thought of retiring after the 1971 World Series. When the Pirates won, however, he decided to stay on. He told a news reporter, "Money means nothing to me, but I love competition."

Besides, he had one more goal to achieve: to have 3,000 hits in his career. He had only 118 hits to go.

So Clemente went back to Pittsburgh for the 1972 baseball season. As he said, "If you have a chance and don't make the most of it, you are wasting your time on this Earth." On the night of September 30, his dream came true. Roberto Clemente got hit number 3,000!

When the season ended, Clemente went home to his wife and three sons in Puerto Rico. One of his many plans was to build a "Sports City," where the children of Puerto Rico could get free training in sports.

Before he could really get started, however, Nicaragua was struck by an earthquake. Thousands of people were without homes, medical help, food, and clothing. Clemente went right to work. He organized a relief operation with his business friends. He found a plane to fly emergency supplies to Nicaragua. For a week, he was so involved in getting emergency supplies to the earthquake victims that he hardly ate or slept. Finally on December 31, 1972, the plane that was to take him to Nicaragua was ready. The cargo was aboard, and the plane was fueled up. Clemente kissed his wife goodbye and boarded the plane. Soon after they parted, the plane took off. Minutes later, Roberto Clemente was dead.

On August 6, 1973, Roberto Clemente was elected to the Baseball Hall of Fame. The first Latino player to be elected, Clemente was chosen for his outstanding baseball achievements and for his inspiring concern for others.

COMPREHENSION

1. Who is the main character of this story?

   _____

   _____

   _____

2. What was the effect of Clemente's long hours of practice as a boy?

   _____

   _____

   _____

3. How was Clemente like his father?

   _____

   _____

   _____

4. List two of Roberto Clemente's major baseball achievements.

   _____

   _____

   _____

5. Number the following events in the order in which they took place.

   _____ a. Clemente gets hit 3,000.

   _____ b. The Pittsburgh Pirates hire Roberto Clemente.

   _____ c. Clemente is chosen the outstanding player of the 1971 World Series.

   _____ d. Clemente becomes the first Latino player elected to the Baseball Hall of Fame.

6. List two details from the story that support this statement. *Roberto Clemente cared about others.*

   _____

   _____

   _____

7. Why was Clemente flying to Nicaragua?

   _____

   _____

   _____

8. Circle the letter of the sentence that best expresses the main idea of this story.

   a. Many Puerto Ricans could be baseball stars.

   b. Hard work and talent helped Clemente achieve his goals.

   c. Talent is more important to success than hard work.

   d. All baseball players are good people.

9. Complete each sentence with the correct word.

   machetes   arduous   exasperated

   a. Chopping sugar cane is a difficult and _____ task.

   b. Large steel _____ are used to cut heavy jungle vines.

   c. The young comedian's constant joking _____ his family.

CRITICAL THINKING

1. Why might it have been important to Clemente to take the artificial legs to the Nicaraguan boy himself?

   _____

   _____

2. Some fans thought Clemente was using his injuries as an excuse not to play. State a fact that proves them wrong.

   _____

   _____

3. Explain why it was so important for Clemente to work harder than anyone else.

   _____

   _____

4. Describe how players might feel after losing the first two of seven games in a World Series.

   _____

   _____

SKILL FOCUS: CHARACTER

To answer questions 1 through 4, choose from among the following character traits: compassion, determination, and pride.

1. a. Which trait does Clemente show by working so hard to achieve his goal of becoming an outstanding baseball player? _____

   b. Which trait is evident in Clemente's feeling about being Puerto Rican? _____

   c. Which trait is evident in Clemente's wanting to help victims? _____

2. **a.** Which trait is demonstrated in the following passage? _____

Clemente also believed that he had a special responsibility. He was a Puerto Rican. He believed that he had to show the world how talented, hard-working, and caring the people of his island were.

b. Go back to the selection and underline another passage that demonstrates this same trait.

3. **a.** Which trait is demonstrated in the following passage? _____

Roberto wanted to throw farther, hit harder, and run faster than other players to prove himself.

b. Go back to the selection and draw a box around another passage that demonstrates this trait.

4. Roberto Clemente made the following statement. What quality or qualities does it reveal about him?

"If you have a chance and don't make the most of it, you are wasting your time on this Earth."

_____

_____

5. Which better demonstrates Clemente's caring, his aiding the Nicaraguan earthquake victims or his ambition to be a great baseball player? Explain.

_____

_____

_____

6. In what ways was Roberto Clemente more than just a baseball star?

_____

_____

_____

7. In a few sentences, tell why you would or would not have liked to have had Roberto Clemente for a friend.

_____

_____

_____

Reading-Writing Connection

In your opinion, what was Roberto Clemente's best quality? On a separate sheet of paper, write a paragraph describing how you could demonstrate this quality in your own life.

Skill: Using Statistics

BACKGROUND INFORMATION

"The Changing Face of America" explains some of the findings of the 2000 Census. According to the U.S. Constitution, the United States must conduct an official population count every 10 years. The first U.S. Census took place in 1790, when the nation's population was less than 4 million. In 2000, Census workers found that the nation's population had grown to more than 280 million people.

SKILL FOCUS: Using Statistics

Statistics are numerical facts, often presented in tables or graphs. People collect statistics on many different topics, from scientific data to population figures to the prices of gasoline and groceries. Since statistics often show important changes or trends, workers in governments and in businesses use them to make predictions and draw conclusions.

Statistics can show important changes, but they do not explain the reasons for the changes. For example, statistics can show that people are moving to a certain area of the country or buying a particular product. By themselves, however, the numbers cannot explain *why* these changes are occurring. Therefore, other information is often needed to interpret and use statistics effectively.

Use these steps when reading and interpreting a selection that includes a table of statistics.

1. Read the title of the table and the labels on its rows and columns to identify the type of information shown in the table.

2. Practice reading the statistics. Statistics often involve numbers in the millions. Make sure you can read these numbers correctly.

3. Find relationships among the numbers on the table. Compare and contrast numbers in different rows and columns.

4. Use the statistics and the text of the selection to draw conclusions. You can also use them to evaluate the conclusions made by the author.

5. Use the statistics to make predictions or forecasts about future trends.

▶ Read the following statistics from the 2000 Census. Then answer the question.

2000 U.S. Census	
Total U.S. population	281,421,906
U.S. population 18 and over	209,128,094

About how many people under the age of 18 were living in the United States in 2000?

_____

CONTEXT CLUES: Appositive Phrases

Sometimes the meaning of a new word follows the word and is set off by commas or dashes. This type of context clue is called an **appositive phrase**.

Find the appositive phrase that explains the meaning of the underlined word in the following sentence.

> *As the United States enters the twenty-first century, its population is more **diverse**, or varied.*

If you don't know the meaning of *diverse*, the appositive phrase that follows it can help you. *Diverse* means "varied."

▶ In the sentence below, circle the appositive phrase that explains the meaning of the underlined word.

> *Census workers make **projections**, or forecasts based on present trends, about future population growth.*

As you read, use appositive phrases to help you understand the meanings of the underlined words *demographers*, *mandated*, and *distribution*.

> ### Strategy Tip
>
> Use the information in "The Changing Face of America" to help you interpret the statistics in the tables and graph.

The Changing Face of America

As the United States enters the twenty-first century, its population is more diverse, or varied, than ever. The American population today is a rich mix of people of different races and national origins. It also spans a broader age range than ever before. The U.S. **Census** (SEN səs) gives a "snapshot" of the people living in the United States. In the year 2000, the total population of the United States was 281.4 million. That was up from 249 million just 10 years earlier.

When filling out Census forms, Americans check a box to indicate their race. Most Americans described themselves as belonging to either the black, white, or Asian races. More than 35 million Americans also described themselves as Hispanic. Hispanics are Americans whose families originally came from Spanish-speaking countries. Hispanic is not a race, but an **ethnicity** (eth NIS ə tee), or a cultural group with a language and customs in common. A Hispanic person can be Hispanic and white, Hispanic and black, or Hispanic and Asian. Figure 1 shows some of the results of the 2000 Census.

2000 U.S. Population by Race and Ethnicity		
Group	**2000 Population**	**Percentage of Growth Since 1990**
Hispanic	35,305,818	57.9%
Black (non-Hispanic)	35,383,751	21.1%
White (non-Hispanic)	198,177,900	5.3%
American Indian/ Alaska Native (non-Hispanic)	3,444,700	92%
Asian (non-Hispanic)	11,579,494	74.3%
Native Hawaiian/ Pacific Islander	748,149	129.6%
Other	1,770,645	610.8%

FIGURE 1. This table shows different groups within the U.S. population in 2000 and how they have grown since 1990.

Hispanic Americans

The number of Hispanic Americans came as a surprise to demographers, scientists who study population statistics. In the 1990 Census, the number of Hispanics was only 22 million. By 2000, the Hispanic population had grown by almost 58 percent to 35.3 million. Hispanics in the United States come from many different countries. In the 2000 Census, Hispanics identified their countries or regions of origin, as shown in Figure 2.

National Origins of Hispanics in the United States, 2000	
Cuba	4%
Puerto Rico	9%
Mexico	66.1%
Central and South America	14.5%
Other	6.4%

FIGURE 2. This table shows the percentage of Hispanics from different parts of the world that lived in the United States in 2000.

Cubans make up 4 percent of the Hispanic population in the United States. In the early 1960s, a revolution brought Fidel Castro to power in Cuba. As a result, hundreds of thousands of Cubans fled their island homeland. Many settled in Florida. By the 1980s, Miami had become the center of the Cuban American community.

Puerto Ricans make up 9 percent of the Hispanic population. The island of Puerto Rico is a territory belonging to the United States. Its residents are U.S. citizens, but they are not represented in Congress. Instead, the island is a commonwealth, a republic with its own government. Many Puerto Ricans moved to the mainland United States after World War II to find jobs. Most often, they settled in New York City, Chicago, or other northern cities.

Mexicans make up more than 66 percent of the Hispanic population in the United States. Mexicans have lived for centuries in the area that is now the southwestern United States. The most important

SOCIAL STUDIES

centers of Mexican American culture are the Southwest and California.

The recent growth in the Hispanic population is mainly due to increasing immigration from Mexico and other countries in Central and South America. In recent years, many people from these countries have come to the United States to find work. Some do not plan to stay. They hope to return to their homelands someday. About 7 percent of those who arrived during the 1990s became U.S. citizens.

Large families have also boosted the Hispanic population. About 31 percent of Hispanic families living in the United States have five or more people in them. Among non-Hispanic whites, only 12 percent of families have more than five members.

The Hispanic population is also young. More than 70 percent of the Hispanics in the United States are under the age of 40. So even if immigration slows, the Hispanic population will continue to rise.

Census workers make projections, or forecasts based on present trends, about future population growth. According to these projections, Hispanics may soon be the nation's largest minority group. By 2050, the number of Hispanics could triple to 98 million people, and Hispanics would make up about 25 percent of the American population.

Asian Americans

Asian Americans are another rapidly growing minority. In 2000, 11.5 million Americans identified themselves as Asian or as Asian and some other race. That was an increase of more than 74 percent from 1990. Chinese Americans make up the largest group of Asians—about 2.4 million people. Their numbers increased 48 percent from 1990 to 2000.

Among Asian Americans, the biggest increase was in people from India. The Census labels this group *Asian Indian*. From 1990 to 2000, the population of Asian Indians in the United States rose 106 percent, to almost 1.7 million. The Vietnamese population in the United States also grew, increasing 83 percent.

According to Census projections, the number of Asian Americans will triple by 2050. If so, about 38 million Asian Americans will live in the United States by then. They will make up about 9 percent of the total population.

African Americans

African Americans have always been the largest minority group in the United States. According to the 2000 Census, the number of non-Hispanic blacks (African Americans) grew by more than 21 percent during the 1990s. The total number was about 35.4 million. About one in 20 African Americans described himself or herself as both black and one other race.

Foreign-Born Americans

Today, about 20 percent of all elementary and high school students in the United States have at least one foreign-born parent. The Census data shows that more than 27 million Americans were born outside the United States. This is about 10 percent of the population. The circle graph in Figure 3 shows where these Americans were born.

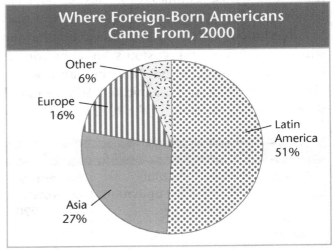

FIGURE 3. This circle graph shows the percentage of foreign-born Americans who come from various places around the world.

Where Americans Live

The American population is growing faster in the West and the South than in other regions of the nation. The western states had the largest percentage growth from 1990 to 2000. In 2000, they had nearly 20 percent more residents than they did in 1990. The South recorded a 17.3 percent growth rate. These two regions outpaced the Midwest's 8 percent growth rate and the Northeast's 5.5 percent. The table in Figure 4 shows the ten fastest-growing states are in the West or the South.

Selected State Populations, 1990 and 2000			
State	1990 Population	2000 Population	% Change
Nevada	1,201,833	1,998,257	66.3
Arizona	3,655,228	5,130,632	40.0
Colorado	3,294,394	4,301,261	30.6
Utah	1,722,850	2,233,169	29.6
Idaho	1,006,749	1,293,953	28.5
Georgia	6,478,216	8,186,456	26.4
Florida	12,937,926	15,982,378	23.5
Texas	16,986,510	20,851,820	22.8
N. Carolina	6,628,637	8,049,313	21.4
Washington	4,866,692	5,894,121	21.1

FIGURE 4. **This table compares the population in 1990 and 2000 in various states.**

How Old Are Americans?

The Census notes the ages of everyone in the United States. In 2000, about 72 million U.S. residents were under the age of 18. That was 26 percent of the total population. Another 35 million—13 percent of the total—were 65 years of age or older. One of the fastest-growing segments of the U.S. population was people over the age of 100. More than 65,000 people over the age of 100 lived in the United States in 2000. This marked an increase of 81 percent from 1990.

The United States has an aging population. By 2050, the number of people over age 65 will more than double, to 82 million. At that time, senior citizens will make up 20 percent of the total population. In 2050, children under 18 will be 24 percent of the total. This is a smaller percentage than today. Today the **median** age in the United States is 35.8 years. That means that half the people are younger than that age and half are older. In 2050, the median age will probably rise to 38.8 years.

Why Is the Census Important?

The writers of the U.S. Constitution mandated, or ordered, that a Census be taken every 10 years. Government officials need up-to-date information about the population to govern well. Census data also determines how the federal government spends its money. States and cities get federal money for education and other services based on their populations. That is why local government officials try to ensure that the Census counts everyone in their community.

The Census can also change the makeup of Congress. The nation has 535 **congressional districts**. Each district elects one representative to the House of Representatives. Since our population is now over 280 million, each House member represents more than half a million people.

✔ After each Census, lawmakers study the population distribution, or how many people live in different areas of the country. Then they draw new lines on a map of the United States to show new congressional districts. They base the districts on each area's population. These changes ensure that each state is represented fairly in Congress. A state like Nevada, which has grown rapidly, might get an additional seat in Congress. That means that another state has to lose a representative, to keep the total number at 535. So changes in population have a major political impact.

Census data also helps businesses make decisions. The booming Hispanic population, for example, might persuade broadcasters to start more radio stations for Spanish-speaking audiences. Developers might build more senior-citizen housing in areas with a rapidly rising elderly population or single-family housing in areas with many young families.

In short, each U.S. Census report provides an important picture of who Americans are and how they are changing. The Census statistics are an essential tool that helps us understand the United States: where it has been, where it is today, and where it might be going in the future.

1. What is the meaning of ethnicity?

   _____

   _____

2. What are two main causes for the increase in the Hispanic population in the United States during the 1990s?

   _____

   _____

3. Look at the paragraph with the ✔ next to it. Underline the sentence that states its main idea.

4. Complete each sentence with the correct word.

   demographers   mandated   distribution

   a. The Constitution _____ a Census of the population every ten years.

   b. The _____ of the U.S. population is changing, with the West gaining population faster than other regions.

   c. Some _____ predict that Hispanics will form 25 percent of the population in 2050.

CRITICAL THINKING

1. Explain why the Hispanic American population is growing so rapidly in the Southwest.

   _____

   _____

   _____

   _____

2. Summarize the benefits Americans will enjoy by being counted in the Census.

   _____

   _____

   _____

3. Describe some effects the growth of the aging American population might have on our country over time.

   _____

   _____

   _____

4. On the line next to each statement, write whether it is a *fact* or an *opinion*.

   _____ a. Puerto Ricans make up 9 percent of the Hispanic population.

   _____ b. An aging population can make better decisions.

   _____ c. Mexicans have lived in the southwestern United States for centuries.

   _____ d. A growth in population is a good trend.

SKILL FOCUS: USING STATISTICS

1. Identify the type of statistical information given in Figure 3 on page 70.

   a. What is the title of the circle graph? _____

   b. What are the four sectors shown on the graph? _____

   c. What percentage of foreign-born Americans were born in Asia? _____

2. Practice reading statistics in a table by looking at Figure 1 on page 69.

    a. What was the white (non-Hispanic) population in 2000? _____

    b. By what percentage did the Hispanic population increase between 1990 and 2000? _____

    c. Which group had about 11.6 million people in 2000? _____

3. Study a table to find relationships among numbers by looking at Figure 1 on page 69.

    a. Which group had the smallest rate of increase in population between 1990 and 2000?_____

    b. Which group had a faster rate of population growth between 1990 and 2000—Asians or

    Hispanics? _____

    c. Which two groups of Americans were almost equal in size in 2000? _____

4. Use statistics and text to draw conclusions.

    Figure 2, on page 69, shows the countries of origin of Hispanics in 2000. Based on what you have read in the selection, how might this table have been different for the year 1990? Give reasons to support your answer.

    _____

    _____

    _____

5. Use statistics to make projections or forecasts.

    On the chart below, predict the population of each state in the year 2010. Assume that each state will grow at the same rate between 2000 and 2010 as it did between 1990 and 2000. Use the following steps. The prediction for Nevada is already done for you.

    a. Change the percentage to a decimal (66% = .66).

    b. Multiply the decimal by the 2000 population (2.0 × .66 = 1.32).

    c. Add your answer for step *b* to the 2000 population (2.0 + 1.3 = 3.3).

State	1990	2000	% Change	2010
Nevada	1.2 million	2.0 million	66	3.3 million
Arizona	3.6 million	5.1 million	40	
Colorado	3.3 million	4.3 million	30	

Reading-Writing Connection

On a separate sheet of paper, make a list of benefits that all Americans enjoy from having people of many diverse backgrounds and nations living together.

Skill: Cause and Effect

BACKGROUND INFORMATION

"The Human Circulatory System" explains the working of the human heart and the circulatory system. For centuries, people observed the regular thumping inside their chests and knew that this thumping was somehow necessary for life. It wasn't until the 1600s, though, that the English physician William Harvey (1578–1657) figured out that the heart is a pump that moves blood in a circular path through the body. Today, doctors can explain how the circulatory system works in great detail.

SKILL FOCUS: Cause and Effect

A **cause** is an event that makes something happen. An **effect** is what happens as a result of the cause. Sometimes, one effect has several causes, as in the following paragraph.

Local blood banks have a shortage of blood. At this time, many donors are on vacation. Other donors are too busy to give blood. Several recent accidents have used up much of the stored blood.

The first sentence states the effect, which is a shortage of blood. The other three sentences give three causes of this effect.

Sometimes, one cause has several effects, as in the following paragraph.

Exercising is good for you. It can take inches off your waistline. It can build muscle. Exercise even helps your heart and lungs work better.

The first sentence states the cause, which is exercising. The other three sentences give the effects of the cause.

Sometimes a cause can lead to an effect, which then causes another effect. This is called a cause-and-effect chain. Read the paragraph below.

Many Americans are jogging. The exercise is making them healthier. As a result, they have lower medical bills.

▶ Complete the cause-and-effect chain in the next column. Use details from the paragraph above. The first part of the chain is done for you.

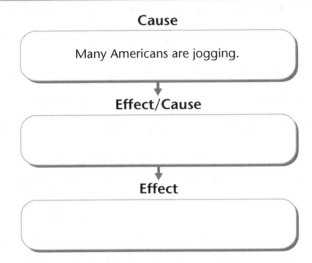

Cause

> Many Americans are jogging.

Effect/Cause

Effect

CONTEXT CLUES: Appositive Phrases

Some context clues are **appositive phrases**. An appositive phrase explains the meaning of a word that comes right before it. The phrase is usually set off from the word by commas and by the word *or*.

Read the sentence below. What appositive phrase explains the meaning of *elastic*?

*Arteries can stand up to this pressure without being damaged because they are **elastic**, or flexible.*

If you don't know the meaning of *elastic*, the phrase *or flexible* can help you. This appositive phrase explains that *elastic* means *flexible*.

▶ Read the following sentence. Circle the appositive phrase that explains the meaning of the underlined word.

*Another condition that affects the circulatory system is **hypertension**, or high blood pressure.*

In the selection, use appositive phrases to figure out the meanings of the underlined words *contraction*, *chambers*, and *pulmonary*.

Strategy Tip

As you read "The Human Circulatory System," look for the chain of causes and effects that pushes blood through the body.

The Human Circulatory System

The heart and the rest of the **circulatory system** (SER kyə lə TOR ee SIS təm) function like a pump that is connected to many tubes. The tubes are filled with a fluid that the pump circulates, or moves in a cycle. The pump is the heart, the tubes are the blood vessels, and the fluid is blood. These are the three main parts of the circulatory system.

Blood Vessels and Blood

There are three types of blood vessels in the human circulatory system: arteries, veins, and capillaries (KAP ə LAIR eez).

Arteries carry blood away from the heart. The heart forces blood into the arteries under great pressure. Arteries can stand up to this pressure without being damaged because they are elastic, or flexible. The walls of arteries are thick and have muscles that help move the blood. Look at Figure 1.

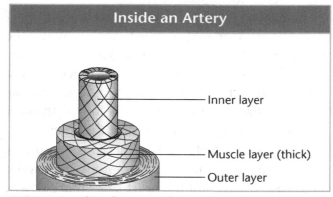

Inside an Artery

- Inner layer
- Muscle layer (thick)
- Outer layer

FIGURE 1. **This diagram shows the three layers of an artery.**

Veins carry blood back to the heart from all parts of the body. Their walls are much thinner than the walls of arteries. Veins have valves that prevent blood from backing up and keep it flowing toward the heart. Veins are located near the muscles of the body, such as those in the arms and legs. As the muscles contract and relax, they help push the blood in the veins toward the heart. Look at Figure 2.

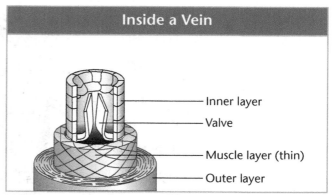

Inside a Vein

- Inner layer
- Valve
- Muscle layer (thin)
- Outer layer

FIGURE 2. **This diagram shows the parts of a vein.**

Capillaries are the smallest blood vessels. They are so narrow that blood cells must travel through them in single file. Capillaries form a network throughout the body that connects small arteries to small veins.

Blood is mainly made up of a watery liquid called **plasma**. In addition to plasma, blood contains three kinds of cells: red blood cells, white blood cells, and platelets (PLAYT lits). **Red blood cells** carry oxygen to all parts of the body. **White blood cells** help the body fight disease. **Platelets** are necessary for blood clotting, so that bleeding stops after an injury.

The Heart

The heart is a muscle about the size of a person's fist, and it is the hardest-working muscle in the body. With each <u>contraction</u>, or beat, the heart moves blood throughout the body. Even when the body is at rest, the heart pumps 5 liters (4.7 quarts) of blood per minute. During strenuous exercise, this rate is increased to 25 liters (23.7 quarts) per minute. In a normal adult, the heart beats about 70 times a minute, 101,000 times a day, 36,800,000 times a year, and about 2.7 billion times in an average lifetime.

The heart is almost centered in the chest between the lungs. It is covered with a sac, called the **pericardium** (pair ə KAHR dee əm). This sac is made up of two membrane layers that are separated

SCIENCE

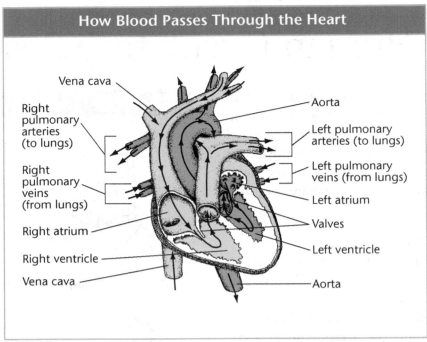

How Blood Passes Through the Heart

Vena cava

Right pulmonary arteries (to lungs)

Right pulmonary veins (from lungs)

Right atrium

Right ventricle

Vena cava

Aorta

Left pulmonary arteries (to lungs)

Left pulmonary veins (from lungs)

Left atrium

Valves

Left ventricle

Aorta

FIGURE 3. Blood enters the heart through the vena cava and leaves through the aorta.

by a fluid. The fluid acts as a cushion to prevent friction between the heart and the rib cage as the heart beats. The pericardium also attaches the heart to the surrounding tissues.

The heart has four <u>chambers</u>, or hollow cavities. The upper chambers are the right and left **atria** (AY tree ə; singular, *atrium*). The lower chambers are the right and left **ventricles** (VEN tri kəlz). Valves between the atrium and ventricle on each side prevent blood from flowing backward. The body's biggest veins, the **venae cavae** (VEE nee KAY vee; singular, *vena cava*), carry blood to the right atrium. This blood does not contain much oxygen because body cells have absorbed the oxygen that it was carrying.

As you read about how blood moves through the heart, trace its path by looking at Figure 3. The right atrium contracts, moving the oxygen-poor blood to the right ventricle. When the right ventricle contracts, it forces blood into the <u>pulmonary</u> (PUL mə NAIR ee) arteries, which carry the blood to the lungs. In the lungs, the blood takes in oxygen and releases carbon dioxide. Oxygen-rich blood then leaves the lungs through the pulmonary veins.

The pulmonary veins carry blood to the left atrium, which moves the blood into the left ventricle by contracting. When the left ventricle contracts, it pushes blood into the **aorta** (ay OR tə), the body's main artery. From here, oxygen-rich blood travels to all parts of the body.

The heart muscles contract and relax in a rhythmic manner that is called beating. When the ventricles contract, they force blood into the arteries. When the ventricles relax, the atria contract, pushing blood from each atrium into each ventricle. In this way, a constant supply of blood is moved through the heart, the lungs, and all parts of the body.

The rate at which the heart beats is not always constant. When resting, a person needs less oxygen than when active, and the heart beats more slowly. As a person becomes more active, the heart beats faster, and the body is provided with more oxygen.

Diseases of the Heart and Circulatory System

Changes in the circulatory system may cause health problems. One such change is atherosclerosis (ATH ə ROH sklə ROH səs), in which fatty material builds up on the inner walls of arteries and blocks blood flow. When this happens, the heart has to work harder to pump blood throughout the body. Sometimes the arteries that supply the heart itself become clogged, eventually causing a heart attack. In a heart attack, part of the heart muscle dies because it does not receive blood.

Another condition that affects the circulatory system is hypertension (HY pər TEN shən), or high blood pressure. Blood pressure is the force exerted against the walls of blood vessels when the heart pumps blood through them. High blood pressure can damage not only the heart and blood vessels but other organs as well.

A stroke occurs when the blood flow to part of the brain is suddenly cut off by a blockage or rupture of a blood vessel. A stroke can cause the loss of the ability to speak or move, or it can even cause death. The effects of a stroke depend on what part of the brain is damaged.

People can reduce their risk of developing circulatory diseases by practicing good health habits. The most important habits to adopt are avoiding smoking, limiting alcoholic drinks, exercising regularly, and eating a diet low in saturated fats and salt.

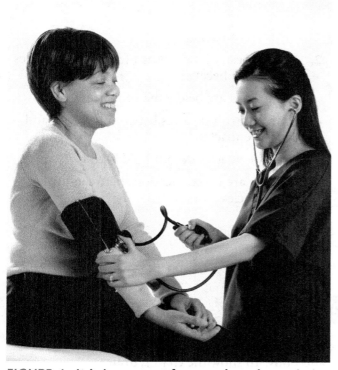

FIGURE 4. It is important for people to have their blood pressure checked regularly.

COMPREHENSION

1. Name the three main parts of the circulatory system.

   _____

2. In which direction from the heart do veins carry blood?

   _____

3. In which direction do arteries carry blood?

   _____

4. Describe how the structure of arteries helps them do their job.

   _____

   _____

5. What do red blood cells do?

   _____

6. What do white blood cells do?

   _____

7. What do platelets do?

   _____

8. Complete each sentence with the correct word.

   contraction   chambers   pulmonary

   a. Each _____ of the heart pumps blood through the body.

   b. The _____ arteries carry blood to the lungs.

   c. The human heart has four hollow cavities, or _____.

CRITICAL THINKING

Circle the letter of the correct answer.

1. How is the heart rate related to the body's need for oxygen?

   a. The heart rate controls the amount of blood going through the lungs to pick up oxygen for the rest of the body.

   b. The heart uses more oxygen when the body is resting than when it is active.

   c. As the heart rate increases, the lungs and the rest of the body need less oxygen.

   d. The heart always beats at the same rate because the lungs always need the same amount of oxygen.

2. Blood doesn't flow upward from the ventricles to the atria because

   a. the atria are below the ventricles.

   b. the heart has valves between the atria and the ventricles.

   c. the ventricles do not hold blood.

   d. there are no connections between the ventricles and the atria.

SKILL FOCUS: CAUSE AND EFFECT

Three chains of causes and effects can be made from the events listed below. Together, these chains describe how blood is circulated through the heart and body. To show the chains, draw an arrow from one event in the first column to an event in the second and third columns.

Cause	Effect/Cause	Effect
1. The venae cavae empty oxygen-poor blood into the right atrium, which contracts.	The blood is pushed into the right ventricle, which contracts.	Blood is forced into the pulmonary arteries, which carry it to the lungs to pick up oxygen.
2. The blood takes in oxygen and is carried to the left atrium by the pulmonary veins.	The blood moves through the capillaries and into veins.	Blood is forced into the aorta.
3. Oxygen-rich blood is carried throughout the body.	The blood is pumped into the left ventricle, which contracts.	Oxygen-poor blood returns to the heart through veins.

Reading-Writing Connection

On a separate sheet of paper, make a poster that persuades people to protect their circulatory system by practicing good health habits.

LESSON 19

Skill: Word Problems

BACKGROUND INFORMATION

"Completing and Solving Word Problems" will help you ask questions and solve problems when you read numerical information. Most math problems provide the question that you must answer. Sometimes, however, you have to pose your own questions about a group of number facts and then figure out the answers to your own questions. For these kinds of problem situations, you must study the information given to determine the most logical question to ask.

SKILL FOCUS: Word Problems

Use the following five steps to complete and solve word problems.

1. **Read the problem situation.** If the problem does not include a question or directions, but describes a problem situation, you have to determine what the problem is yourself. To do so, you need to understand all the information given. Think about how the various facts are related.

2. **Decide on a question to ask and how to find the answer.** Usually, it is helpful to write a mathematical sentence about each fact that is given. Then write a question that logically connects the number facts. Finally, decide what operation or operations to use to answer the question you have written.

3. **Estimate the answer.** This is one way to be sure that the question can be answered by using the information given in the problem.

4. **Carry out the plan.** Solve the mathematical sentence or sentences that you wrote in Step 2.

5. **Reread the problem situation and your question.** Is the answer to the question logical? Is it close to your estimate?

▶ Read the following data about the 2000 Census.

The Census Bureau states that the population of the United States in the year 2000 was 281,400,000. The total Hispanic population was 35,300,000—a big jump from 22,400,000 in 1990.

1. Write a question about the above information that logically connects the facts.

_____

_____

_____

2. Write your question as a mathematical sentence.

_____

_____

WORD CLUES

Difficulties with word problems often involve key words. Sometimes the solution involves a rate, such as kilometers *per* hour or a *percent* of a whole. The word *per* always means that a rate is involved. Rates are found by division. For example, *kilometers per hour* is a rate that is found by dividing a number of kilometers by a number of hours.

A percent is a rate found by dividing a portion of the total amount by the total amount. In percent problems, you need to divide sometimes and multiply at other times. The operation that you use depends on whether you want to figure out the percentage or the total amount.

▶ Circle the key word that signals what operation to use in order to solve the following word problem. Then on the line, solve the word problem.

Miguel drove 1,600 kilometers from El Paso, Texas, to Mexico City. The whole trip took three days. How many kilometers did he travel per day?

_____

Completing and Solving Word Problems

If you travel in the countries that border or are located in the Caribbean Sea, you may need to know many facts. Although a map or other reference gives you important facts, it may not give the fact that you need. You first have to determine what fact you want to figure out from the information that you have, and then decide how to find the answer. In other words, you make up a question, or problem, whose answer will give you the fact that you need.

Use these five steps to solve word problems.

1. Read the problem situation.
2. Decide on a question to ask about the facts in the situation and how to find the answer.
3. Estimate the answer.
4. Carry out the plan.
5. Reread the problem situation and your question.

Read the Problem Situation.

You learn from a map that it is 402 kilometers from Nogales to Guaymas, 193 kilometers from Guaymas to Navojoa, 161 kilometers from Navojoa to Los Mochis, and 209 kilometers from Los Mochis to Culiacán.

Nogales, Guaymas, Navojoa, Los Mochis, and Culiacán are the names of cities in Mexico. After reading the information, think about what problem you could solve using the information provided.

Decide on a Question to Ask and How to Find the Answer.

The problem situation gives you four facts. Write a short sentence about each.

1. *It is 402 kilometers from Nogales to Guaymas.*
2. *It is 193 kilometers from Guaymas to Navojoa.*
3. *It is 161 kilometers from Navojoa to Los Mochis.*
4. *It is 209 kilometers from Los Mochis to Culiacán.*

You want to make up a question that uses all four facts. Therefore, you need to find a mathematical operation that connects the four facts. When you want to connect more than two facts, the operation you use is often addition. If you add the four distances, you know the distance from Nogales to Culiacán. The question you want to answer, then, is *How far is it from Nogales to Culiacán?*

Write a mathematical sentence, or equation, connecting the four facts by addition.

$$402 + 193 + 161 + 209 = d$$

Estimate the Answer.

Round each number to the nearest hundred.

$$400 + 200 + 200 + 200 = 1,000$$

Carry Out the Plan.

$$402 + 193 + 161 + 209 = 965$$

Reread the Problem Situation and Your Question.

After rereading the problem situation, write out a complete answer to the question that you wrote in the second step. *The distance from Nogales to Culiacán is 965 kilometers.* Then check to see that your answer is close to your estimate. If not, start over with Step 1. The answer 965 is close to the estimate of 1,000, so it is probably correct.

Decide on a question to ask from the following facts and solve the word problem.

Read: *From 1493 until 1897, or for 404 years, Puerto Rico was a colony of Spain. From 1898 until 1951, Puerto Rico was a possession of the United States.*

Make sure that you know what all the words mean. If you do not know the meaning of the word *colony*, for example, look it up in a dictionary.

Decide: From the information given, you know that Puerto Rico was a colony of Spain.

You also know that Puerto Rico was a possession of the United States for a number of years. What question does this information suggest? A logical question would be *How much longer was Puerto Rico a colony of Spain than it was a possession of the United States?*

This problem requires two operations. First you have to find how long Puerto Rico was a possession of the United States. Then you have to find how much longer Puerto Rico was a colony of Spain than it was a possession of the United States.

Choose variables, such as U and t, to stand for the answer to each step. Write equations that connect the information. Use a word clue in your question to help you figure out what operations to use. Problems that ask *how much longer* or *how much more* can usually be solved by subtraction.

$$1951 - 1898 = U$$
$$404 - U = t$$

Estimate: Since the smallest number in the problem has three places, you round all the numbers to the nearest hundred and estimate.

$$2000 - 1900 = 100$$
$$400 - 100 = 300$$

Carry Out: $1951 - 1898 = 53$
$$404 - 53 = 351$$

Reread: *Puerto Rico was a colony of Spain for 351 years longer than it was a possession of the United States.* The answer is close to your estimate.

COMPREHENSION

1. To connect more than two numbers in a problem, which operation do you often use?

   _____

2. If a problem contains the word clue *how much more*, which operation do you most often use to solve the problem?

   _____

3. The reread step involves two important parts in addition to rereading. What are they?

   a. _____

   b. _____

4. What should you do if you do not understand a word in the problem?

   _____

CRITICAL THINKING

1. In the first problem situation in the selection, why would the question probably not be *How much farther is it from Nogales to Guaymas than it is from Guaymas to Navojoa?*

   _____

2. In the second problem situation in the selection, what can you infer about the status of Puerto Rico after 1951?

   _____

3. In the selection, the variables *d*, *U*, and *t* were used. What did they stand for?

   _____

4. What can you infer about the difference between the number of years Puerto Rico was a colony of Spain and the years since Puerto Rico ceased to be a U.S. possession?

   _____

Write the question you think should be asked for each problem situation below. Then write one or two equations as a plan, make an estimate, carry out your plan, and state the answer to the question in a complete sentence.

1. **Read:** On a road map of Cuba, José found that it was 96.5 kilometers from Havana to Matanzas and 35.5 kilometers from Matanzas to Varadero.

   Decide: _____

   Estimate: _____

   Carry Out: _____

   Reread: _____

   _____

2. **Read:** In Puerto Rico, the entrance to the Rio Abajo Commonwealth Forest is at kilometer 70.2 on Route 10. Dos Bacos Lake, in the forest, can be reached at kilometer 68 on Route 10.

   Decide: _____

   Estimate: _____

   Carry Out: _____

   Reread: _____

   _____

3. **Read:** From Tamazunchale in Mexico, the road climbs steadily into the mountains. You reach an elevation of 2,044.8 meters in 96.54 kilometers of driving.

   Decide: _____

   Estimate: _____

   Carry Out: _____

   Reread: _____

   _____

Reading-Writing Connection

Think of a problem situation based on numbers related to your class, school, or community. On a separate sheet of paper, describe the problem situation, and write a question based on those numbers. Ask a partner to solve your problem.

Skill: Accented Syllable and Schwa

When words contain two syllables, one of the syllables is stressed, or accented, more than the other. In dictionaries, the **accent mark** (') is placed at the end of the syllable that is said with more stress. For example, the first syllable in the word *carrot* is said with more stress.

car' rot

In words with three syllables, the accent is usually on one of the first two syllables. When you are trying to pronounce a word with three syllables, such as *tradition,* try saying the first syllable with more stress. If the word does not sound right, say it again, stressing the second syllable.

tra di' tion

A. Say each of the following words to yourself. Write an accent mark after the syllable that should be stressed.

1. reg u lar	**3.** wal rus	**5.** con di tion	**7.** fi nal
2. ad di tion	**4.** pol i tics	**6.** dra mat ic	**8.** par ti tion

Words of four or more syllables usually have two accented syllables. In the word *composition*, the third syllable has the most stress. This syllable has the **primary accent mark** ('). The first syllable has more stress than the remaining two syllables but less than the third syllable. The **secondary accent mark** (') is placed after that syllable.

com' po si' tion

B. Say each of the following words to yourself. Write a primary accent mark after the syllable that has the most stress. Say the word again. Write a secondary accent mark after the syllable that has the second-most stress.

1. in for ma tion	**3.** pan o ra ma	**5.** per son al i ty	**7.** a vi a tor
2. nav i ga tor	**4.** com pli ca tion	**6.** sal a man der	**8.** en thu si as tic

The vowels *a, e, i, o,* and *u* can all have the same sound. This is a soft sound like a short *u* pronounced lightly. This short, soft *u* sound is called the **schwa** sound. In dictionary respellings, the symbol ə stands for the schwa sound. If you look up the word *compete* in the dictionary, you will find it respelled this way.

kəm pēt'

C. Say each of the words below to yourself. Write an accent mark after the syllable that is stressed. Then circle the letter that stands for the schwa sound.

1. sec ond	**3.** haz ard	**5.** pi o neer	**7.** or i gin
2. ac count	**4.** ca det	**6.** dec o rate	**8.** fam i ly

Look at the words in the list above. Notice that the schwa sound always falls in an unaccented syllable of a word.

A **prefix** is a word part that is added to the beginning of a word to change its meaning. Eight prefixes and their meanings are given below.

Prefix	Meaning	Prefix	Meaning
bi-	having two, or happening every two	*non-*	not
dis-	away or opposite of	*pre-*	before
mid-	middle	*semi-*	half or partly
mis-	wrong or badly	*trans-*	over, across, or beyond

A. Read each word below and the meaning that follows it. Write the correct prefix on the line before each word.

1. _____ comfort — opposite of comfort

2. _____ monthly — happening every two months

3. _____ pay — pay before

4. _____ stop — no stops

5. _____ pacific — across the Pacific

6. _____ school — before regular school

7. _____ circle — half a circle

8. _____ week — middle of the week

9. _____ loyal — opposite of loyal

10. _____ spell — to spell incorrectly

11. _____ sweet — partly sweet

B. Use one of the words from Part A to complete each sentence below.

1. This picture book is for _____ children.

2. _____ meetings will be held every Wednesday.

3. An aching tooth causes a lot of _____.

4. Proofread your paragraph to make sure that you did not _____ any words.

5. The team sat in a _____ around the coach.

6. A _____ magazine comes out six times a year.

7. The _____ ship left Los Angeles for Tokyo.

8. A traitor is _____ to his or her country.

9. The plane will fly _____ from New York to San Francisco.

10. We had to _____ our order from the Clarkstown Mail-Order Company.

11. The recipe calls for honey and _____ chocolate.

Skill: Suffixes

A **suffix** is a word part that is added to the end of a word to change its meaning. When a word ends in *y* preceded by a consonant, change the *y* to *i* before adding suffixes that begin with a vowel.

defy + ance = defiance

When a word ends in *e,* drop the *e* before adding suffixes that begin with a vowel.

desire + able = desirable

Below are four suffixes and their meanings. Study them carefully.

Suffix	Meaning	Suffix	Meaning
-able	that can be	-ance	the act of
-al	the process of	-ant	that has or shows

A. Write the correct suffix after each word below. If the word ends in *y*, cross out the *y* and add *i* before the suffix. If the word ends in *e*, cross out the *e* before adding the suffix. The first one is done for you.

1. compl~~y~~ _iance_   the act of complying
2. vary_____   that shows variety
3. compare_____   that can be compared
4. arrive_____   the process of arriving
5. defy_____   that shows defiance

6. envy_____   that can be envied
7. please_____   that shows pleasure
8. endure_____   the act of enduring
9. bury_____   the process of burying
10. rely_____   that can be relied on

B. Use one of the words from Part A to complete each sentence below.

1. Rugby is a game _____ to football.

2. Mr. Matsumi and his children spent a(n) _____ day in the park.

3. A runner must have great _____ to run 10 miles each day.

4. Lucia and Tomas are waiting for the _____ of their parents' plane.

5. This barometer gives a(n) _____ weather forecast.

6. Carol appreciated the salesperson's _____ with her request for a refund.

7. The volcano's eruption caused the _____ of an entire village.

8. Mike has an _____ record of achievement in Spanish.

9. *Theatre* is a _____ spelling of *theater.*

10. LaTeena told us in a _____ manner that she was against our plans.

Skill: Main Idea and Supporting Details

The **main idea** is the most important idea in a paragraph. It states what the paragraph is about. Supporting details give more information about the main idea.

There are two kinds of **supporting details**. The most important details, called **major details,** develop the main idea of a paragraph. Less important details, called **minor details,** give more information about the major details.

As you read each of the following paragraphs, look for the main idea, major details, and minor details.

Puerto Rico and Its Economy

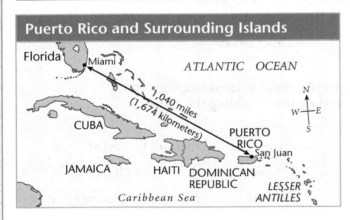

Puerto Rico and Surrounding Islands

Florida · Miami · ATLANTIC OCEAN · 1,040 miles (1,674 kilometers) · CUBA · PUERTO RICO · San Juan · N W E S · JAMAICA · HAITI · DOMINICAN REPUBLIC · LESSER ANTILLES · Caribbean Sea

1. The island of Puerto Rico covers 3,515 square miles (9,103 square kilometers). The only two states that are smaller than Puerto Rico are Delaware and Rhode Island. Puerto Rico's 2000 population was about 3.8 million. About 71 percent of all Puerto Ricans live in urban areas. More than half live in the metropolitan areas of San Juan, Ponce, Caguas, Mayaguez, Arecibo, and Aquadilla. Only 29 percent inhabit the rural areas. Indeed, Puerto Rico is a small but crowded island.

2. About 60 percent of Puerto Rico's land is used for farming. Coffee, sugar cane, and tobacco are the island's leading crops. Most of the tobacco is used for cigars. Many fruits are also grown commercially for export. Such fruits include bananas, plantains, pineapples, avocados, coconuts, and oranges.

3. Puerto Rico's economy used to be based primarily on farm products, but today manufacturing is the main source of income. Agriculture accounts for only a small percentage of the value of goods produced in Puerto Rico annually. Manufactured products include petrochemicals, medicinal drugs, clothing, electronic equipment, and machinery. There are about 2,000 factories in Puerto Rico, with both American and Puerto Rican owners. The factories employ about 162,000 workers.

Sugar cane is one of Puerto Rico's leading crops.

More than half of Puerto Ricans live in metropolitan areas like San Juan.

Complete the diagram for each paragraph. In the box labeled *Main Idea,* write the sentence that states the main idea as it appears in the paragraph. Use your own words when filling in the boxes labeled *Major Details* and *Minor Details.* Some of the boxes are filled in for you.

Paragraph 1:

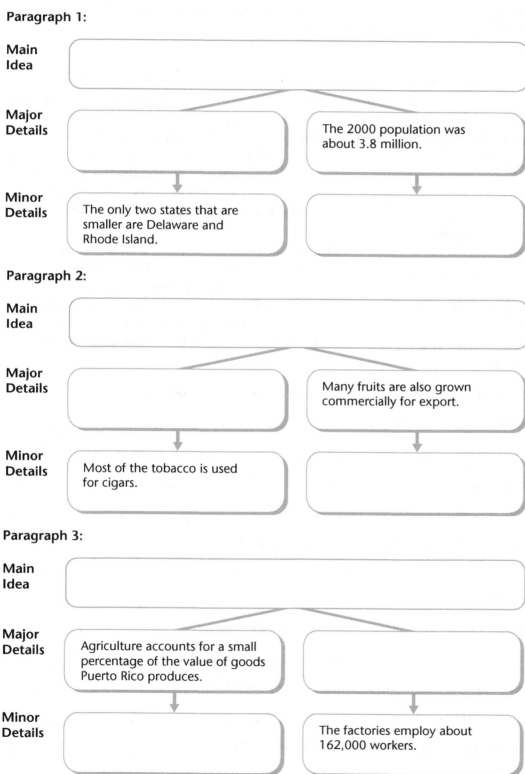

Main Idea

Major Details

The 2000 population was about 3.8 million.

Minor Details

The only two states that are smaller are Delaware and Rhode Island.

Paragraph 2:

Main Idea

Major Details

Many fruits are also grown commercially for export.

Minor Details

Most of the tobacco is used for cigars.

Paragraph 3:

Main Idea

Major Details

Agriculture accounts for a small percentage of the value of goods Puerto Rico produces.

Minor Details

The factories employ about 162,000 workers.

Skill: Using a Dictionary

Each word, abbreviation, prefix, suffix, or group of words that your dictionary explains is called an **entry word.** The entry word and all the information about it is called an **entry.** All entries are arranged in alphabetical order.

To help you find an entry quickly, **guide words** are printed in the upper left-hand and right-hand corners of each page. The upper left-hand guide word tells the first full entry on that page. The upper right-hand guide word tells the last entry on the page.

In many dictionaries, dots divide entry words into **syllables.** Syllabication shows you where to divide a word when you cannot write it all on one line.

Respellings appear in parentheses after most entry words. The **key** to pronunciation is in the front or back of most dictionaries, and a shortened version appears at the bottom of every other page. A key word accompanying each symbol shows you how to pronounce the symbol correctly.

The definitions, or meanings, of entry words are grouped according to **parts of speech.** Some entry words appear as only one part of speech, as does *tractor,* which is a noun. Many words, however, can be used as several parts of speech. For example, *range* can be a verb, a noun, or an adjective.

If entry words can be used as more than one part of speech, abbreviated labels identify the group of meanings for each. For example, all the noun meanings of an entry word follow the abbreviation for noun, **n.**

Idioms are included at the end of any entry that is a key word in an idiom. An idiom is a group of words that has a different meaning from the meanings of the individual words by themselves. For example, the entry for the word *take* includes the idioms *take after, take off,* and *take it out on.*

On page 89 is part of a page from a dictionary. Use it to answer the following questions.

1. What are the guide words for this page? _____

2. What is the respelling of *plow*? _____

3. What is the fourth entry word on this page? _____

4. What is the second noun meaning of *plot*? _____

5. What sentence is given for the third transitive verb (*vt.*) meaning of *plow*?

_____

6. How big does a plover grow to be? _____

7. What two idioms are given for the word *plow*? _____

8. What are three types of pliers? _____

9. What key word is given in the pronunciation key for the long *e* sound? _____

10. What is the adjective form of the word *plow*? _____

11. Which two entry words are homographs, words with the same spelling but

    different meanings? _____

12. Which entry word means a pedestal? _____

13. Which entry word can be used only as an adjective? _____

14. How do you spell the past tense of *plot*? _____

15. How would you divide the word *plumage* into syllables? _____

---

pliers

pli·ers (plī´ərz) *n. pl.* [<PLY¹] small pincers for gripping small objects, bending wire, etc.

plight¹ (plīt) *n.* [< Anglo-Fr. plit, for OFr. pleit, a fold] a condition or state of affairs; esp., an awkward, sad, or dangerous situation [the *plight* of the men trapped in the mine]

plight² (plīt) *vt.* [OE, plihtan, to pledge < pliht, danger] to pledge or promise, or bind by a pledge —**plight one's troth** to make a promise of marriage.

Plim·soll mark (or **line**) (plim´ səl, -säl, -sôl) [after S. Plimsoll (1824-98), English statesman] a line or set of lines on the outside of merchant ships, showing the water level to which they may be legally loaded

☆**plink** (pliŋk) *n.* [echoic] a light, sharp, ringing or clinking sound –*vt.*, *vi.* 1 to make such sounds on (a piano, banjo, etc.) 2 to shoot at (tin cans, etc,)

plinth (plinth) *n.* [<L.< Gr. *plinthos*, a brick, tile] 1 the square block at the base of a column, pedestal, etc. 2 the base on which a stature rests

Plin·y (plin´ē) 1(L. name *Gaius Plinius Secundus*) 23-79 A.D.; Rom. naturalist & writer called *the Elder* 2 (L. name *Gaius Plinius Caecilius Secundus*) 62?-113? A.D.; Rom. writer & statesman: called *the Younger*: nephew of *Pliny the Elder*

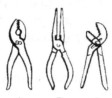

PLIERS
(A, slip joint; B, needle nose; C, arc joint)

plover (pluv´ər, plo´vər) *n., pl.* **plov´ers, plov´er**: see PLURAL, II, D, l [<OFr.,ult. < L. *pluvia*, rain] a shore bird with a short tail, long, pointed wings, and a short beak

plow (plou) *n.* [MEE. *ploh* < Late OE.] 1 a farm implement used to cut and turn up the soil 2 anything like this; specif., a SNOW-PLOW —*vt.* 1 to cut and turn up (soil) with a plow ☆2 to make furrows in with or as with a plow 3 to make as if by plowing [he **plowed** his way through the crowd] 4 to cut a way through (water) —*vi.* 1 to use a plow in tilling the soil. 2 to cut a way (through water, etc.) 3 to go forward with effort, plod 4 to begin work vigorously (with into) 5 to strike against forcefully (with *into*) —**plow back** to reinvest (profits) in the same business enterprise —**plow up** 1 to remove with a plow 2 to till (soil) thoroughly —**plow´a·ble** *adj.* —**plow´er** *n.*

plow·boy (plou´boi´) *n.* 1 formerly, a boy who led a team of horses drawing a plow 2 a country boy

plow·man (plou´ mən) *n., pl.* –men 1 a man who guides a plow 2 a farm worker

plow·share (-sher´) *n.* the share, or cutting blade, of a mold-board plow.

ploy (ploi) *n.*, [? < (EM)PLOY] an action or maneuver intended to outwit or confuse another person in order to get the better of him

PLOVER
(to 11 in. high)

---

plot (plät) *n.* [OE., a piece of land] 1 a small area of ground [a garden *plot*] 2 a chart or diagram, as of a building or estate 3 a secret, usually evil, scheme 4 the plan of action of a play, novel, etc. — *vt.* **plot´ted, plot´ting** 1 a) to draw a plan of (a ship's course, etc.) b) to mark the position of course of on a map 2 to make secret plans for [to *plot* a robbery} 3 to plan the action of (a story, etc.) 4 a) to determine the location of (a point) on a graph by means of coordinates b) to represent (an equation) by joining points on a graph to form a curve — *vi.* to plan together secretly; scheme [to *plot* against the king] **plot´less** *adj.* —**plot´less ness** *n.* —**plot´ter** *n.*

plum (plum) *n.* [OE. *plume*] 1 a) any of various small trees bearing a smooth-skinned fruit with a flattened stone b) the fruit eaten as food 2 a raisin, when used in pudding or cake [*plum* pudding] 3 the dark bluish-red or reddish-purple color of some plums 4 something excellent or desirable [the new contract is a rich *plum* for the company]

plum·age (ploo´mij) *n.* [MFr. <L. *pluma*, a feather] a bird's feathers

plu·mate (-māt, -mit) *adj.* [,L. *pluma*, a feather] *Zool*, resembling a feather, esp. in structure

---

fat, āpe, cär; ten, ēven; is, bīte; gō, hôrn, tōōl, loͻk; oil, out; up, fur; get; joy; yet; chin; she; thin, *then*; zh, leisure; ŋ, ring; ə for *a* in *ago*, e in *agent*, *i* in *sanity*, *o* in *comply*, *u* in *focus*; ' as in *able* (ā´b'l); Fr. bål; ë, Fr. coeur; ö, Fr. feu; ô, Fr. moŋ; ō, Fr. coq; ü, Fr. duc; r, Fr, cri; H, G. ich; kh, G. doch; ‡ foreign; ☆Americanism; < derived from. See inside front cover.

Skill: Reading a Social Security Application Form

Everyone in the United States who is planning to work is required to have a **Social Security number.** Children who have bank accounts also must have a Social Security number. Assigned to you for life, the number belongs only to you. Because you must write your Social Security number on job applications, it is wise to get your number before applying for a job. Your Social Security number is needed for many other forms that you are required to complete, such as income tax forms.

The Social Security program is supported by money that is deducted, or taken out, from each of your paychecks. When you stop working because your health is poor or you reach retirement age, you receive money from the Social Security program each month. Also, if a working parent dies, the children in the family receive monthly Social Security checks for a set period.

To apply for a Social Security number, call, write, or visit the nearest Social Security office to get an **application form** like the one shown on page 91. You can also download an application at the Social Security administration Web site: www.ssa.gov. To obtain a card, you must also present documents that prove your age, identity, and U.S. citizenship or lawful alien status. After you fill out the form and return it to the office, your Social Security card, with your number on it, will be mailed to you.

A. Use the Social Security application form on page 91 to answer the following questions. Fill in the circle next to the phrase that correctly completes each sentence.

1. When filling out a Social Security application, you print the name that you now use in
   ○ item 1.   ○ item 2.   ○ item 3.   ○ item 4.

2. You print the names of the city and state or foreign country where you were born in
   ○ item 2.   ○ item 3.   ○ item 7.   ○ item 11.

3. Item 1 asks for your full name at birth, which according to this form means
   ○ your first name.   ○ your first, middle, and last names.
   ○ your first and last names.   ○ your first name, middle initial, and last name.

4. If the person applying for the card is a boy or a man, he would complete item 4 by
   ○ printing the word *male* in the box.   ○ checking the box next to *Female*.
   ○ checking the box next to *Male*.   ○ writing his age in the box.

5. If you give false information when applying for a Social Security number, you may have to
   ○ pay a fine.   ○ pay a fine, go to prison, or both.
   ○ go to prison.   ○ go without getting a Social Security number.

6. Which is the only voluntary item on the form?
   ○ item 3.   ○ item 5.   ○ item 11.   ○ item 17.

B. Write the answer to each question on the line provided. Use complete sentences.

1. Where is the only place on the application that you should not write anything?

_____

2. What information does item 8 require?

_____

3. What two dates does everyone need to include on the application?

_____

4. If a father is filling out the form for his daughter, how would he respond to item 17?

_____

5. When would the information on the first line of item 1 differ from the information on

the second line? _____

SOCIAL SECURITY ADMINISTRATION
Application for a Social Security Card

Form Approved
OMB No. 0960-0066

		First	Full Middle Name	Last
1	**NAME** TO BE SHOWN ON CARD			
	FULL NAME AT BIRTH IF OTHER THAN ABOVE	First	Full Middle Name	Last
	OTHER NAMES USED			

		Street Address, Apt. No., PO Box, Rural Route No.		
2	**MAILING ADDRESS** Do Not Abbreviate	City	State	Zip Code

3	**CITIZENSHIP** (Check One)	☐ U.S. Citizen	☐ Legal Alien Allowed To Work	☐ Legal Alien **Not** Allowed To Work (See Instructions On Page 1)	☐ Other (See Instructions On Page 1)

4	**SEX**	☐ Male	☐ Female

5	**RACE/ETHNIC DESCRIPTION** (Check One Only - Voluntary)	☐ Asian, Asian-American or Pacific Islander	☐ Hispanic	☐ Black (Not Hispanic)	☐ North American Indian or Alaskan Native	☐ White (Not Hispanic)

6	**DATE OF BIRTH** Month, Day, Year	**7**	**PLACE OF BIRTH** (Do Not Abbreviate) City State or Foreign Country FCI	Office Use Only

8	**A. MOTHER'S MAIDEN NAME**	First	Full Middle Name	Last Name At Her Birth
	B. MOTHER'S SOCIAL SECURITY NUMBER	☐☐☐ – ☐☐ – ☐☐☐☐		

9	**A. FATHER'S NAME**	First	Full Middle Name	Last
	B. FATHER'S SOCIAL SECURITY NUMBER	☐☐☐ – ☐☐ – ☐☐☐☐		

10	Has the applicant or anyone acting on his/her behalf ever filed for or received a Social Security number card before? ☐ Yes (If "yes", answer questions 11-13.) ☐ No (If "no", go on to question 14.) ☐ Don't Know (If "don't know", go on to question 14.)

11	Enter the Social Security number previously assigned to the person listed in item 1.	☐☐☐ – ☐☐ – ☐☐☐☐

12	Enter the name shown on the most recent Social Security card issued for the person listed in item 1.	First	Middle Name	Last

13	Enter any different date of birth if used on an earlier application for a card.	Month, Day, Year

14	**TODAY'S DATE** Month, Day, Year	**15**	**DAYTIME PHONE NUMBER** ( ) Area Code Number

DELIBERATELY FURNISHING (OR CAUSING TO BE FURNISHED) FALSE INFORMATION ON THIS APPLICATION IS A CRIME PUNISHABLE BY FINE OR IMPRISONMENT, OR BOTH.

16	**YOUR SIGNATURE** ▶	**17**	**YOUR RELATIONSHIP TO THE PERSON IN ITEM 1 IS:** ☐ Self ☐ Natural Or Adoptive Parent ☐ Legal Guardian ☐ Other (Specify)

Egypt and the Nile

LESSON 26

Skill: Imagery

BACKGROUND INFORMATION

"Hymn to the Nile" is an ancient Egyptian poem whose words were sung in praise of the Nile river. Egypt is one of the world's first civilizations. It arose some 5,000 years ago in the valley along the Nile river. This fertile river valley was enriched by yearly flooding of the Nile and produced fine crops. The Nile helped Egypt become a wealthy and highly advanced culture.

SKILL FOCUS: Imagery

Imagery is language that appeals to the senses. Many images create pictures in the reader's mind by appealing to the sense of sight. Other images appeal to the senses of hearing, touch, taste, and smell.

Read these lines. What pictures do you see in your mind?

You create the golden kernels of corn.
You bring forth the pearls of barley.

The poem uses visual images to help readers see the grain as gold and pearls. These images suggest the richness of the foods that the river helps to grow.

To which sense does the following line appeal?

Your waters caress all growing things....

The word *caress* creates an image that appeals to the sense of touch. Readers can feel the waters gently stroking the growing things.

▶ Read the following lines of poetry. Then fill in the Idea Web in the next column with words that appeal to different senses.

If you did not nourish us, the country would fall exhausted;

the bitter taste of gall would fill our mouths,
our dwellings would fall silent,
and the dank smell of death would fill the land.

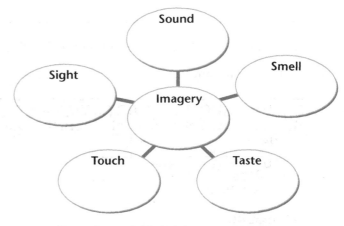

CONTEXT CLUES: Footnotes

Footnotes are explanations of names and other special words in a selection. A footnote might give information about an unfamiliar person, place, or thing. Words with footnotes have a small raised number next to them. Each footnote appears at the bottom of the same page where the numbered word appears.

Read the following line and footnote.

*We adore you, O **Nile**![1]*

[1]Nile: a river in Africa that runs north from Uganda through Egypt to the Mediterranean Sea; one of the world's longest rivers.

The raised number is a signal to look at the bottom of the page for a footnote with the same number.

▶ Read the following sentence. Circle the details in the footnote that tell you the meaning of Ra.

*This day we celebrate the flood which overtakes our land, nourishing the orchards created by **Ra**.[2]*

[2]Ra: the Egyptian god of the sun.

As you read, use footnotes to find the meanings of the underlined words *Seb*, *royal city*, and *gall*.

Strategy Tip

As you read the poem, look for imagery to see, hear, smell, touch, and taste ancient Egypt.

HYMN TO THE NILE

We adore you, O Nile![1]
We adore you, O Nile!
You spread yourself over this land, embracing the Earth.
You come to give life to Egypt!
You spring from a dark, mysterious source.   (5)
    This day we celebrate the flood which overtakes our land, nourishing the
    orchards created by Ra.[2]
Your waters give life to the cattle and slake the thirst of the Earth.
There is no end to your gifts. O inexhaustible one!
Your waters caress all growing things; even the gods depend on your bounty.

    You are the mighty Lord of the Fish—   (10)
    Your waters whisper along their course....
    The birds fear your anger,
    and dare not disturb the growing seedlings and crops.
You create the golden kernels of corn.
You bring forth the pearls of barley.   (15)
On your banks the temples stand strong to welcome your worshippers.
If your waters do not rise and ebb each season,
If you cease your toil and work,
    then all that exists cries in anguish,
    the gods in heaven will suffer,   (20)
    and the faces of your worshippers will waste away.

    If the Nile smiles, the Earth is joyous;
    Every stomach is full of rejoicing,
    Every spine is happy,
    Every jawbone crushes its food.   (25)
Nimble fingers strum songs to you on the harp.
Women clap their hands and chant.
The feet of young men beat the Earth in a gleeful dance of praise.
As the sunlight glints on your waters, the people rejoice ... with great feasts
    they celebrate.

    You are the greatest jewel of Seb[3]   (30)
You are a ship with great sails, advancing with the wind...
    when men and women see you rise before them, their hearts beat with joy.
As you flow in a molten silver stream through the royal city,[4]
    the rich grow content with their good life;
    the poor are satisfied with their lot.   (35)

---

[1]Nile: a river in Africa that runs north from Uganda through Egypt to the Mediterranean Sea, one of the world's longest rivers.

[2]Ra: the Egyptian god of the sun.

[3]Seb: according to the ancient Egyptians, another name for Earth.

[4]royal city: Cairo.

You make everything grow to full measure,
    and all that grows is for us, your children.
    If you did not nourish us, the country would fall exhausted;
    the bitter taste of <u>gall</u>[5] would fill our mouths,
    our dwellings would fall silent,   (40)
    and the dank smell of death would fill the land.

    O flood time of the Nile!
    O giver of Life!
We shall make offerings to you.
We shall give up great oxen.   (45)
We shall sacrifice birds to you.
For you our warriors will hunt down swift-footed gazelles.
We shall prepare a pure bright flame to praise you.
    O Nile, come and prosper!
We cannot live without our flocks.   (50)
Our flocks must feed in the orchards.
Only you can nourish them all.
    Come and prosper, come,
    O Nile, come and prosper!

———————
[5]gall: bile, a bitter fluid secreted by the liver.

COMPREHENSION

1. Is this hymn being sung during or before the Nile flood? Support your answer by referring to lines in the poem.

_____

_____

_____

2. According to line 22, what happens when the Nile smiles?

_____

_____

_____

3. How do people celebrate the flooding of the Nile?

_____

_____

_____

4. In line 30, to what is the Nile compared?

_____ In line 31? _____

5. Name the animals offered to the Nile.

_____

_____

_____

_____

_____

6. Decide if each statement is true or false. Write *true* or *false* on the line.

_____ **a.** <u>Seb</u> was the ancient Egyptian name for Earth.

_____ **b.** The <u>royal city</u> referred to in the poem is Rome.

_____ **c.** <u>Gall</u> is a type of honey.

CRITICAL THINKING

1. Why did the ancient Egyptians believe that the Nile deserved a song of praise?

   _____

   _____

2. The statements below are either facts or opinions. Fill in the circle next to each statement that expresses a fact.

   ○ **a.** The Nile is a river in Africa.

   ○ **b.** The Nile is the source of happiness and joy for all Egyptians.

   ○ **c.** The ancient Egyptians depended on the Nile's flood waters for survival.

   ○ **d.** The Nile is the most beautiful river in the world.

3. Does the poet identify the source of the Nile? Identify a line in the poem that supports your answer.

   _____

   _____

4. Summarize what would happen if the Nile did not overflow its banks as expected.

   _____

   _____

5. Explain why the Nile was the "giver of Life" to Egypt.

   _____

   _____

SKILL FOCUS: IMAGERY

1. The lines below are from the poem. In the space provided, identify the sense to which the image in each line appeals.

   sight   sound   touch   taste   smell

   _____ **a.** Your waters whisper along their course....

   _____ **b.** Your waters give life to the cattle and slake the thirst of the earth.

   _____ **c.** ... sunlight glints on your waters....

   _____ **d.** The feet of young men beat the Earth....

   _____ **e.** Nimble fingers strum songs to you on the harp.

   _____ **f.** ... the dank smell of death would fill the land.

2. In each of the following lines, circle the word or phrase that creates a sense image. Then describe in one sentence what each image means or suggests to you.

   a. As you flow in a molten silver stream through the royal city . . . (line 33)

   _____

   _____

   b. For you our warriors will hunt down swift-footed gazelles. (line 47)

   _____

   _____

   c. the bitter taste of gall would fill our mouths . . . (line 39)

   _____

   _____

3. The imagery in this poem helps the reader see the Nile as the poet saw it. Of all the images in the poem, which one gives you the clearest picture of some aspect of the Nile? Give reasons to support your choice.

   _____

   _____

4. **a.** In three or four sentences, write a factual description of the Nile, based on the information in the poem. Do not use any sense images.

   _____

   _____

   _____

   _____

   b. Reread the poem and your paragraph. Which evokes stronger feelings or emotions, the poem or your paragraph? Explain.

   _____

   _____

5. What emotional effect did the Nile have on the poet?

   _____

   _____

Reading-Writing Connection

Write a descriptive paragraph about an area in your community, without naming the actual place. Use words that appeal to the senses. Read your description to other students. Have them identify the place you have described by naming it or drawing it.

Skill: Comparing and Contrasting

BACKGROUND INFORMATION

"Egypt: Gift of the Nile" compares and contrasts the role of the Nile river in ancient Egypt and in modern Egypt. Like many civilizations, ancient Egypt arose along the banks of a great river. The Nile, bringing water and life to the dry desert land, has always been Egypt's chief natural resource. With modern advances in technology, Egyptians can now use and control the Nile's flow as never before.

SKILL FOCUS: Comparing and Contrasting

Comparing and contrasting are important ways to understand what you read. **Comparing** means noticing how two or more things are alike. **Contrasting** means noticing how they are different.

Writers often use comparison and contrast to show relationships between two topics. The writer may present information about the two topics separately. The first part of an article, for example, might tell about one place. The next part of the article might tell about a different place.

When an article is organized in this way, the writer does not tell readers directly how the two topics are similar and how they are different. Readers must read about each topic and then look for the similarities and differences themselves.

▶ Use details from the paragraphs below to complete the Comparison-and-Contrast Chart about ancient and modern Egypt.

Scholars believe that between 1 million and 4 million people lived in ancient Egypt. The vast majority of them lived in the Nile Valley. The rest of the population lived in the Nile Delta and on oases west of the river.

Today, Egypt has more than 60 million people. Almost all of them live on just 4 percent of the nation's land—along the Nile river and the Suez Canal. Only 1 out of 100 Egyptians lives in the deserts or mountains east and west of the Nile.

Place	Population	Where People Lived
Ancient Egypt		
Modern Egypt		

CONTEXT CLUES: Details

When you read a word that you don't know, look for context clues to help you understand the word's meaning. Often these clues are **details**, small pieces of information that make the meaning of a new word clear.

Read the sentences below.

*In both ancient and modern times, the Nile river has been the source of Egypt's **prosperity**. The Nile has brought Egypt good fortune, wealth, and power.*

If you don't know the meaning of *prosperity*, the details *good fortune*, *wealth*, and *power* can help you figure it out. *Prosperity* means "wealth and well-being."

▶ Circle the details that help you figure out the meaning of the underlined word below.

*In addition, the year-round plantings **deplete** minerals in the soil, further reducing its fertility.*

As you read, use details to help you understand the meaning of the underlined words *silt*, *famine*, and *feluccas*.

Strategy Tip

As you read "Egypt: Gift of the Nile," look for comparisons and contrasts. Look back and forth between the sections to see how ancient Egypt and modern Egypt are alike and different.

Egypt: Gift of the Nile

Ancient Egypt was a great civilization that arose more than 5,000 years ago. Modern Egypt is one of the most powerful and most influential countries of the Arab world. In both ancient and modern times, the Nile river has been the source of Egypt's prosperity. The Nile has brought Egypt good fortune, wealth, and power.

The Nile River: Giver of Life

The Nile is the longest river in the world. From its source in the mountains of central Africa to its mouth at the Mediterranean Sea, the river flows northward for almost 4,150 miles (6,640 kilometers). Lake Victoria in Tanzania feeds one branch of the river. This branch is called the White Nile because of the color of the limestone particles that it carries. Another branch of the Nile begins in the highlands of Ethiopia. It is called the Blue Nile because its pure water reflects the color of the sky. These two branches meet at Khartoum (kar TOOM) in Sudan.

As the river flows north, it crosses 950 miles (1,520 kilometers) of Egypt's barren desert land. In the far south of Egypt, the Aswan (AS wahn) High Dam, built across the river, has helped to control the waters of the Nile. Behind the dam lies Lake Nasser (NAS ər), a huge lake created by engineers.

From the Aswan High Dam north to Cairo, the river winds through the desert. It supports life along its banks and farming in the Nile Valley. Fertile strips of land lie on both sides of the Nile. These strips of land, sometimes as wide as 14 miles (22.4 kilometers) or as narrow as 3 miles (4.8 kilometers), support nearly half of Egypt's population.

At Cairo, Egypt's capital and Africa's largest city, the Nile fans out into a fertile triangle of small **tributaries** (TRIB yə TAIR eez), or streams. This area of soil is called the Nile Delta. Stretching 90 miles (144 kilometers) from Cairo to the Mediterranean Sea, the **delta** is 150 miles (240 kilometers) wide at the coast. Yet this small area of rich land supports the other half of the nation's population. In fact, the valley and the delta of the Nile together support

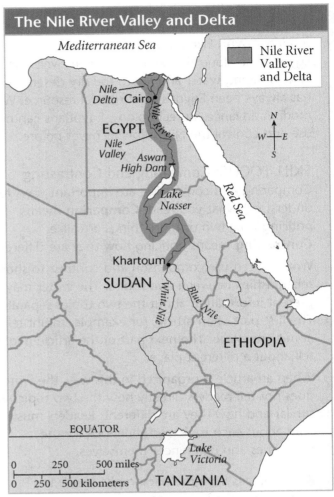

The Nile river irrigates long, narrow strips of land along its banks.

almost the entire Egyptian population. Of Egypt's 386,000 square miles (1,003,600 square kilometers), only one-thirtieth is inhabited.

Ancient Egypt and the Nile

The Nile river enabled the ancient Egyptians not only to survive but also to develop an advanced civilization. Because the Nile brought water into the parched desert, the people there could grow crops and raise livestock. The river was also important for travel, communication, and trade.

Early Agriculture During a visit to ancient Egypt, the Greek historian Herodotus (hə RAHD ə təs) declared that the land was "wholly the gift of the Nile." Every year Egyptian farmers worked the land according to seasons that were based on the flow of the Nile. From June to September was the Flood. During this time, the Nile reached its highest level. It flooded the **irrigation** (IR ə GAY shən) systems that the farmers had built to supply water to their crops.

The second season, called the Emergence, lasted from October to February. During this time, the flood waters subsided, leaving behind a rich, black silt. At the beginning of the season, farmers planted their crops in this layer of fertile soil. At the end of the season was the harvest.

The last season, from March to May, was called the Drought. During this hot, dry season, nothing grew. Once again, farmers waited for the floods to arrive and the cycle to begin all over again.

Wheat was the most important crop for the ancient Egyptian farmer. It was used to make bread and to fatten cattle. Small plots of land were also planted with vegetables, such as beans, onions, garlic, and lentils. In addition to food, flax and **papyrus** (pə PY rəs) reed grew along the banks of the Nile. Flax was used to make clothing and papyrus reed to make paper.

✔ Farmers developed systems of ditches and basins to trap the river's water. They invented water wheels to carry water from the river to the land. They learned to estimate the time and height of the Nile's floods. Yet the river was still beyond their control. Some years it rose to enormous heights, washing away homes and killing livestock. Other years it did not flood at all, bringing famine (FAM ən) to the land. This severe shortage of food often resulted in starvation and misery.

Transportation and Trade For the early Egyptians, the Nile was a natural highway that linked the villages along its banks. The Nile was so important that even the language of ancient Egypt reflected the river's influence. The word for *travel* was either *khed*, to go downstream, or *khent*, to go upstream.

To travel on the Nile, the Egyptians built sailboats, called feluccas (fə LUK əz). Because the river flowed from south to north, these small, narrow boats could follow the river's current northward. Because the winds of the Mediterranean Sea blew north to south, the feluccas were propelled southward by their triangular sails. Merchants sailed from village to village with their wares. Grain barges floated north to the delta. During the construction of the great pyramids, river barges carried heavy stones to building sites.

The river also provided Egypt with a major route for trade with other countries. Egyptian traders sailed the Nile to do business with merchants from Syria and Mesopotamia (mes ə pə TAY mee ə). The Nile was a lifeline of commerce.

Modern Egypt and the Nile

The Nile is still the country's primary resource. Egypt's rapidly growing population remains concentrated along the Nile Valley and the Nile Delta. However, the Aswan High Dam, completed in 1970, has changed the relationship between the Nile river and the Egyptian people. Not only has it affected farming in the Nile Valley, but it has also transformed the country's economy.

Modern Agriculture Built across the Nile river in southern Egypt, the Aswan High Dam now controls the mighty river. Lake Nasser, extending 300 miles (480 kilometers) behind the dam into Sudan, collects the river water that the dam holds back.

The dam has affected Egypt's agriculture in several ways. The dam holds back the river during the high-water season. It then releases the water in a constant flow to the north. Thus, the dam has eliminated the annual flood and drought cycle along the Nile Valley. During several dry years in the 1970s, the dam provided Nile water to irrigate farmland and thereby prevented widespread famine.

Farmers can now rely on a steady, year-round supply of water to their land. To make use of the Nile's changed flow, new irrigation systems have been built. Modern diesel pumps bring the river water to the land. Large, heavy-duty tractors till and plant the earth. However, in some places, Egypt's farming traditions remain unchanged. Some farmers still turn the soil with ancient plows and irrigate the land with water wheels.

In modern times, cotton has become Egypt's most important crop. In fact, Egypt leads the world

Even today, some feluccas sail the Nile as they did 4,000 years ago.

in cotton production. Cotton plants require a steady supply of water. So the Aswan High Dam has made cotton growing possible. In recent years, the Egyptian government has encouraged farmers to grow other crops, too. Today Egypt also produces beans, corn, rice, sugar cane, and wheat.

The Aswan High Dam has also caused some problems for the Egyptian farmer. Besides water, the dam holds back the rich silt that the Nile floods used to carry into the Nile Valley. Because this silt is rich in nutrients, it once acted as a natural fertilizer for crops. Now farmers have to enrich the soil with costly chemical fertilizers. The absence of silt is also seriously damaging the environment by causing the erosion of land along the Mediterranean coast near the Nile. In addition, the year-round plantings deplete minerals in the soil, further reducing its fertility.

Transportation, Commerce, and Industry The Nile is still Egypt's most convenient means of transportation. Feluccas like those of ancient times still sail up and down the river. In addition, the barges and steamers that carry much of Egypt's commercial freight clog the great waterway. Construction materials, iron ore, agricultural products, and industrial equipment are all transported along the Nile. A network of highways and railroads also crisscrosses the Nile Valley.

In recent years, the power of the Nile has been harnessed for uses other than agriculture. Generators at the Aswan High Dam have tripled Egypt's output of electricity. This increased output has revolutionized Egypt's manufacturing capability. Electric power is vital to industrial production and has helped the country develop as a modern nation.

From ancient times to modern, Egypt has prospered. The Nile river has given the Egyptian people the gift of water and thereby the gift of life.

COMPREHENSION

1. Use the map on page 98 to help you fill in the blanks in the passage below.

   The Nile begins as two separate

   branches, called the _____ Nile and the

   _____ Nile. These two branches meet in

   _____ and then flow _____

   together until they reach the mouth of the river

   in the city of _____ on the

   _____ Sea.

2. Describe the sequence of the three seasons in ancient Egypt, and explain how they affected farmers.

   _____

   _____

   _____

   _____

   _____

   _____

3. How does the Aswan High Dam prevent famine in Egypt during dry years?

_____

_____

4. Write two causes for the effect below.

Cause 1: _____

_____

Cause 2: _____

_____

Effect: Egyptian farmers now need to fertilize their soil.

5. Reread the paragraph that has an ✘ next to it. Then underline the sentence that states the main idea of the paragraph.

6. Write the letter of the correct meaning on the line next to each word.

_____ silt

_____ famine

_____ feluccas

a. small, narrow boats propelled by triangular sails

b. grains of fertile soil carried by moving water

c. severe shortage of food, often resulting in starvation

CRITICAL THINKING

1. What sort of land lies beyond the strips of fertile soil along both sides of the Nile Valley?

_____

_____

2. Reread the paragraph with a ✔ next to it. Write a sentence that states its main idea.

_____

_____

3. List two facts about the Nile that make it ideal for transportation.

_____

_____

4. Identify each of the following statements as a fact or an opinion. Fill in the circle next to each statement that expresses a fact.

○ **a.** The Nile river crosses 950 miles (1,520 kilometers) of Egypt.

○ **b.** Egypt should not have built the Aswan High Dam.

○ **c.** The Aswan High Dam tripled Egypt's output of electricity.

5. Write the cause for the following effect.

Cause: _____

_____

Effect: Egypt has become a leading world producer of textiles.

6. Explain the major drawback of the Aswan High Dam for Egypt's agriculture.

_____

_____

SKILL FOCUS: COMPARING AND CONTRASTING

The two charts below outline similarities and differences between ancient and modern Egypt. Look at the general topics listed in the center column of these charts. Then reread the selection, looking for information about how ancient Egypt and modern Egypt compare and contrast on these topics. When you have collected this information, write one sentence for each topic under each heading. The first sentence on each chart is done for you.

Comparisons		
Ancient Egypt	**Topic**	**Modern Egypt**
The Nile was Egypt's main source of water.	**Source of Water**	The Nile is still Egypt's main source of water.
	Location of Population	
	Means of Transportation	

Contrasts		
Ancient Egypt	**Topic**	**Modern Egypt**
Wheat was the main crop.	**Major Crop**	Cotton is the main crop.
	Growing Season	
	Industry	

Reading-Writing Connection

On a separate sheet of paper, write two paragraphs comparing and contrasting ancient and modern Egypt. In the first paragraph, explain similarities, using the Comparisons Chart above for details. In the second paragraph, explain differences, using the Contrasts Chart for details.

Skill: Main Idea and Supporting Details

BACKGROUND INFORMATION

"Hot Deserts" explains how plants and animals survive in hot deserts. Any structure or response in an organism's body that helps it survive is called an adaptation (ad ap TAY shən). Plants and animals in the desert are well adapted to their harsh environment. A camel's hump and a cactus's spines are two familiar desert adaptations.

SKILL FOCUS: Main Idea and Supporting Details

A paragraph's **main idea** is its overall subject, or what the paragraph is all about. In some paragraphs, the main idea is stated directly. In other paragraphs, it must be inferred. The **supporting details** in a paragraph tell more about the main idea.

A paragraph may include two different kinds of supporting details. **Major details** give important information to support the main idea. **Minor details** provide information of less importance. They often support the major details with examples.

As you read the following paragraph, look for its main idea, its major details, and its minor details.

Dry, desertlike areas occur in both hot and cold regions of North America. In the Arctic, northern Canada, and Alaska, there are cold, dry areas called tundras. Hot desert regions cover parts of the southwestern United States. Hot desert areas get very little rain during their short, mild winters.

You can show the paragraph's main idea and supporting details in a chart, as the one below.

Main Idea: Dry desertlike areas occur in both hot and cold regions of North America.

Major Details: Arctic tundras in northern Canada, Alaska | hot deserts in parts of southwestern United States

Minor Details: little rain during short, mild winters

Read the paragraph below. Circle the sentence that states the main idea. Next, draw a line under the major details. Finally, draw two lines under any minor details.

The seeds of many desert plants have chemical coatings, which help the plants survive. These chemicals keep the seeds from sprouting when conditions are too dry. Only a heavy rainfall will wash away the chemicals so the seeds can sprout. After a heavy rain, a desert comes alive with new sprouts and flowers.

CONTEXT CLUES: Synonyms

Synonyms are words with similar meanings. When you read an unfamiliar word, look for a synonym nearby that is used in a similar way. It may help you figure out the meaning of the new word.

Read the following sentences. Look for a synonym for the underlined word.

The Empty Quarter, which is located in southeastern Saudi Arabia, is the largest __expanse__ of sand in the world. Its spread covers almost a million square kilometers.

If you don't know the meaning of *expanse*, the synonym *spread* can help you figure it out. An *expanse* is a "spread of land."

Read the following sentences. Circle a synonym for the underlined word.

In the future, more desert may be __transformed__ into farmland. Advanced new irrigation techniques have already changed some desert sand into crop-producing soil.

As you read, use synonyms to find the meanings of *transient, dense,* and *germinating.*

Strategy Tip

As you read "Hot Deserts," identify the main idea and supporting details of each paragraph. Decide which details are major details and which are minor details.

HOT DESERTS

1. During summer days, temperatures in hot desert regions may soar to well over 38 degrees Celsius. However, as the sun sets, the temperature drops sharply. At night, temperatures may be more than 30 degrees lower than during the day. In the winter, deserts may even have freezing temperatures. In addition, the air is very dry. Over an average year, no more than 25 centimeters (10 inches) of rain falls. The desert's extreme environment is one of the most difficult areas on Earth in which to live.

2. Hot deserts exist in several parts of the world. In the Middle East there are two desert regions. The Sahara, which stretches the full width of northern Africa, is the largest desert in the world. It covers more than 9 million square kilometers. A number of rivers flow into the Sahara, forming "islands" of living things throughout this barren region. The Empty Quarter, which is located in southeastern Saudi Arabia, is the largest expanse of sand in the world. Its spread covers almost a million square kilometers. Unlike the Sahara, the Empty Quarter has no rivers flowing into it. However, it does have <u>transient</u> streams. These temporary streams dry up and disappear during periods of drought.

3. Many kinds of **organisms** (OR gə niz əms), or living things, survive in the world's hot deserts. At nightfall, birds, lizards, snakes, and small mammals scurry about in search of food. After a spring rain, the desert bursts into life as wildflowers quickly grow and blossom. How living things survive and reproduce in the desert has long fascinated scientists. By carefully studying and observing desert organisms, scientists can learn their secrets.

Desert Animals

4. Both warm-blooded and cold-blooded desert animals have ways to escape the desert heat. Warm-blooded animals are those that maintain a constant body temperature. The body temperature of cold-blooded animals rises and falls, depending on the temperature of their surroundings. Warm-

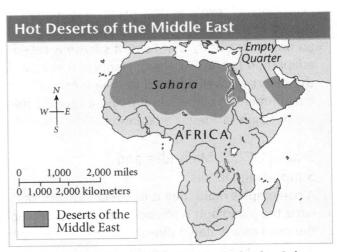

Hot Deserts of the Middle East

Empty Quarter

Sahara

N
W—E
S

AFRICA

0   1,000   2,000 miles
0 1,000 2,000 kilometers

▨ Deserts of the Middle East

The deserts of the Middle East include the Sahara and the Empty Quarter.

blooded desert animals, such as rats and mice, rest during the day, often staying in cool underground burrows. At night, they search for food. Animals that are out during the day, such as cold-blooded lizards and snakes, are active only for short periods. As their body temperature rises, these reptiles move into the shade in order to cool down. In the early evening, when the sun grows weaker, the reptiles become more active and resume their search for food.

5. Getting enough water to survive is a major problem for all desert animals. Some desert animals, such as desert birds and bats, manage to find water holes. Other desert animals, such as the kangaroo rat and the related **jerboa**, get water only from the food they eat. Because these animals eat mainly dry seeds, they must survive on a tiny amount of water.

This jerboa can survive on the tiny amounts of water it gets from the seeds it eats.

6. Most deserts have only a small number of frogs and toads because these animals must be near water to survive. Yet even these creatures have adapted to desert conditions. When small amounts of water collect in temporary streams, the desert-living frogs and toads become active. After a rainfall, they lay their eggs. The eggs grow into tadpoles in a few days and into adults in just four weeks. When the puddles dry up, the adult frogs or toads dig into the ground. Their metabolism (mə TAB ə LIZ əm), or rate of using energy, slows, and they stay beneath the ground until the next rain. That may be as much as a year away. Until then, their bodily activities continue at a reduced rate.

7. The camel—often called the ship of the desert—is one of the most successful desert animals. Camels can go for long periods without water, but eventually they must drink. When water becomes available to them after a long drought, they may drink 95 liters of water or more. When water is not available, camels can survive the desert heat because of the fat stored in their humps. A camel's hump contains about 12 kilograms of fat. Fat is rich in

The acacia has a taproot that extends deep into the ground to find water.

(ə KAY shəz), have a thick **taproot** that grows deep into the ground until it reaches water. The taproots of some plants go down more than 30 meters. While the taproot is growing toward water, plant growth aboveground is not thick. However, after the taproot reaches water, the growth aboveground often becomes quite <u>dense</u>. Other desert plants have shallow roots that grow just below the surface of the ground and extend out from the plant for many meters. When rain comes, the root system acts like a large sponge, capturing most of the water that falls on it.

Hydrogen from the fat in a camel's hump combines with oxygen to form water.

hydrogen. As the fat is digested, hydrogen from the fat combines with oxygen in the air that the camel breathes. The result is H_2O, or water. Each kilogram of fat that a camel digests yields about a liter of water.

Desert Plants

8. Desert plants have different kinds of root systems that help them survive in an environment with little water. Some plants, such as acacias

Some desert plants, like the cactus, store water in their fleshy stems during dry periods.

9. Other desert plants have different ways to survive despite the lack of water. The seeds of annuals, which grow, flower, and die in one season, are coated with a natural chemical that prevents them from <u>germinating</u>. However, when water washes away this chemical, the seeds can begin sprouting. The amount of water necessary to wash away the chemical is the same amount that the seed needs to sprout, grow, flower, and make new seeds for the next generation. **Succulents** (SUK yoo lənts), such as cactus, store water in their thick, fleshy stems for use during dry periods.

10. Plants need leaves to make food, but they lose much water through their leaves. Desert plants have different ways to reduce this loss. The leaves of many desert plants are small and covered with a waxy layer. Both the small leaf size and the waxy covering reduce water loss. Other desert plants grow leaves only after a rainfall. Then when dry weather comes again, the leaves are quickly dropped, before much water is lost through them. Some plants, such as cactus, exhibit an extreme way to reduce water loss through leaves. They don't have leaves at all. Their stems carry out the food-producing function of leaves.

11. In spite of the harsh conditions of deserts, many organisms can survive in them, including human beings. In the future, more desert land may be transformed into farmland. Advanced new irrigation techniques have already changed some desert sand into crop-producing soil.

COMPREHENSION

1. What is a desert's average yearly rainfall?

   _____

   _____

2. How many square kilometers does the Sahara desert cover?

   _____

   _____

3. Where is the Empty Quarter?

   _____

   _____

4. How do camels get water without drinking?

   _____

   _____

5. Explain how rats escape daytime desert heat.

   _____

   _____

6. Where do jerboas get the water they need?

   _____

   _____

7. What do desert frogs and toads do during a drought?

   _____

   _____

8. How are frogs and toads able to reproduce in deserts?

   _____

   _____

9. Which desert has permanent rivers, the Sahara or the Empty Quarter?

   _____

   _____

10. Explain how a taproot helps an acacia survive in the desert.

   _____

   _____

   _____

11. Where is most water lost from a plant?

   _____

   _____

12. Complete each sentence with the correct word.

transient   dense   germinating

a. Luckily, the unseasonable weather was

_____ and passed quickly.

b. The seeds are _____ in the field.

c. The fog was so _____ that we couldn't see the road.

CRITICAL THINKING

Fill in the circle next to the correct phrase to complete each sentence.

1. If the Sahara covers about nine times more area than the Empty Quarter, but the Empty Quarter has a larger expanse of sand, then
   - ○ a. part of the Empty Quarter must be swamp.
   - ○ b. part of the Sahara must be rocky or hilly.
   - ○ c. part of the Sahara must be cold.
   - ○ d. part of the Empty Quarter must have trees.

2. Desert animals are usually more active at night because
   - ○ a. it is cooler at night.
   - ○ b. they like the dark.
   - ○ c. they are less likely to be attacked at night.
   - ○ d. it rains only at night.

3. If you were stranded in a desert, your easiest water source would be plants that
   - ○ a. have a taproot.
   - ○ b. lose their leaves.
   - ○ c. had died.
   - ○ d. are succulents.

4. Desert mammals are more active
   - ○ a. after dusk.
   - ○ b. after dawn.
   - ○ c. after a drought.
   - ○ d. at noon.

SKILL FOCUS: MAIN IDEA AND SUPPORTING DETAILS

When completed, the charts on the next page will show how the ideas in each paragraph of the selection are related. For each numbered paragraph, copy the sentence that states the main idea. Then write the major details that support or develop the main idea, using only key words or phrases. Finally, write the minor details, using only key words or phrases. Some parts are done for you.

Paragraph 2

Main Idea

Major Details

Sahara Desert in northern Africa—the largest desert

Empty Quarter in southeastern Saudi Arabia—the largest expanse of sand

Minor Details

almost a million square kilometers

Paragraph 4

Main Idea

Major Details

warm-blooded animals stay in cool underground burrows

Minor Details

such as rats and mice

Paragraph 9

Main Idea

Major Details

Minor Details

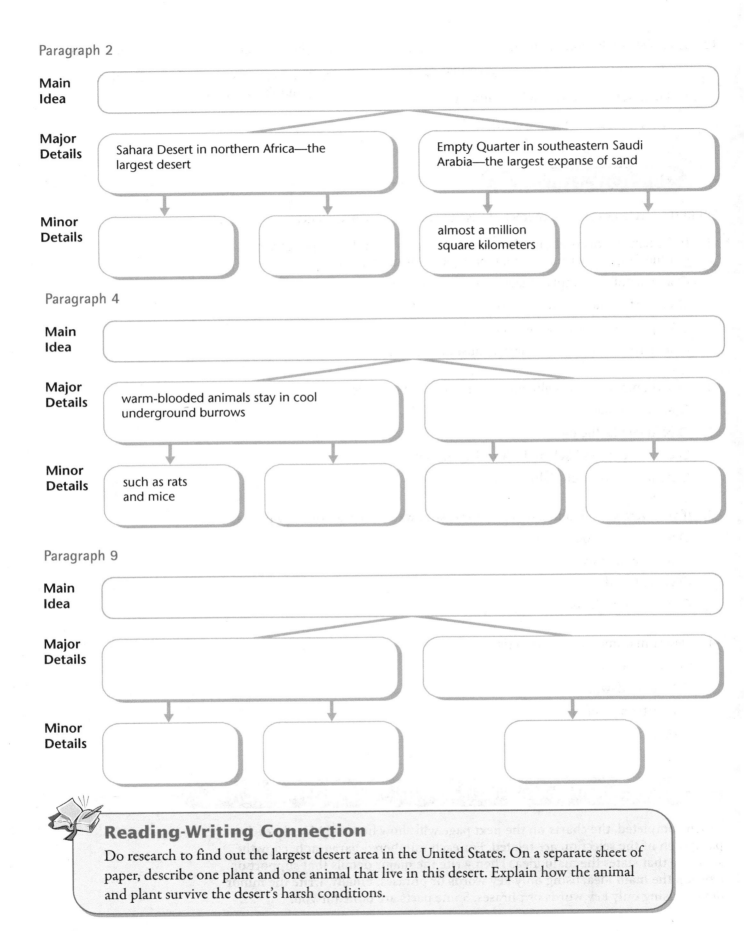

Reading-Writing Connection

Do research to find out the largest desert area in the United States. On a separate sheet of paper, describe one plant and one animal that live in this desert. Explain how the animal and plant survive the desert's harsh conditions.

Skill: Understanding Geometric Terms

BACKGROUND INFORMATION

In "Geometric Terms," you will learn some mathematical terms that will help you when you study geometry. Geometry is a branch of mathematics that deals with shapes and sizes. Geometry dates back at least 5,000 years to ancient Egypt. There, architects used geometry to build the pyramids.

SKILL FOCUS: Understanding Geometric Terms

Mathematics is concerned with more than just numbers. It also deals with shapes and sizes. This branch of mathematics is called **geometry**. In geometry, you learn about different kinds of shapes and the terms used to name them. You also learn how to measure the shapes.

You probably already know the names of certain geometric figures—triangles, rectangles, and circles, for example. You can use geometry to solve problems related to different kinds of shapes. For example, you can figure out the perimeter of a figure. The perimeter of a figure is the total distance around it. You can also figure out a figure's area. The area of a figure is the total amount of space it covers.

It is also important to be able to recognize whether the two halves of a geometric figure are symmetrical (si MET ri kəl). The two halves of a symmetrical figure match each other exactly. A symmetrical figure may have straight or curved sides. It may have three, four, or more sides.

▶ Look at the triangle below. The length of each side is given. Then answer the questions in the next column.

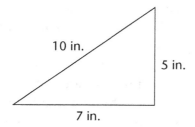

10 in.

5 in.

7 in.

1. What is the perimeter, or distance around the triangle? _____

2. Is this triangle symmetrical? How do you know?

_____

WORD CLUES

In "Geometric Terms," you will see many words with special **math prefixes**. Learning these prefixes and their meanings will help you understand the names of geometric terms.

Prefix	Meaning
tri-	three
quad-	four
pent-	five
hex-	six

▶ Use math prefixes to answer these questions.

1. How many sides does the Pentagon in Washington, D.C. have? _____

2. How many legs does a tripod have? _____

3. If a mother has quadruplets, how many babies does she have? _____

4. How many feet does a hexapod have? _____

Strategy Tip

When you read "Geometric Terms," study the diagrams carefully. Be sure that you understand the meaning of each geometric term before going on to the next one. Compare and contrast the geometric figures to understand how each one is similar to and different from other kinds of figures.

Geometric Terms

If you fold a piece of paper in half and cut out a shape from the folded side, then unfold the paper, the two halves of the paper will be **symmetrical** (si MEH tri kəl). In a symmetrical shape, the two halves match exactly. Here is a symmetrical geometric figure made by cutting folded paper.

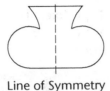

Line of Symmetry

In the picture, the fold is shown as a dotted line, called the **line of symmetry** for the figure. The two halves on the sides of the line of symmetry match exactly. However, each half is a mirror image of the other half.

Some figures have more than one line of symmetry. Drawings of symmetrical figures usually show all the lines of symmetry. The circle is an exception to this rule because every line through the center of a circle is a line of symmetry.

Drawings give the properties, or characteristics, of some of the figures. One property of a figure is the distance around it, known as its **perimeter**. Another property is the amount of space it covers, or its **area**. For most geometric figures, there is a rule, or **formula**, that tells how to find the area.

A figure with three straight sides is called a **triangle**. If two of the sides have the same length, the triangle is **isosceles** (eye SAHS ə leez). An isosceles triangle has only one line of symmetry.

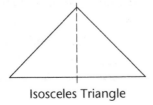

Isosceles Triangle

When all three sides of a triangle have the same length, it is **equilateral** (EE kwə LAT ər əl). An equilateral triangle has three lines of symmetry.

In the equilateral triangle below, each side has a length of 3 meters. The label on each side is *3m*, which tells you the length of the side (*m* is the abbreviation for *meter*). Because the perimeter is the distance around a figure, the perimeter of this triangle is 9 meters.

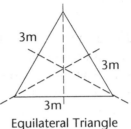

3m   3m

3m

Equilateral Triangle

Fold a sheet of paper diagonally, or from corner to corner. Then fold it diagonally again, making sure that the two edges of the first fold meet. The result of the two folds is a right angle. In a **right triangle**, one of the three angles of the triangle is a right angle. A right triangle with two equal sides is also isosceles.

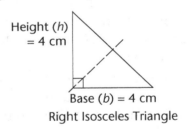

Height (*h*)
= 4 cm

Base (*b*) = 4 cm

Right Isosceles Triangle

The sides of this right triangle are each 4 centimeters long (*cm* is the abbreviation for *centimeter*). If you know the length of the base of a triangle, as well as its height, you can figure out its area. Area is the space inside the lines of a figure.

Area is measured in square units. The formula for the area of a right triangle is $A = \frac{1}{2}bh$. The letter A stands for the number of square units in the area. The letter b stands for the length of the base, 4 centimeters. The letter h stands for the height, also 4 centimeters. To find the area of a right triangle, substitute numbers for the letters in the formula $A = \frac{1}{2}bh$. When two letters are written next to each other, or when a number is written next to a letter, they are multiplied.

$$A = \frac{1}{2} \times b \times h$$

Include the measurements in the formula.

$$A = \frac{1}{2} \times 4 \times 4$$
$$= 8$$

The area of the right triangle shown is 8 square centimeters, or 8 cm².

A figure with four straight sides and four right angles is a **rectangle**. The formula for the area of a rectangle is $A = lw$. Again, A stands for the number of square units in the area. The letter l stands for the number of units in the length. The letter w stands for the number of units in the width.

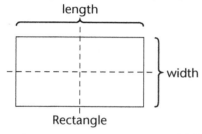
Rectangle

If the sides of a rectangle are the same length, the figure is a **square**.

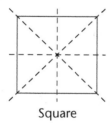
Square

A **rhombus** (ROM bəs) is like a square because it has four sides of the same length. It is different from a square because none of the angles is a right angle.

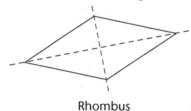
Rhombus

Rectangles, squares, and rhombuses are called **quadrilaterals** (kwod rə LAT ər əls). Any figure with four straight sides is a quadrilateral.

A **pentagon** (PEN tə gon) is any figure with five straight sides. This figure is a regular pentagon. A figure is regular if all the sides are the same length and all the angles are the same size.

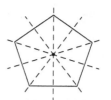
Regular Pentagon

A **hexagon** (HEK sə gon) is any figure with six straight sides.

All figures that have straight sides are called **polygons** (POL i gonz).

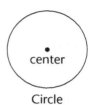
Circle

A **circle** does not have straight sides. Therefore, it is not a polygon. All the points in a circle are the same distance from a single point, called the center. Every line through the center of the circle is a line of symmetry.

Not every geometric figure has a line of symmetry. The following three figures are examples of polygons that are not symmetrical.

A **scalene** (skay LEEN) triangle is a triangle in which no two sides are the same length.

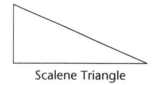
Scalene Triangle

A **trapezoid** (TRAP ə zoyd) is a quadrilateral in which two sides are parallel. Parallel sides do not meet no matter how far they are extended. The other two sides are not parallel.

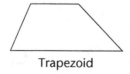
Trapezoid

A **parallelogram** (pahr ə LEL ə gram) is a quadrilateral in which both pairs of sides are parallel.

Parallelogram

MATHEMATICS

1. What is the distance around a geometric figure called?

_____

_____

2. Look at all the diagrams in the selection. Name the figures that have exactly two lines of symmetry.

_____

_____

3. Which figures in the selection have straight sides that are all the same length?

_____

_____

4. Which figures in the selection are quadrilaterals?

_____

_____

5. What is a circle?

_____

_____

6. Look at all the diagrams in the selection. Which figures have two or more sides that are parallel?

_____

_____

CRITICAL THINKING

1. Identify the kind of triangle this is. _____

2. A kite is a geometric figure with two equal short sides and two equal long sides, but it is not a rectangle. How would you classify a kite? _____

5 m   5 m

4 m

3. What is another name for a regular quadrilateral? _____

SKILL FOCUS: UNDERSTANDING GEOMETRIC TERMS

A. Draw a line of symmetry through each of the letters below. If a letter has two lines of symmetry, draw both of them. If a letter has no line of symmetry, circle it. The first one has been done for you. Then answer the questions below.

A B C D E F G H I J K L M
N O P Q R S T U V W X Y Z

1. Which letters have vertical lines of symmetry? _____

2. Which letters have horizontal lines of symmetry? _____

3. Which letters have two lines of symmetry? _____

4. Which letters have no lines of symmetry? _____

B. Answer the following questions about the perimeters of the geometric figures below. Remember to use units in your answers.

1. What is the perimeter of the rectangle shown below? _____

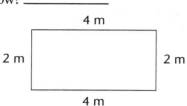

2. The polygon below is an equilateral triangle. What is its perimeter? _____

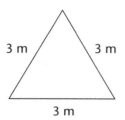

3. What is the perimeter of the rhombus below? _____

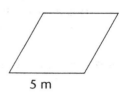

4. What is the perimeter of the parallelogram below? _____

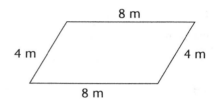

C. Answer the following questions about the areas of the geometric figures below.

1. What is the area of the right triangle below?

$A = \frac{1}{2}bh$ _____

2. What is the area of the rectangle below?

$A = lw$ _____

3. What is the area of the rectangle below?

$A = lw$ _____

4. What is the area of the right triangle below?

$A = \frac{1}{2}bh$ _____

Reading-Writing Connection

On a separate sheet of paper, write a paragraph explaining how you would go about finding the perimeter of your school building.

Skill: Synonyms and Antonyms

A **synonym** is a word having the same or nearly the same meaning as another word. An **antonym** is a word that is opposite in meaning to another word.

A. Underline the word that is the best *synonym* of the italicized word.

1. *apparent*
   a. amazing   **c.** alarming
   b. visible   **d.** impossible

2. *cautious*
   a. burning   **c.** careless
   b. clean   **d.** watchful

3. *challenge*
   a. dare   **c.** flavor
   b. change   **d.** plan

4. *detach*
   a. connect   **c.** warn
   b. poison   **d.** separate

5. *fascinate*
   a. charm   **c.** sweeten
   b. horrify   **d.** look

6. *mammoth*
   a. tiny   **c.** loud
   b. wicked   **d.** huge

7. *portion*
   a. ownership   **c.** section
   b. painting   **d.** covering

8. *rehearse*
   a. practice   **c.** command
   b. warn   **d.** relax

B. Underline the word that is the best *antonym* of the italicized word.

1. *bright*
   a. dull   **c.** short
   b. shiny   **d.** forceful

2. *build*
   a. raise   **c.** add
   b. grow   **d.** destroy

3. *filth*
   a. dirt   **c.** soap
   b. cleanliness   **d.** refuge

4. *necessary*
   a. unimportant   **c.** fancy
   b. needed   **d.** required

5. *continue*
   a. maintain   **c.** begin
   b. end   **d.** remain

6. *disgrace*
   a. shame   **c.** honor
   b. disease   **d.** ugly

7. *quarrel*
   a. argue   **c.** agree
   b. grow   **d.** calm

8. *reduced*
   a. shrunk   **c.** correct
   b. increased   **d.** lowered

Skill: Taking Notes and Summarizing

One way to take notes is to write a summary. A **summary** tells the most important ideas in as few words as possible. Before writing a summary, carefully read the selection. Because a summary is much shorter than the whole selection, you need to decide which details are important. A good summary should include only the main ideas and major details in a selection.

Read the following selection. Underline the main ideas and major details that you think should be included in your summary. Then write a one-paragraph summary in your own words.

In recent years, Egyptian women have won new rights and have taken a greater role in public affairs. Some people credit this change to Jehan Sadat, wife of the late Egyptian president, Anwar Sadat. A well-known leader in the women's movement, Jehan Sadat encouraged her husband to take steps to improve the position of Egyptian women.

In 1979, President Sadat announced new laws giving women additional political and legal rights. He added 30 seats to the 360-seat Egyptian parliament. All the new seats were to be reserved for women representatives. At the same time, he decreed that one-fifth of the members of local city councils should be women. When the newly elected women entered parliament, Jehan Sadat arranged a series of meetings for them. She encouraged the new members to ask a lot of questions and to raise issues that concerned them. "I'm very satisfied," Jehan Sadat said after the meetings, "because I fought for many, many years for this."

Jehan Sadat was not the only woman to influence public policy. Women gained important positions in several areas. Sadat appointed another

Jehan Sadat

woman, Amina el-Said, chairperson of the board of the largest state-run Egyptian publishing company. Sadat had met el-Said in the early 1950s, when they were both on the staff of the publishing company.

Educated Egyptian women have moved into leading positions in a number of areas, including medicine, media, and education. For example, Dr. Haifaa Shanawany has won international recognition for her family-oriented medical services throughout Asia, Africa, and Europe. The success of women leaders in Egypt has set an example for women in other Middle Eastern nations and has helped them counter opposition to their new roles.

_____

_____

_____

_____

_____

Skill: Outlining

An **outline** shows how the main idea and supporting details in a selection are organized.

Read the following paragraph. Then look at the outline next to it.

In 1922, archaeologist Howard Carter entered the four-room tomb of the Pharoah Tutankhamun, who had been buried almost 3,300 years earlier. The largest room, the Antechamber, was 26 by 12 feet. Its contents included both everyday and religious objects. The Burial Chamber was 17 by 11 feet. It held objects for the last rites and the afterlife. Next to this room was the Treasury, which was 16 by 12$\frac{1}{2}$ feet. This room contained mostly funerary equipment. The smallest room was the 14-by-8$\frac{1}{2}$-feet Annex. Provisions for the dead king were kept here.

The Tomb of Tutankhamun

I. Four rooms of the tomb
   A. Antechamber
      1. Largest room—26 by 12 feet
      2. Everyday and religious objects
   B. Burial Chamber
      1. 17 by 11 feet
      2. Objects for the last rites and afterlife
   C. Treasury
      1. 16 by 12$\frac{1}{2}$ feet
      2. Funerary equipment
   D. Annex
      1. Smallest room—14 by 8$\frac{1}{2}$ feet
      2. Provisions for the king

Notice that *Four rooms of the tomb*, the main idea of the paragraph, is written next to Roman numeral I. *Antechamber*, written next to capital letter A, is the first major detail about the rooms. Next to number 1 is the phrase *Largest room—26 by 12 feet*, a minor detail about the Antechamber. Notice that the outline uses only words and phrases—not full sentences.

Every outline should have a title. It should always include at least two main ideas; it can never have a Roman numeral I without a II. There should be at least two major details under each main idea and at least two minor details under each major detail.

Use the information in the next four paragraphs to complete the outline on page 117.

As Carter entered the Antechamber, he thought it looked like a rummage sale. His procedure was to assign a number to each object for photographing and record keeping. It took seven weeks to record and remove small objects, just to make room for dismantling larger things. Three large animal-shaped couches, royal thrones, and stools lined one wall. Four dismantled chariots were piled in a corner. Guarding a doorway were two life-sized statues of the king.

Carter went to work next in the Burial Chamber. Taking apart the shrines, which almost filled the room, involved modern scaffolding and took four months. An elaborate pulley system was devised to open the coffins. Studying the king's mummy took eight months. In all, four shrines were nested inside one another, protecting a stone sarcophagus. This held the outer coffin, which had two smaller coffins inside. Within the inner coffin lay the king. Covering his head was a great treasure, the Gold Mask.

Carter delayed work in the Treasury until the Burial Chamber had been emptied. It took a full winter to clear out small objects to make room for dismantling the Canopic shrine. Removal of the shrine revealed a chest holding the king's internal organs. Of the many ritual images, 413 were *shawabtys*—workers to serve the king in the afterlife.

The Annex was discovered first but was cleared last. The clutter made clearing work space a complicated procedure. Using rope slings, archaeologists swung over the threshold to remove the objects. They found baskets and pottery jars filled with provisions for the king. Royal furniture and urns were among these common objects.

II. Antechamber _____

   A. Procedure _____

      1. Assigned each object a number _____

      2. _____

   B. Objects _____

      1. Three animal-shaped couches, royal thrones, and stools _____

      2. _____

      3. _____

III. _____

   A. _____

      1. Took apart shrines with scaffolding (4 months) _____

      2. _____

      3. _____

   B. _____

      1. Four shrines with sarcophagus inside _____

      2. _____

      3. _____

IV. _____

   A. _____

      1. _____

      2. _____

   B. _____

      1. _____

      2. _____

V. _____

   A. _____

      1. _____

      2. _____

   B. _____

      1. _____

      2. _____

Skill: Improving Reading Rate

A good reader reads at several speeds, depending on the material. When reading difficult or unfamiliar material, a good reader reads more slowly. For example, social studies, science, mathematics, and poetry are often read more slowly than short stories or novels. Sometimes a reader needs to reread a paragraph to understand a complex idea. A good reader also slows down to read diagrams and maps. You should adjust your **reading rate** to the difficulty of the reading.

Read the following selection to check your reading rate. Use a watch or a clock with a second hand to time yourself. Start right on a minute, and write your starting time at the beginning of the selection. Write your ending time at the end of the selection.

The Temple of Dendur

Starting time _____

The Temple of Dendur is one of the ancient monuments of the Nile river. It was built by the Emperor Augustus around 15 B.C., during the Roman occupation of Egypt. Between 1891 and 1902, a dam was built at Aswan, the ancient frontier between Egypt and Nubia. The dam regulated the water level of the Nile. By raising the water level, the dam caused some of the monuments at Dendur to be underwater for nine months each year.

In the 1950s, a decision was made to build a new dam at Aswan. The Aswan High Dam would create a 3,000-square-mile lake. The advantages of the dam included providing more fertile land and hydroelectric power to Egypt's growing population. One disadvantage was that the lake would flood part of the Nubian Desert, and the people living there would have to move elsewhere. Also, the ancient monuments at Dendur would be lost forever under the raised waters of the Nile.

To save the temples, shrines, and early Christian churches at Dendur, UNESCO, a division of the United Nations, began a worldwide campaign to move and reassemble as many of the buildings as possible. The United States contributed $16 million to help save the monuments. To show its appreciation, Egypt offered the United States the 2,000-year-old Temple of Dendur as a gift.

The Egyptian Department of Antiquities took apart the Temple of Dendur in 1965. Due to the fragile nature of the stone, the masons carefully took the temple apart block by block, numbering each one.

Detailed drawings of every part of the temple recorded the level, position, and number for each block, so that reassembling the temple would be simplified. The blocks were packed, loaded onto a barge, and floated to Elephantine Island. The temple that had stood on the banks of the Nile had been reduced to 640 crates that weighed more than 800 tons.

In 1967, a committee appointed by President Johnson suggested that the temple should go to New York City's Metropolitan Museum of Art. The temple would be a significant addition to the museum's already impressive Egyptian collection. In the summer of 1968, the crates containing the temple were put aboard the freighter *Concordia Star*, headed for the United States. Once the crates arrived at the Metropolitan Museum, they were stored in a large, inflated canvas and vinyl structure in a parking lot. They remained there for six years, until 1974, when they were transported by truck to their final home at the north end of the museum. Construction had begun that year on the Sackler Wing, an all-glass wing designed specifically to house the temple. By the end of the year, the first phase of construction— the platform for the temple with a garage and service area below it—was complete.

As each block was repaired, it was brought up to the platform to be assembled. The masons assembling the temple exhibited the same care as those who had dismantled it. They used padded pulleys to protect each stone while putting it into its proper place. When the temple had been set up, it was enclosed in a steel scaffold and covered as protection from the major construction going on around it.

Dendur is the only complete ancient Egyptian temple in the Western Hemisphere. It has a gateway and a temple with floral columns on the front and three rooms beyond. The gateway and temple are made of pink sandstone.

The temple was reassembled in the Sackler Wing to appear as it once did on the banks of the Nile. The platform it stands on looks much like an ancient wharf. A reflecting pool surrounds the platform, showing how the temple must have appeared in its original location on the Nile. Visitors to the museum have been admiring the Temple of Dendur since September of 1978.

Words in selection: 658

Ending Time _____

	Hr.	Min.	Sec.
Ending time			
Starting time			
Total time			

$$\frac{\text{No. of words } 658}{\text{No. of seconds}} = \quad \times 60 = \quad \text{WPM}$$

To find the total time that it took you to read the selection, first subtract your starting time from your ending time. Then divide the number of words in the selection by the remainder expressed in seconds.

For example, if it took you 3 minutes and 5 seconds ($3 \times 60 + 5 = 185$ seconds) to read the selection, you would have read 3.6 words per second ($658 \div 185 = 3.6$). To find the number of words per minute (WPM), multiply your rate per second by 60. Your answer would be 216 WPM.

To check your understanding of the selection, underline the answer to each question.

1. When was the Temple of Dendur built?
   a. around 15 B.C.
   b. from 1891 to 1902
   c. in 1974
   d. in the 1950s

2. Why was the temple moved?
   a. It was taking up too much space.
   b. It was falling apart.
   c. It would have been underwater.
   d. The government hated it.

3. Why did Egypt give the Temple of Dendur to the United States?
   a. The United States started a campaign to move the temple.
   b. The United States helped dismantle Nubian monuments.
   c. The United States contributed money to save the Nubian monuments.
   d. The United States asked for it as payment of debts.

4. Why were drawings made as the temple was dismantled?
   a. They would be sold to museums.
   b. They would make reassembly easier.
   c. They would remain in Egypt.
   d. They would be studied by school children.

5. Where does the temple now stand?
   a. on the banks of the Nile
   b. in an art museum in New York City
   c. on Elephantine Island
   d. in the Nubian Desert

Skill: Reading a Bank Statement

If you have a checking account, you receive a **statement** every month from your bank. The statement shows the two main types of activities that occurred during the month. The first is **deposits**, or the money that has been put into your account. The second is **withdrawals**, or the money that has been paid out of the account.

The statement also shows the **balance**, or the amount of money remaining in your account, and **charges**, such as the service charge by the bank for processing checks. Canceled checks, or the checks that have been cashed, are noted in your statement.

Every time you write a check, you should record the following information in the checkbook register: the check number; the date; the person, business, or organization to whom the check is issued; and the amount of the check. You should also record the amount and date of any deposits made into your checking account. Accurate record keeping is essential for keeping track of your checking account. If your records are done correctly, the balance in your checkbook register should match the balance on the checking account statement exactly. Getting these figures to match is called balancing a checking account.

Study the checking account statement below, and compare it to the checkbook register.

FROM:	Big City Bank 111 E. Capital St., S.E. Washington, D.C. 20003	TELEPHONE ASSISTANCE NUMBER: 202-555-8002	ACCOUNT NUMBER: 2840264 FOR THE PERIOD: 11/17/07-12/17/07
TO:	Francine Harris 466 25th Street, N.W. Washington, D.C. 20020	ACTIVITY ON THIS STATEMENT: DEPOSITS 2 | CHECKS 6	

ENDING BALANCE ON PREVIOUS STATEMENT	DEPOSITS AND OTHER CREDITS	WITHDRAWALS AND FEES	BALANCE AS OF THIS STATEMENT DATE
$222.40	$1,308.35	$645.80	$884.95

DATE	DESCRIPTION	OTHER ACTIVITY	DEPOSITS	WITHDRAWALS	BALANCE
11/19	CHECK PAID-302			22.10	200.30
11/23	CHECK PAID-303			5.00	195.30
11/23	CHECK PAID-304			110.10	85.20
11/29	DEPOSIT		25.00		110.20
12/4	CHECK PAID-305			10.00	100.20
12/6	CHECK PAID-306			45.00	55.20
12/14	DEPOSIT		1283.35		1338.55
12/16	CHECK PAID-307			450.00	888.55
12/17	SERVICE CHARGE			3.60	884.95

		PLEASE BE SURE TO DEDUCT CHARGES THAT AFFECT YOUR ACCOUNT BALANCE FORWARD				BALANCE FORWARD	
NO.	DATE	ISSUED TO OR DESCRIPTION OF DEPOSIT	AMOUNT OF PAYMENT	OTHER DEDUCT	AMOUNT OF DEPOSIT	222	40
302	11/17	TO R & B GROCERIES FOR	22 | 10			22 200	10 30
303	11/17	TO SECOND ST. CINEMA FOR TICKET FOR MOVIE	5 | 00			5 195	00 30
304	11/20	TO MORGAN'S DEPT. STORE FOR	110 | 10			110 85	10 20
	11/29	TO DEPOSIT FOR BIRTHDAY GIFT			25 | 00	25 110	00 20
305	12/1	TO GIFTS & GAGS FOR GIFT-GRANDPA	10 | 00			10 100	00 20
306	12/2	TO DR. AUSTIN PHILLIPS FOR	45 | 00			45 55	00 20
	12/14	TO DEPOSIT FOR PAYCHECK			1283 | 35	1283 1338	35 55
307	12/14	TO BARNSTONE REALTY FOR RENT	450 | 00			450 888	00 55
		TO SERVICE CHARGE FOR	3 | 60			3 884	60 95

A. **Circle the letter next to the correct answer to each question.**

1. Which check number was written for the amount of $450.00?
   a. 1216   **b.** 307   **c.** 306   **d.** 183.46

2. On what date was there a balance of $110.20?
   a. November 17   **b.** November 23   **c.** November 29   **d.** December 4

3. What was the amount of check 305 to Gifts & Gags?
   a. $10.00   **b.** $46.05   **c.** $25.00   **d.** $110.10

4. On which date were two checks paid by the bank?
   a. November 19   **b.** November 23   **c.** November 29   **d.** December 16

5. What was the balance in the account after check 304 was paid?
   a. $85.20   **b.** $110.10   **c.** $110.20   **d.** $222.40

6. What was the period of time covered by this checking account statement?
   a. from Nov. 19, 2007 to Dec. 17, 2007   **c.** from Nov. 17, 2007 to Dec. 17, 2007
   b. from Nov. through Dec. 2007   **d.** from Nov. 19, 2007 to Dec. 19, 2007

7. Under which heading do you find out how much money is in the account on the day the statement was prepared?
   a. balance   **c.** balance as of this statement date
   b. ending balance on previous statement   **d.** withdrawals and fees

8. Why was $25.00 added to the balance of $85.20 in the BALANCE column?
   a. A $25.00 check was paid.   **c.** The bank made an error of $25.00.
   b. A $25.00 service charge was added.   **d.** A $25.00 deposit was made.

B. **Read the sentences below, and write *true* or *false* on each line.**

1. There was a balance of $85.20 on November 29. _____

2. The deposits that were made total $1,308.35. _____

3. The balance as of this statement date is $222.40. _____

4. The total of the checks paid and of other charges equals $645.80. _____

5. A check for the amount of $5.00 was paid on November 23. _____

6. After check 305 was paid, the balance in the account was $10.00. _____

7. Check 302 for $200.30 was paid on November 19. _____

8. Check 304 for $110.10 was paid on November 23. _____

9. Check 307 for $1,283.35 was paid on November 16. _____

Forces of Nature

LESSON 35

Skill: Setting

BACKGROUND INFORMATION

"The Life Jacket" is a story about a girl's brush with death in a dangerous setting. People who have near-death experiences often recall vivid memories of the event, even if it lasted only a few seconds. Some people have even claimed to see their entire lives "flash before their eyes" when death seemed near.

SKILL FOCUS: Setting

Setting is the time and place in which story events occur. The setting of a story can be as ordinary as your classroom or as dramatic as a battlefield. The time of the setting can be the present, the past, or many years into the future.

A story's setting often creates its mood. Mood is the overall feeling of a story or part of a story. You can describe a story's mood in one or two adjectives, such as *happy, scary, threatening, sad,* or *peaceful.* An author creates mood by using sensory details and words that convey emotion to describe the setting.

The following questions will help you understand how a story's setting helps create its mood.

- Where and when do the story events take place?
- What details describe the setting?
- What kind of feeling do these details create?
- How does the story's mood change as the plot develops?

▶ Read the following description of a prairie. On the Idea Web on this page, write important details the author uses to describe the setting. In the center, write what mood these details create.

No air moved under the swollen gray sky. The sounds on the prairie were unnaturally stilled. A bird darted on silent wings across the driveway. A worried woman came to the door of her tiny house. Her eyes searched the dark horizon. Was a tornado on the way?

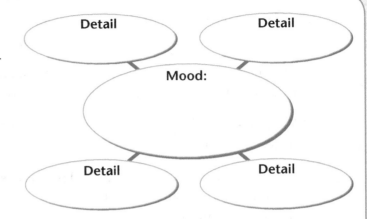

Detail · Detail · Mood: · Detail · Detail

CONTEXT CLUES: Details

Details can help you figure out the meanings of new words.

In the sentences below, look for details that show the meaning of the underlined word.

*Instead of shouting back, though, I looked down and decided to tighten the drawstring of my pullover jacket. I pulled it **taut** at the bottom and knotted it.*

Details in the first sentence show the meaning of *taut.* From these details you can figure out that *taut* means "tight."

▶ Read the following sentences. Circle the details that help you figure out the meaning of the underlined word.

*Then Sandy came by and tried to **prod** me into action. "Come on, Maisie—let's go down to the beach and look for shells," she insisted.*

As you read, use details to figure out the meanings of the underlined words *spasm, briny,* and *frigid.*

Strategy Tip

In "The Life Jacket," look for details that describe the setting. Figure out how the mood of the story changes as the setting changes.

THE LIFE JACKET

Just ahead of me was a small island, not much more than a rocky outcropping, several hundred yards offshore. It was a secluded island, difficult to get to. You couldn't land a boat on it since the only way to approach it was by crossing the causeway, a rocky path between it and the tip of Mosquito Head. It was a wild, free place that always thrilled me with the awesome power of its crashing waves and winds.

The wind whistled in gusts, plucking at me as I picked my way along the causeway's rocks. If I had been alone, I probably would have felt great. I like that kind of weather. Thick clouds raced in from the ocean's horizon. The wild wind and salty spray were refreshing and challenging as the coming storm made the ocean leap and churn. You could feel in your bones that something exciting was about to happen. I love that kind of day.

Earlier, I had been bored. The sky had been a carnival blue, with cotton candy clouds floating in it. It had been almost too perfect. Then Sandy came by and tried to prod me into action. "Come on, Maisie—let's go down to the beach and look for shells," she insisted. I wasn't interested.

"Then let's walk over to the island off Mosquito Head. Aren't you supposed to make a count of nesting sea birds for your science project?" she asked. Sandy had a point.

The island wasn't much to look at, I knew. It was just a mounded tumble of gray boulders and a few weeds. You'd never plan a picnic there, but it was a perfect spot for sea birds to build their nests. If I were looking for a variety of nesting sea birds to report on—and I was—that was the place to look.

So I laced on my thick-soled climbing boots, grabbed my pullover jacket, and started off with Sandy. I soon found myself relishing the salt spray on my face as I clambered over rocks at a leisurely pace.

The wind caught my hair, and I felt it whip around my face. I turned into the wind, so that the jet-black strands blew off my face and streamed behind me. Just then, a voice broke into my daydream, calling, "Hurry up, Maisie! Come on!"

It's Mei Ling, not Maisie, I thought. I hate my nickname because it makes me think of a doll with blue eyes and bouncy blonde ringlets in her hair, instead of me—Mei Ling, with my shiny, straight black hair and dark eyes that people say are beautiful. Sandy could really get on my nerves. Besides, right now my mind was set on enjoying the world around me, not on racing with Sandy.

Instead of shouting back, I looked down and decided to tighten the drawstring of my pullover jacket, so I pulled it taut at the bottom and knotted it. Tying the drawstring gave me a reason for staying where I was for a moment. As things turned out, it probably saved my life.

"What's the rush?" I said when I was close enough for Sandy to hear me over the whistling wind.

"I thought you had to check the island for your science project," Sandy said. "Let's keep together. In case you slip, I can help you."

"I can take care of myself."

Sandy was only two years older, but somehow she felt responsible for me.

"Look," she said, "the tide's starting in. A storm's blowing up, and pretty soon the waves will be rolling in over the causeway. It wouldn't be smart to get stuck on the island." She held up her fingers and counted off her points one by one, as if she were explaining something to a child. I'm fifteen, I thought. I'm not a child.

Sandy didn't notice my glare. She spun around suddenly and started toward the island. "Come on! Hurry!"

Between us and the mainland, waves thundered against the causeway. Sandy was already way ahead of me. Now I'm supposed to run along and catch up, I thought angrily. Catching up was the last thing on my mind as I crossed the slippery rocks. Suddenly, a tremendous wave crashed over me, knocking me off the causeway and dragging me down.

The icy wave shocked me like a jolt of electricity. I gasped, expecting to hit the rocks below. The next thing I knew, I was plunging down through murky green water, and my world suddenly became a dark, underwater nightmare.

A huge fist seemed to be pressing on my chest. I wanted to breathe, but I couldn't. I kicked my feet and struggled toward the surface, the dim light above me. At last I struggled to the surface about a hundred feet from the island—gagging, choking, and gasping for breath. A strong, deadly current was relentlessly dragging me out to sea, and my heavy, water-soaked climbing boots continued to pull me toward the bottom. I was absolutely terrified.

I tried to think, but my mind sputtered like a live wire. My heart thudded, and my whole body went into a spasm of panic, as all my muscles contracted at once, trying to find a way to escape this watery grave. The weight of my boots made it difficult to keep kicking, and I was too numb to untie them. "Help," I cried, "I don't want to die!" My eyes stung. I thought, how silly to spill salty tears into the briny ocean.

A gull appeared above a storm-tossed wave. Its eyes swept over me and dismissed me from its search. It vanished beyond another foaming crest, and then I was completely alone.

Suddenly, I realized that I was floating on my back. An air bubble was trapped inside my nylon jacket—a miracle was keeping me afloat.

The seconds passed, each one an eternity. When the churning swells lifted me skyward, I tried to catch sight of land. I did once, just long enough to see that I was being pulled farther out to sea. Unfortunately, I didn't see Sandy, and I hoped the wave hadn't knocked her into the water, too. I hoped she'd been too fast for it.

With each minute, the precious air bubble grew smaller. Was I still kicking my legs? I thought so, but my whole body was numb from the cold as I swallowed more and more of the salty, frigid water.

Another gull streaked across my sight, low on the water, like an arrow. I started to cry again. I wanted to finish my research paper, talk with Mother, tell jokes with Father—a million things. I wondered: If I drowned, would anyone ever find my body? I'd never felt so alone, so helpless, so abandoned. I think at that point I started to give up. I let my mind drift off to avoid thinking all those terrible thoughts, and I must have closed my eyes.

Something powerful clamped around my body. Sharks! I opened my eyes, started to scream, and looked straight up at the strangest of all birds, a helicopter. It hovered 50 feet above me, with a line dangling down to the rolling sea. The Coast Guard rescuer had an arm around my chest and bobbed next to me like a cork. In a minute or two, I was buckled into a harness. He signaled, the rope pulled taut, and slowly, it lifted me from my watery grave, plucking me from the sea that had plucked me from the rocks.

Not until the next day did I learn that Sandy was also rescued by the Coast Guard. Fortunately, the Coast Guard, patrolling the coast for boaters in distress, had seen Sandy signaling for help. Sandy immediately told them that I had been swept into the sea.

It was a while before I ventured out again to the island off Mosquito Head to count nesting sea birds. Before I went, I checked the weather bureau to be sure that there were no storms in the day's forecast. Also, I asked Sandy to go with me, having learned my lesson well.

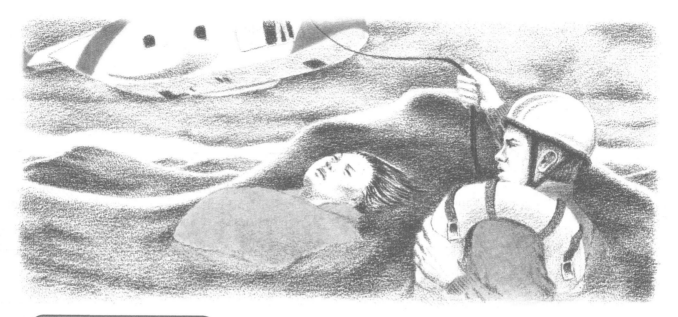

COMPREHENSION

1. From what point of view—first-person or third-person—is this story written? Who is the narrator?

   _____

   _____

2. Number the following events in the order in which they occur in the story.

   _____ **a.** Mei Ling, knocked over by a tremendous wave, plunges down through the water.

   _____ **b.** Mei Ling and Sandy go to the island off Mosquito Head.

   _____ **c.** Mei Ling floats on her back.

   _____ **d.** Mei Ling is rescued by the Coast Guard.

   _____ **e.** Mei Ling's whole body grows numb from the cold.

3. **a.** With what does Mei Ling come into conflict?

   _____

   _____

   _____

   b. How is Mei Ling's conflict resolved?

   _____

   _____

4. Answer each question by writing yes or no on the line provided.

   a. Is a <u>spasm</u> a calm, regular movement? _____

   b. Is lake water usually <u>briny</u>? _____

   c. Is <u>frigid</u> water cold enough to chill

   someone? _____

CRITICAL THINKING

1. In what season of the year does the story take place? Give two or three details from the story to support your answer.

   _____

   _____

   _____

2. **a.** Describe Mei Ling's personality.

   _____

   _____

   _____

   _____

b. Why do you think Mei Ling thinks about her family as she is pulled underwater?

_____

_____

_____

_____

3. Why does Mei Ling resent Sandy's helping her?

_____

_____

_____

_____

4. Why does Mei Ling gag and choke when she struggles to the surface?

_____

_____

_____

_____

5. Explain how pulling her jacket's drawstring taut saves Mei Ling's life.

_____

_____

_____

6. Mei Ling learns that it is foolish to go out to the island when a storm is approaching. What else does she learn?

_____

_____

_____

_____

7. Think about the point of view from which this story is told. Explain why it is a good point of view for this story.

_____

_____

_____

_____

SKILL FOCUS: SETTING

1. When you first meet Mei Ling, she and a friend are on their way to a small island, several hundred yards offshore. Mei Ling loves the "wild, free place that always thrilled me with the awesome power of its crashing waves and winds." She adds that "you could feel in your bones that something exciting was about to happen" as storm clouds came racing in.

a. What is the setting in this part of the story?

_____

_____

b. What is the mood, or atmosphere, in this part of the story?

_____

_____

2. Circle the letter next to each detail of setting that adds to the mood at the beginning of the story.

    a. The wild wind and salty spray are refreshing and challenging.

    b. The coming storm makes the ocean leap and churn.

    c. Earlier in the day, Mei Ling had been bored.

    d. Waves crash and clouds race in.

    e. The wind whips around Mei Ling's face.

3. What suddenly happens to change the setting and the mood of the story?

_____

4. Mei Ling suddenly finds herself "plunging down through murky green water," feeling as if a huge fist pressed against her chest. Swept out to sea by a strong current, she feels her heart begin to thud, and her body goes into a spasm.

    a. What is the setting in this part of the story?

_____

    b. What kind of mood does the author create in describing this incident?

_____

5. Circle the letter next to each detail of setting that adds to the story's changed mood.

    a. Mei Ling is pulled under by her heavy, water-soaked climbing boots.

    b. A strong, deadly current drags her out to sea.

    c. Her body grows numb in the frigid seawater.

    d. The sky had been a carnival blue, with cotton candy clouds floating in it.

    e. With each minute, the precious air bubble grows smaller.

6. **a.** How does the arrival of the storm influence the story's setting?

_____

    b. What happens to the mood when the setting changes?

_____

Reading-Writing Connection

On a separate sheet of paper, write a paragraph describing a natural setting that you enjoy. Use details of the setting to convey a mood.

Skill: Reading a Map

BACKGROUND INFORMATION

"Russia's Icy Defender" describes how Russia's harsh winters helped that country defeat two invading armies. Throughout history, nations have invaded other nations to gain land and power. Most nations maintain strong armies and navies to protect and defend themselves against invaders. A country's geography and climate can also be natural defenses against invading armies that are not used to these weather conditions.

SKILL FOCUS: Reading a Map

Maps can provide historical information. One type of historical map is a **battle map**. A battle map usually shows the path of an army's attack. It might also show the sites of major battles and list their dates. A battle map can give you a clear picture of the troop movements and fighting in a war.

Battle maps use colors and symbols to represent information. Colors often show the territory an army wins or loses in the fighting. Arrows show the direction of an army's advance or retreat. A map key shows what the colors and symbols mean.

To read a battle map, ask yourself these questions.

- What geographic area does the map show?
- What events and time period are depicted?
- Whose movements does the map trace?
- What symbols indicate the direction of these movements?
- What geographic features (rivers, regions) do the troop movements cross?
- What does the map show about the success or failure of a military campaign?

▶ Look at the battle map of some early battles of the American Revolution. Then answer the questions below.

1. From which direction did British troops travel to reach Saratoga in 1777?

   _____

2. Who won the battle that was fought there?

   _____

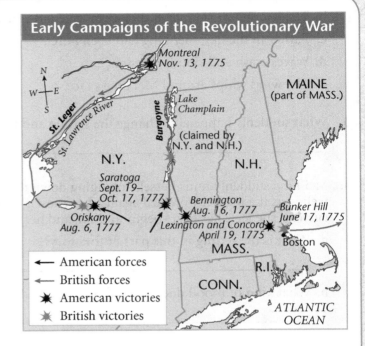

Early Campaigns of the Revolutionary War

Montreal Nov. 13, 1775

MAINE (part of MASS.)

Lake Champlain

St. Leger

St. Lawrence River

Burgoyne

(claimed by N.Y. and N.H.)

N.Y.

N.H.

Saratoga Sept. 19– Oct. 17, 1777

Bennington Aug. 16, 1777

Oriskany Aug. 6, 1777

Lexington and Concord April 19, 1775

Bunker Hill June 17, 1775

Boston

MASS.

R.I.

CONN.

ATLANTIC OCEAN

← American forces
← British forces
✴ American victories
✴ British victories

CONTEXT CLUES: Word Groupings

A **word grouping** is a series of words in a sentence that are related in meaning. The words that you know in the grouping can help you figure out the meaning of an unfamiliar word in the same series.

Use the words in the grouping below to help you figure out the meaning of the underlined word.

> *However, he was not prepared for the devastating enemy that met him in Moscow— the raw, bitter, **bleak** Russian winter.*

If you don't know the meaning of *bleak*, *raw* and *bitter* can help you infer that it means "cold and dreary."

▶ Read the following sentence. Circle the words in the word grouping that can help you figure out the meaning of the underlined word.

> *The German trucks, tanks, and **artillery** lay buried in the heavy snowbanks.*

As you read, use word groupings to help you figure out the meanings of *efficient*, *maimed*, and *quarter*.

> **Strategy Tip**
>
> In "Russia's Icy Defender," use the maps on pages 129 and 131 to follow the Russian military campaigns of Napoleon and Hitler.

RUSSIA'S ICY DEFENDER

In 1812, Napoleon Bonaparte, Emperor of France, led his Grand Army into Russia. He was prepared for the fierce resistance of the Russian people defending their homeland. He was prepared for the long march across Russian soil to Moscow, the capital city. However, he was not prepared for the devastating enemy that met him in Moscow—the raw, bitter, bleak Russian winter.

In 1941, Adolf Hitler, leader of Nazi Germany, launched an attack against the Soviet Union, as Russia was then called. Hitler's military might was unequaled. His war machine had mowed down resistance in most of Europe. Hitler expected a short campaign. However, like Napoleon before him, he was taught a painful lesson. The Russian winter again came to the aid of the Soviet soldiers.

Napoleon's Grand Army

In 1804, Napoleon Bonaparte crowned himself Emperor of France. The son of a minor noble family, Napoleon had gained power in France during the years of its bloody revolution. From 1807 to 1812, he established an empire that stretched from the Atlantic Ocean to the borders of Russia.

Napoleon was a military genius who created his empire through wars of **conquest** (KAHN kwest). He used his armies to overrun neighboring countries and take them over. In 1812, however, Napoleon undertook a campaign that was to turn the tide of his fortunes.

For several years, Napoleon had kept an uneasy truce with Czar Alexander I of Russia. Yet Alexander would not totally submit to the power-hungry Napoleon. In the spring of 1812, Napoleon decided to teach the Russians a lesson. He assembled an army of 600,000 men on the borders of Russia. The soldiers were recruited from 20 different nations in Napoleon's empire. They were well trained, <u>efficient</u>, and well equipped. This military force was called the Grand Army. Napoleon, confident of a quick victory, predicted the conquest of Russia in five weeks.

Empty Victory for Napoleon

In the spring of 1812, Napoleon's army crossed the Neman River into Russia. The quick, decisive victory that Napoleon expected never happened. To his surprise, the Russians refused to stand and fight. Instead, they retreated eastward, burning their crops

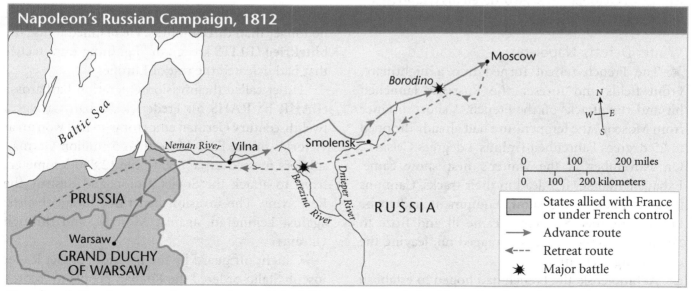

Napoleon's Russian Campaign, 1812

- Baltic Sea
- Moscow
- Borodino
- Neman River
- Vilna
- Smolensk
- Berezina River
- Dnieper River
- RUSSIA
- PRUSSIA
- Warsaw
- GRAND DUCHY OF WARSAW

0   100   200 miles
0   100   200 kilometers

States allied with France or under French control
→ Advance route
◄--- Retreat route
✷ Major battle

Napoleon's Russian campaign was doomed to failure because of the bitter Russian winter. In October 1812, Napoleon ordered the Grand Army to retreat from Moscow.

SOCIAL STUDIES

and homes as they went. The Grand Army followed, but its advance march soon became bogged down by slow-moving supply lines.

In August, the French and Russian armies fought at Smolensk. It was a battle that left more than 10,000 dead on each side. Yet the Russians were again able to retreat farther into Russian territory. Napoleon had won no decisive victory. He was now faced with a crucial decision. Should he continue to pursue the Russian army, or should he keep his army in Smolensk for the approaching winter?

Napoleon took the gamble of pressing on to Moscow, 280 miles (448 kilometers) away. On September 7, 1812, the French and Russian armies met in fierce battle at Borodino, 70 miles (112 kilometers) west of Moscow. By nightfall, 30,000 French and 44,000 Russians lay dead, wounded, or <u>maimed</u> on the battlefield.

Again the Russian army retreated to safety. Napoleon had a clear path to Moscow. His troops took over the city, but the **occupation** of Moscow became an empty victory. The Russians fled their capital. Soon after the French arrived, a raging fire destroyed two-thirds of the city. Napoleon offered a truce to Alexander I, but the Russian czar knew he could simply wait. "We shall let the Russian winter fight the war for us," he declared.

Napoleon soon realized he could not feed, clothe, and <u>quarter</u> his army in Moscow during the winter. In October 1812, he ordered his Grand Army to retreat from Moscow.

Winter Defeats Napoleon

✘ The French retreat turned into a nightmare. From fields and forests, the Russians launched hit-and-run attacks on the French. A short distance from Moscow, the temperature had already dropped to 25 degrees Fahrenheit (minus 4 degrees Celsius). On November 3, the winter's first snow came. Exhausted horses fell dead in their tracks. Cannons became stuck in the snow. Equipment had to be burned for fuel. Soldiers became ill and froze to death. The French soldiers dragged on, leaving the dead along every mile.

✔ At Smolensk, the French had hoped to establish winter quarters, but now Napoleon was in a race against time. The Russian army was gathering its strength. The French had to flee Russia to avoid certain defeat. At the Berezina (bə REZ i nə) River, the Russians nearly trapped the retreating French by burning the bridges over the swollen river. By a stroke of luck, however, Napoleon was able to build two new bridges. Thousands of French soldiers escaped, but at the cost of 50,000 dead. Once across the Berezina, the tattered survivors limped toward Vilna.

On December 5, Napoleon left his soldiers to return to Paris. Of the 600,000 soldiers he had led into Russia, fewer than 100,000 came back.

The weakened French army continued its retreat westward across Europe. Soon Britain, Austria, Russia, and Prussia formed a powerful **alliance** (ə LY əns) and attacked these stragglers. In March 1814, Paris was captured. Napoleon gave up his power and went into exile. The Napoleonic empire was at an end.

Hitler's Operation Barbarossa

By early 1941, Adolf Hitler, leader of Nazi Germany, had seized control of most of Europe. To the east of Hitler's German empire was the Soviet Union. On June 22, 1941, without a declaration of war, Hitler began an invasion of the Soviet Union. It was the largest military land campaign in history. The time had come, Hitler believed, to seize the rich farmlands and oil fields in the western part of the Soviet Union. Confident of a quick victory over the Soviet Union, Hitler expected the campaign to last no longer than three months. He planned to use the **blitzkrieg** (BLITS kreeg), or "lightning war," tactics that had defeated the rest of Europe.

Hitler called the invasion Operation Barbarossa (BAHR bə RAHS ə). Frederick Barbarossa was a twelfth-century German emperor who had won great victories in the East. More than 3 million German soldiers massed on a 1,800-mile (2,880-kilometer) front to attack the Soviet Union and destroy the Red Army. The invasion had three broad thrusts: against Leningrad, against Moscow, and through Ukraine.

Caught off guard by the invasion, Soviet leader Joseph Stalin ordered the Russian people to "scorch the earth" in front of the German invaders. Farms and factories were burned, destroyed, or rendered useless. During the first ten weeks of the invasion, the Germans pushed the front eastward, and the Russians suffered more than a million casualties.

The German Siege of Leningrad

In the north, the Germans closed in on Leningrad. Despite great suffering, however, the people of Leningrad refused to surrender. As the battle of Leningrad dragged on into winter, the city's situation became desperate. The people of the city were trapped—surrounded on three sides by German soldiers. As food ran out, people died of starvation and disease. By the middle of the winter of 1941–1942, nearly 4,000 people were starving to death every day. Close to 1 million people died as a result of the siege.

In the center of Russia, Hitler's goal was to capture Moscow. Because the Germans had expected a quick victory, they had made no plans for winter supplies.

October arrived with heavy rains. Mud slowed down the movement of the Germans' lightning attack. In charge of the defense of Moscow was Marshal Georgi Zhukov. He successfully used attack-and-retreat tactics against the Germans, just as the Russians had against Napoleon. Moscow would never be taken.

The Harshest Winter in Years

As Hitler's armies drew closer and closer to Moscow, an early, severe winter settled over the Soviet Union. In fact, the winter of 1941–42 was the harshest winter in years. Temperatures dropped to minus 65 degrees Fahrenheit (minus 48 degrees Celsius). Heavy snows fell. The German soldiers, completely unprepared for the Russian winter, froze in their light summer uniforms. The German tanks, trucks, and artillery lay buried in the heavy snowbanks. The Russian winter brought the German offensive, or attack, to a halt.

Hitler's Russian Campaign, 1941–1944

Baltic Sea

Leningrad
August 1941–January 1944

Volga River

Moscow
October 1941

SOVIET UNION

0   200   400 miles
0   200   400 kilometers

N
W—E
S

Vilna

Smolensk

East Prussia

Warsaw

POLAND

Stalingrad
August 1942–January 1943

UKRAINE

HUNGARY

CRIMEA

ROMANIA
Black Sea   Sevastopol
June 1942–May 1944

German-occupied countries allied with Hitler
← Army Group North
←--- Army Group Center
←--- Army Group South

The five-month battle of Stalingrad was a turning point in World War II. This German defeat ended Hitler's advance into the Soviet Union. After this victory, the Russian army advanced across eastern Europe. Berlin fell on May 2, 1945. Five days later, Germany surrendered.

The Offensive Renewed

By the summer of 1942, Hitler had launched two new offensives. In the south, the Germans captured Sevastopol. With the fall of this city, the Germans had control of the Black Sea and were within striking distance of the Russian oil fields. Hitler then pushed east to Stalingrad, a great industrial city that stretched for 30 miles (48 kilometers) along the Volga River. Despite great suffering, Soviet defenders refused to give up Stalingrad.

In November 1942, the Russians launched a counterattack. With little or no shelter from the cold, German troops were further weakened by a lack of food and supplies. Not until January 1943 did the Germans give up their siege. Of the 300,000 Germans attacking Stalingrad, only 90,000 starving soldiers were left. The loss of the battle for Stalingrad finally turned the tide against Hitler. The German victories were over, thanks in part to the Russian winter.

The German Retreat

During 1943 and 1944, the Soviet armies pushed the German front back toward the west. In the north, the Russian Red Army broke the three-year siege of Leningrad with a surprise attack on January 15, 1944. Within two weeks, the survivors of Leningrad saw their invaders depart. By March 1944, the Ukraine farming region was again in Soviet hands. On May 9, 1944, Sevastopol was liberated from the Germans. The Russians were now heading for Berlin.

For Hitler, the invasion of the Soviet Union had turned into a military disaster. For the Russian people, their country's military victory was accompanied by unspeakable suffering. The Soviet death toll in World War II reached almost 23 million.

The elements of nature must be reckoned with in any military campaign. Napoleon and Hitler both underestimated the severity of the Russian winter. Snow, ice, and freezing temperatures took their toll on both invading armies. For the Russian people, the winter was an icy defender.

COMPREHENSION

1. Write two causes for the effect below.

   Cause: _____

   _____

   Cause: _____

   _____

   Effect: Napoleon's occupation of Moscow was an empty victory.

2. Reread the paragraph that has an ✘ next to it. Underline the sentence that states the main idea. Then circle at least three details that support the main idea of the paragraph.

3. What name did Hitler give to his invasion of the Soviet Union? Explain the meaning of this name.

   _____

   _____

   _____

4. What did the Germans call their war tactics?

   _____

   _____

5. What similar tactics did the Russian army use against Napoleon and Hitler?

   _____

   _____

6. Circle the correct meaning of the underlined word in each sentence.

   a. The relay team had developed an <u>efficient</u> way of working together.

      effective   wasteful

   b. The driver was <u>maimed</u> in the car accident.

      crippled   responsible

   c. The commander decided where to <u>quarter</u> the new troops.

      send   shelter

1. Write the cause for the following effect.

   Cause: _____

   _____

   Effect: Hitler and Napoleon both failed to consider the Russian winter as an important factor in planning their campaigns.

2. Explain why the Russian winter was harder on the invading armies than on the Russian army.

   _____

   _____

3. Who was probably responsible for setting the fire that destroyed two-thirds of Moscow soon after Napoleon occupied the city? Give reasons to support your answer.

   _____

   _____

4. Explain how the geography of the Soviet Union made Hitler's blitzkrieg attack less successful there than it had been in the rest of Europe.

   _____

   _____

5. What might have happened if there had been a late, mild winter in Russia in 1941?

   _____

   _____

6. Summarize how the Russian campaigns of both Hitler and Napoleon contributed to the eventual defeat of their entire empires.

   _____

   _____

7. Reread the paragraph with a ✔ next to it. Write a sentence stating its main idea.

   _____

   _____

SKILL FOCUS: READING A MAP

Use the maps on pages 129 and 131 to answer the following questions.

1. **a.** What area of the world is shown on the first map? _____

   b. What area of the world is shown on the second map? _____

2. **a.** What is the time period of the first map? _____

   b. What is the time period of the second map? _____

3. **a.** What army's route is traced on the first map? _____

   b. What army's route is traced on the second map? _____

4. **a.** Draw the symbol that shows Napoleon's advance to Moscow. _____

   b. Draw the symbol that shows Napoleon's retreat from Moscow. _____

   c. Draw the three symbols that show Hitler's offensives in the Soviet Union. _____

5. **a.** From where did Napoleon begin his invasion of Russia? _____

   b. During his advance, in what town did Napoleon battle the Russians? _____

   c. Approximately how far was Napoleon in his retreat out of Russia when he was

   almost captured at the Berezina River? _____

   d. What city was the goal of Hitler's northern attack? _____

   e. In which direction does Stalingrad lie from Moscow? _____

   f. What region did the Germans have to cross to get to Stalingrad? _____

6. **a.** Which campaign was more ambitious in its attack, Napoleon's or Hitler's? Explain.

   _____

   _____

   b. Which campaign lasted longer? Explain.

   _____

   _____

   c. Which campaign seems to have been more nearly victorious? Explain.

   _____

   _____

Reading-Writing Connection

Find an up-to-date map of Russia and the surrounding countries. On a separate sheet of paper, write a paragraph describing how the boundaries of countries in Eastern Europe have changed since 1944.

Skill: Cause and Effect

BACKGROUND INFORMATION

"Causes of Changing Weather" explains some of the causes of our ever-changing weather. People have always tried to understand and predict the weather, but weather forecasting is a relatively new science. Until the mid-1800s, people could not communicate quickly enough to make weather predictions useful. Today, however, with the rise of electronic communications and satellites, scientists can instantly provide up-to-the-minute and long-range weather forecasts to people all over the globe.

SKILL FOCUS: Cause and Effect

A **cause** is an event that makes something happen. An **effect** is what happens as a result of the cause. When one event causes another event to happen, the process is called **cause and effect**.

To find an effect, ask, "What happened?" To find a cause, ask, "Why did it happen?" The words *because*, *since*, *due to*, and *as a result* often signal cause-and-effect relationships.

Sometimes causes and effects are not stated directly. In these cases, you need to infer, or figure out, a cause or an effect from the context.

Read the following paragraph.

The weather report said that the hurricane would reach our beach area by 7:00 P.M., with winds up to 90 miles per hour by midnight. It was the height of the tourist season, and police warned that traffic would be heavier than usual on the roads leading to the highway.

If you think of the coming storm as the cause, you can infer its effects. People will flee the beach area to escape the hurricane. As a result, the highways will be crowded. You can show this chain of cause and effects in a graphic organizer.

▶ Read the following paragraph. Circle the cause. Underline the effect.

In recent years, hurricanes have done more and more damage. The storms themselves are not more powerful than in the past. People, however, are building more and more homes and businesses along beaches.

CONTEXT CLUES: Appositive Phrases

An **appositive phrase** is a group of words that explains the meaning of a new word. The appositive phrase usually follows the new word and is set off with commas or dashes. An appositive phrase often starts with the word *or*.

In the following sentence, find the appositive phrase that tells the meaning of the underlined word.

As light, warm air __ascends__, or rises, cooler air moves in to takes its place.

If you don't know the meaning of *ascends*, the appositive phrase *or rises* tells you the meaning.

▶ Read the following sentence. Circle the appositive phrase that explains the meaning of the underlined word.

__Meteorologists__, or scientists who study weather, collect data on temperature, humidity, wind speed, wind direction, and air pressure.

In the selection, look for appositive phrases that explain the meanings of the underlined words *spiral*, *descend*, and *diminishes*.

> ### Strategy Tip
>
> As you read "Causes of Changing Weather," look for the causes and effects of different kinds of weather systems. Try to infer causes and effects that are not stated directly.

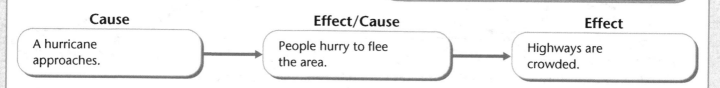

Cause	Effect/Cause	Effect
A hurricane approaches.	People hurry to flee the area.	Highways are crowded.

Causes of Changing Weather

To understand weather patterns, think of the blanket of air surrounding the Earth as a liquid that can flow from place to place. Air does not have exactly the same characteristics everywhere on the globe. The air is cold in some places and hot in others. In some places, the air contains a lot of water vapor and is humid, while elsewhere it contains little water vapor and is dry.

A large body of air with certain characteristics, such as warmth and humidity, is known as an **air mass**. The amount of moisture in an air mass depends on where it develops, so air masses are classified according to where they are formed. Some air masses are formed above continents, and others are formed over oceans. Air masses usually cover thousands of square kilometers.

At any given time, there are several air masses over the United States, and their movement is a major cause of our changing weather. The air masses over the United States also change their characteristics as they move from place to place. The four major air masses that affect the weather on the North American continent are shown in Figure 1.

Fronts

Where two air masses with different characteristics meet, a boundary, or **front**, forms, often causing

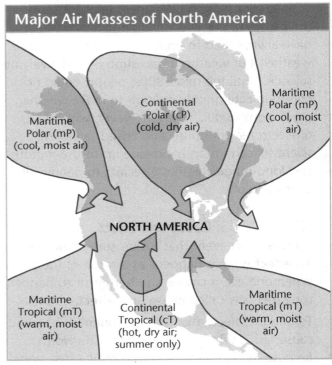

FIGURE 1. This diagram shows the air masses that affect weather in North America.

unsettled weather. Where a mass of warm air meets and rides over a mass of cold air, a **warm front** is created, and showers usually occur. Where a mass of cold air meets and slides under warm air, a **cold front** forms, and violent storms may occur. In this

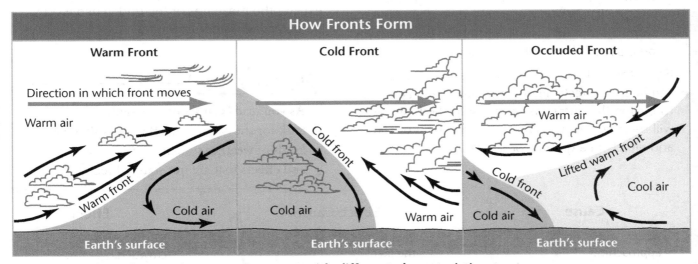

FIGURE 2. A front forms when two air masses with different characteristics meet.

case, the cold air pushes the warm air upward. If a cold front overtakes a warm front, the warm air is pushed up, forming a boundary called an **occluded** (ə KLOOD id) **front**. The occluded front occurs where the coldest air in the cold front meets cool air under the warm front. This type of front usually causes steady rain. Look at Figure 2 on page 136.

If a warm air mass meets a cold air mass and neither of them moves, the resulting front is called a **stationary front**. This condition often results in rainfall throughout the area of the front.

Cyclones and Anticyclones

Another factor affecting weather is air pressure. Warm air is lighter than cold air and, as a result, has lower pressure than cold air. As light, warm air ascends, or rises, cooler air moves in to take its place. This movement causes air currents. These wind currents <u>spiral</u>, or circle, around and into the centers of the areas where warm air is rising. The spiraling winds create what is called a **low** or a **cyclone**.

An area with cold, dry air has high pressure. It is called a **high** or an **anticyclone**. Wind currents in a high-pressure area <u>descend</u>, or fall, toward the Earth and outward from the center of the anticyclone area. In North America, the wind currents in cyclones spiral in a counterclockwise direction. Those in anticyclones spiral in a clockwise direction.

Storms

Fronts and cyclones can result in severe weather called **storms**. The meeting of a warm front and a cold front can result in a storm with heavy rain, lightning, and thunder. If a cold front meets a warm front in winter, there may be a heavy snowfall. If the temperature is less than −7 degrees Celsius (19 degrees Fahrenheit) and the wind speed is above 56 kilometers (35 miles) per hour, a blizzard occurs.

When very strong cyclones develop over tropical oceans, they give rise to **hurricanes**. As the warm, moist air rises rapidly, cooler air moves in, and the air begins to spin. Air pressure in the center drops, more cool air is drawn in, and the air spins even faster. This spinning system of rising air forms a cylinder of clouds, rain, and strong winds that may reach speeds of 120 to 130 kilometers (75 to 80 miles) per hour. At the center of a hurricane is an area of calm air called the eye. Look at Figure 3. As hurricanes move from the ocean onto land, they lose their source of warm, moist air, and their force <u>diminishes</u>, or decreases.

Tornadoes are among the most violent storms on Earth. A tornado is a whirling, funnel-shaped cloud with wind speeds of over 350 kilometers (217 miles) per hour. These storms are most common during the summer in the states of the Great Plains.

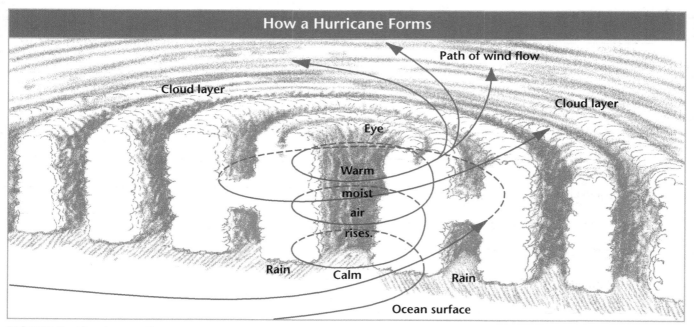

How a Hurricane Forms

Path of wind flow

Cloud layer

Cloud layer

Eye

Warm moist air rises.

Rain   Calm   Rain

Ocean surface

FIGURE 3. Hurricanes form over warm oceans.

There, cool, dry air from the west meets warm, moist air from the Gulf of Mexico.

Tornadoes form high above the ground, and most of them stay in the sky. However, when a tornado touches down on the Earth's surface, it leaves a path of destruction that averages about 6 kilometers (4 miles) long. The tornado causes this destruction in only a few minutes.

Weather Prediction

A major goal of weather science is to predict the weather, both for next week and for next year. Meteorologists (MEET ee ə RAHL ə jəsts), or scientists who study weather, collect data on temperature, humidity, wind speed, wind direction, and air pressure. Their sources of information are weather stations all over the world, weather balloons high in the atmosphere, and weather satellites in space. Today, scientists use computers to analyze data and make predictions.

From their data, scientists make weather maps, such as those that you see in newspapers and on television weather reports. The maps show highs (anticyclones), lows (cyclones), and fronts, as well as the direction in which the weather systems are moving. The maps are the basis for weather predictions. For example, fronts are associated with changing weather. Determining how fast a front is moving toward an area lets a weather forecaster predict when that area will be affected by the front.

Knowing future weather conditions is often very important. Farmers need to know about weather conditions in order to decide when to plant and harvest their crops. Many outdoor sports events depend on clear weather. Airports use weather forecasts in scheduling takeoffs and landings, as well as in planning flight paths. Accurate weather forecasts also alert people to severe weather conditions that could endanger their lives or property.

COMPREHENSION

1. What is a large body of air called?

_____

_____

2. What is a front?

_____

_____

3. What is an occluded front?

_____

_____

4. What is a cyclone?

_____

_____

5. What is an anticyclone?

_____

_____

6. In North America, does the air in an anticyclone move clockwise or counterclockwise?

_____

_____

7. Under what conditions does a blizzard occur?

_____

_____

_____

8. What must happen for a hurricane to form?

_____

_____

_____

_____

9. Where are tornadoes most common in the United States?

_____

_____

_____

10. Name five weather features that forecasters collect data on to make weather predictions.

_____

_____

_____

11. What are some sources of weather data?

_____

_____

_____

12. Look at Figure 1 on page 136. Which air masses affect the weather on the West Coast of the United States?

_____

_____

_____

13. Complete each statement with one of the words below. Write the words on the lines.

spiral   descend   diminishes

a. An early frost _____ the chance of a good orange crop.

b. The elevator will _____ from the top floor.

c. A snake can _____ around the tree.

CRITICAL THINKING

Circle the letter next to the correct answer.

1. Which of the four types of fronts would probably cause the longest period of rainy weather?

a. cold
b. warm
c. stationary
d. occluded

2. If air pressure dropped steadily, you could expect the weather to

a. become warmer.
b. become cooler.
c. remain the same.
d. become sunnier.

SKILL FOCUS: CAUSE AND EFFECT

A. Write the effect for each of the following causes.

1. Cause: Two air masses with different characteristics meet.

Effect: _____

2. Cause: A body of air is warmed.

Effect: _____

3. Cause: A body of air is cooled.

Effect: _____

4. **Cause:** A cold front meets a warm front in winter.

   Effect: _____

5. **Cause:** A warm front meets a cold front in summer.

   Effect: _____

B. **Write the cause for each of the following effects.**

   1. **Cause:** _____

      Effect: A warm front forms, and showers usually occur.

   2. **Cause:** _____

      Effect: A cold front forms, and violent storms may occur.

   3. **Cause:** _____

      Effect: A stationary front forms, and rain may occur.

   4. **Cause:** _____

      Effect: A hurricane may occur.

C. **Sometimes causes or effects are not stated directly in a selection. They have to be figured out, or inferred. For each cause given below, infer an effect and write it on the line provided. For the effect given, infer a cause and write it on the line provided.**

   1. **Cause:** _____

      Effect: Weather forecasting is more accurate now than it was 20 years ago.

   2. **Cause:** _____

      Effect: A warm air mass contains a great deal of water vapor.

   3. **Cause:** _____

      Effect: Cold air pushes up warm air.

   4. **Cause:** As hurricanes move away from water, they lose their power.

      Effect: _____

Reading-Writing Connection

Listen to a local weather forecast for today. On a separate sheet of paper, write a paragraph describing what kind of weather is expected. Explain the causes of the day's weather.

Skill: Reading a Graph

BACKGROUND INFORMATION

"Bar, Circle, and Line Graphs" describes different kinds of graphs to compare average temperatures and amounts of precipitation in two European cities—Rome and Moscow. Rome, the capital of Italy, has January temperatures that can reach 54 degrees Fahrenheit (12 degrees Celsius) and July temperatures as high as 88 degrees Fahrenheit (31 degrees Celsius). Moscow, the capital of Russia, has high temperatures of only 21 degrees Fahrenheit (−6 degrees Celsius) in January and 76 degrees Fahrenheit (24 degrees Celsius) in July.

SKILL FOCUS: Reading a Graph

Graphs show information in a clear, easy-to-read way. They also compare two or more sets of information more easily than lists or charts full of numbers do. There are three commonly used types of graphs.

1. **Bar graphs** are used to compare numbers that show information about the same thing at two or more different times. They can also show information about two or more different things at the same time.

2. **Circle graphs** are used to compare the parts of a whole, often using percents.

3. **Line graphs** show how information changes over time.

To understand a graph, you need to read its title and its labels. They tell the type of information that is shown on the graph. A graph may also have a key. The key explains the meaning of different colors, shadings, or lines shown on the graph. Also, read any text that comes before or after a graph. It may contain information that will help you interpret the graph.

▶ Which type of graph would be best to show the type of information below?

1. the percentages of students studying different

   foreign languages in one school _____

2. the populations in 1980, 1990, and 2000 of two

   Midwestern cities _____

WORD CLUES

When reading the selection, look for the words *data*, *axis*, *vertical*, *horizontal*, and *sectors*. Knowing these words will help you to understand and read graphs.

Strategy Tip

When reading "Bar, Circle, and Line Graphs," use a ruler to figure out what number is represented by a bar or point on a graph.

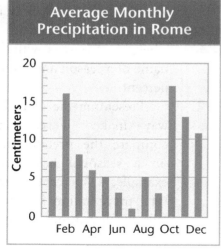

Bar Graph

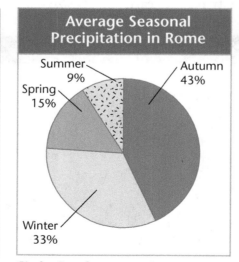

Circle Graph

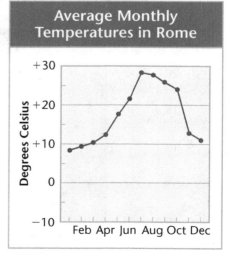

Line Graph

Bar, Circle, and Line Graphs

The information shown in a graph is called **data**. **Double bar graphs** compare two sets of data in the same graph. The double bar graph in Figure 1 compares the average monthly precipitation (prə SIP ə TAY shən) in Rome, the capital of Italy, with the precipitation in Moscow, the capital of Russia. Precipitation is rain, snow, sleet, or hail.

First read the title of the graph. The title tells you the kind of data that the graph shows. The title of this graph is *Average Monthly Precipitation in Rome and Moscow.*

Because this is a double bar graph, it has two sets of bars. One set represents the precipitation in Rome, and the other represents the precipitation in Moscow. You can learn what the bars stand for by looking at the **key**.

To find out the meaning of the data in the graph, read the labels on the **axes** (AK seez), the perpendicular lines that form the left side and the bottom of the graph. The **vertical axis** is labeled *cm*. This label means that the precipitation is given in centimeters. The marks and numbers on the vertical axis show the number of centimeters. The **horizontal axis** has abbreviations for the names of the months.

By combining the information from the two axes with the information from the key, you can find out how much precipitation each city receives each month. For example, the amount of precipitation in Rome is about 7 centimeters in January. You can compare that with about 5 centimeters of precipitation in Moscow for the same month. (Most of the precipitation in Moscow in January is snow, and it is measured by melting it.)

Even without looking at the numbers on the vertical axis, you can learn a great deal from comparing the relative heights of the gray bars and the blue bars. For example, you can see that most of the precipitation in Rome occurs in the autumn and winter (October through February), but most of the precipitation in Moscow occurs in the spring and early summer (May through July). You can also see that the average precipitation in both cities is the same in April. The most precipitation in a single month occurs in Rome in October. In Moscow, the lowest average monthly precipitation occurs in September and December.

Sometimes it is helpful to look at the same information in more than one way. **Circle graphs** can be used to show the percentage of the total annual precipitation that occurs in the two cities during each of the four seasons.

Read the title of the circle graphs in Figure 2 on page 143. Each circle graph is separated into four parts, called **sectors**. Each sector represents a season. Its size depends on how much of the precipitation for the whole year falls in that season. Each sector is labeled in two ways, with the name of a season and with a percent.

Presenting the data this way makes it easy to compare the precipitation on a seasonal basis. For example, 43 percent of the total precipitation in Rome falls during autumn, while in Moscow only 16 percent of the total precipitation occurs

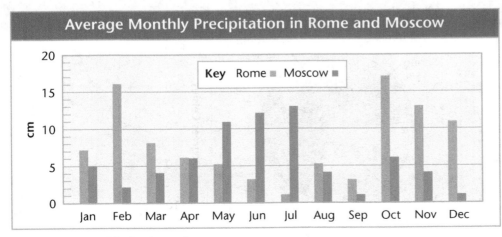

FIGURE 1. Double bar graph

in autumn. You can see that autumn brings the most precipitation to Rome, while spring brings the most to Moscow. Circle graphs are therefore useful for showing how certain parts are related to the whole.

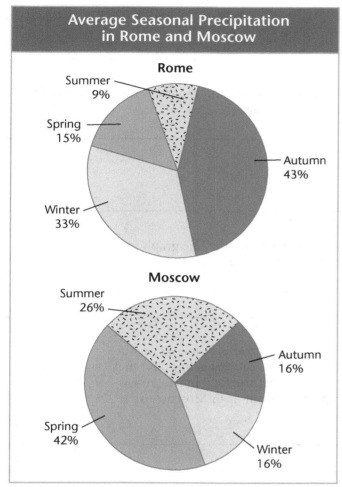

FIGURE 2. **Circle graphs**

Notice that the circle graphs do not show the amounts of precipitation. You can see that 16 percent of Moscow's precipitation occurs in autumn and 15 percent of Rome's precipitation occurs in spring. However, without knowing the amounts in centimeters, you cannot conclude from these percentages that Moscow gets slightly more precipitation in autumn than Rome does in spring. By looking at the double bar graph, you can see that Rome actually gets more precipitation in spring than Moscow does in autumn.

A third type of graph is a **line graph**. Like the bar graph, a line graph can be used to show two related sets of data. To do so, two lines are used. The double line graph in Figure 3 below compares another aspect of the climates of Rome and Moscow.

Read the title to find out the subject of the graph. The label on the vertical axis tells you that temperatures are measured in Celsius units. The labels on the horizontal axis are the same as in the double bar graph on page 142. The key tells you which line shows temperatures in Rome and which shows temperatures in Moscow.

The graph shows that the average temperature in Moscow for a particular month is never as high as the average temperature in Rome for the same month. Summer in Moscow, however, is warmer than winter is in Rome.

The steepness of a line tells you how fast the data is changing. For example, in Moscow, the steep parts of the line show that the temperature rises rapidly from February to May and falls rapidly from August to November. In Rome, the temperature changes more gradually during the whole year. The steepest temperature rise is from June to July, while the steepest decline is from October to November.

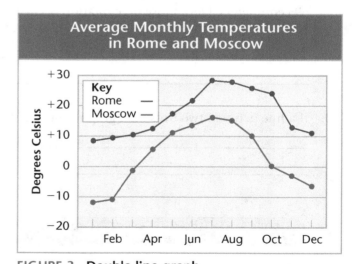

FIGURE 3. **Double line graph**

1. What is the information in a graph called?

_____

2. For any kind of graph, what should you read first?

_____

3. When a bar or line graph presents information about two places, how can you tell which bar or line represents which place?

_____

4. What do the labels on the axes tell you?

_____

5. In a circle graph, what does the size of a sector show?

_____

6. In a line graph, what does the steepness of a line show?

_____

CRITICAL THINKING

1. Combine the information from the double bar graph in Figure 1 and the line graph in Figure 3. Describe what kind of weather probably occurs in Moscow in October.

_____

_____

2. From the circle graphs, you can tell what percent of the precipitation in Rome occurs in autumn and what percent of the precipitation in Moscow occurs in spring. Suppose that the total annual precipitation in Rome is 95 centimeters and that the total in Moscow is 69 centimeters. Does more precipitation occur in Rome in autumn or in Moscow in spring? Explain how you figured out your answer.

_____

_____

3. If a line between two dots on a graph is horizontal, what does that tell you about the data?

_____

_____

SKILL FOCUS: READING A GRAPH

A. Read the graphs in the selection to answer the following questions.

1. On the average, about how many centimeters of precipitation does Rome

receive in February? _____

2. In July, how many more centimeters of precipitation occur in Moscow

than in Rome? _____

3. Which month shows the lowest amount of average precipitation in Rome? _____

4. In the hottest month, about how much hotter is it in Rome than in Moscow? _____

5. In the coldest month, about how much colder is it in Moscow than

in Rome? _____

6. Which season has the lowest amount of precipitation in Rome? _____

B. People who study climate sometimes use a combination line and bar graph, as shown below. The line graph uses the vertical axis on the left, and it shows temperatures. The bar graph uses the vertical axis on the right, and it shows precipitation. Use the climate graph below to answer the following questions.

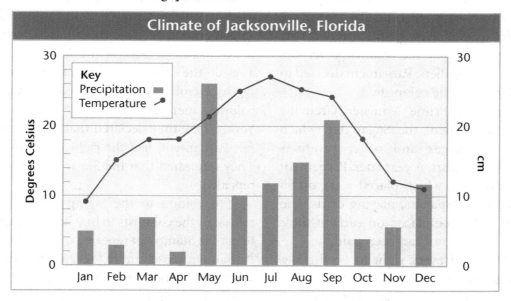

1. What is the subject of the graph? _____

2. In which month does the most precipitation occur in Jacksonville? _____

3. In which month is the temperature the highest in Jacksonville? _____

4. Which month has the least amount of precipitation? _____

5. Which month has the lowest temperature? _____

6. How much precipitation occurs in September? _____

7. What is the average temperature in November? _____

Reading-Writing Connection

Record the hourly temperature changes during a day, from 8:00 a.m. to 8:00 p.m. Then on a separate sheet of paper, make a line graph to show your data in degrees.

Skill: Distinguishing Fact From Opinion

As you read books, newspapers, and magazines, you need to be able to distinguish facts from opinions. A statement of **fact** is information that can be proven to be true. A statement of **opinion** is a personal belief. There can be many different opinions on the same issue.

Read the following paragraphs. Decide which statements are facts and which are opinions.

The Stamp Act

The English government had great expenses as a result of the French and Indian War. Ruling the 13 colonies and other areas, such as Canada, was a financial drain, as well. The British needed new sources of revenue to pay the colonial governors and to support their soldiers. Parliament decided to raise money by taxing the colonists.

In 1764, British Prime Minister Grenville introduced to Parliament the Sugar Act, which placed a tax on sugar and other products imported by the colonists. A year later, Parliament passed the Stamp Act, which placed a tax on all legal documents, newspapers, playing cards, and dice. A stamp had to be placed on each of these items to show that the tax had been paid.

The colonists had every right to be furious. They were angered not so much over the cost of the tax as over the fact that they had no representatives in Parliament. The colonists believed that Parliament did not have the right to pass tax laws affecting them. Therefore, the Stamp Act was unfair. They argued that there could be "no taxation without representation." To the colonists, this was a valid argument. Because British subjects could not be taxed without the agreement of their representatives, why should the colonists be taxed without representation? As a result, the colonists did not accept these taxes.

In October 1765, representatives from nine colonies met at a Stamp Act Congress in New York. There they declared that only the colonists, not Parliament, had the right to tax the colonies. They requested that the Sugar and Stamp acts be repealed.

Opposition to the Stamp Act, especially the refusal of the colonists to buy British goods, helped to get the Stamp Act repealed in 1766. Even though Parliament passed more tax laws the next year, the colonists' reaction to the Stamp Act had important consequences. It helped to unite the colonists, who had formerly been unable to agree. Also, people who had voiced their opinions, such as Samuel Adams, John Adams, Patrick Henry, and George Washington, became America's greatest heroes.

On the line next to each statement, write _F_ if it is a fact or _O_ if it is an opinion.

_____ **1.** Parliament decided to raise money by taxing the colonists.

_____ **2.** In 1764, Prime Minister Grenville introduced the Sugar Act to Parliament.

_____ **3.** The colonists had every right to be furious.

_____ **4.** Parliament did not have the right to pass laws affecting the colonists.

_____ **5.** The colonists had no representation in Parliament.

_____ **6.** The Stamp Act was unfair.

_____ **7.** The Stamp Act Congress met in October 1765.

_____ **8.** Samuel Adams and Patrick Henry were two of America's greatest heroes.

Skill: Making Inferences

Sometimes you can **infer**, or figure out, information that is not stated in a selection.

1. Read carefully.

2. Think about what you have read. Be sure you understand the information stated.

3. Read again. Look for clues to information that is not stated but might follow logically from what is stated.

4. Put together what is stated with information you already know. Use clues to help you make inferences.

As you read the following selection about weather forecasting, pay close attention to the facts. Use the facts to infer information that is not directly stated.

Weather Forecasting

1. People can forecast weather conditions in their area for the next half hour or so just by looking at the sky. To make accurate predictions for the next day and beyond, however, meteorologists need information about a larger geographical area. For example, a good three-day forecast for the eastern United States requires information about today's weather for the entire Northern Hemisphere. Meteorologists get this information from technological devices, such as radar and satellites.

2. One new technology for forecasting weather more accurately is Doppler radar. The old type of radar used in the past could show the location, movement, strength, and type of precipitation (rain, snow, or sleet) approaching an area. Doppler radar not only provides that information but also measures wind speed and direction and detects winds in clear air. It also can identify fronts— boundaries between masses of cool and warm air— even when they are not yet producing precipitation.

Put a ✔ next to the statement that can be inferred from each paragraph. Then write the information that is a clue for each inference. Explain how you made your inference.

Paragraph 1 (check one)

_____ **a.** Three-day and five-day weather forecasts are not very accurate.

_____ **b.** Meteorologists use technological devices to study and forecast weather conditions.

_____ **c.** Weather satellites and radar provide information about large areas of the Earth.

Clue: _____

Explanation: _____

Paragraph 2 (check one)

_____ **a.** Identifying fronts helps meteorologists develop more accurate weather forecasts.

_____ **b.** Wind speed and direction could be measured with the old type of radar.

_____ **c.** Weather forecasters have stopped using the old type of radar.

Clue: _____

Explanation: _____

The quickest way to find information in a text or reference book is to use the **index**. An index alphabetically lists the book's topics.

On page 149 is part of an index from a science textbook. Find the topic *vegetables*. Below it, two subtopics are listed alphabetically: *source of Vitamin C* and *vitamins in*. Subtopics tell the specific kinds of information about the main topic that are discussed.

The numbers after each topic or subtopic are the page numbers on which that information can be found. Numbers separated by commas indicate that the information appears only on the pages given. Numbers separated by dashes indicate that the topic is discussed on all the pages that come between the two numbers. Notice that some subtopics have words like *in* and *of* before them. These short words do not affect the alphabetical order of the subtopics.

Study the index on the next page. Then answer the following questions.

1. On which page(s) would you find information about weather balloons? _____

2. How many subtopics are listed under the topic *Time*? _____

3. On which page(s) would you find information about wood pulp? _____

4. On how many pages does the book have information on time zones? _____

5. On which page(s) would you find information about how water evaporates? _____

6. Information about which two types of vitamins is found on page 65? _____

7. On which page(s) would you find information about removing wax from cloth? _____

8. Which five subtopics are listed under *Water Routes*? _____

9. On which page(s) would you find information about the effects of the moon on the tides? _____

10. Which topic comes between *Vegetables* and *Venom, snake*? _____

11. On which page(s) would you find information about Daylight Saving Time? _____

12. If you wanted information about how moisture affects weather, which page would you

    not look at between 248 and 253? _____

13. On which page(s) would you find information about materials suspended in water? _____

14. If the book had information about Telstar 1, after which major topic would

    it be listed? _____

15. If the book had information about the Triassic period, before which major topic

    would it be listed? _____

16. On which page(s) would you find information about the composition of seawater? _____

17. On which page(s) would you find information about air pollution caused by volcanoes? _____

Tear gas, 192
Telescopes, 212–214
   Hale (Mount Palomar), 214–217
   Hubble, 215–217
Television, 101
Temperature zones, 206
Temperature, 248–249
   abnormally high, 111
   effect on solutions, 152
   of body, 34, 104
Terracing, 161
Thermometers, 31, 34, 249, 250
Thermostat, 161
Thiamine, 63, 64
Tides, moon and, 208–209
Time:
   Daylight Saving, 213
   International Date Line, 212–213
   measurement of, 211–213
   zones, 211–213
Tincture solution, 153
Tobacco, 121–122
Today's Health, 20
Tongue, and sense of taste, 97–98
Torricelli, Evangelista, 235
Touch, sense of, 88, 99, 102
Transplanting seedlings, 70
Transportation, water, 133–134
Trees, materials from, 194–195
Tropical air masses, 255
Tropic of Cancer, 206
Tropic of Capricorn, 206
Tuberculosis, 34, 116
Turbines:
   steam, 157
   water, 155–156
Turpentine, 71, 195
Typhoid fever, 148
   bacteria, 33

V

Vaccination, 22, 197
   of cows, 23
Vacuum, 235
Vapor, water, 137–138
Vegetables, 51
   source of Vitamin C, 65
   vitamins in, 62
Veins, 107, 113
   valves in, 62
Venom, snakes, 74
Venus, planet, 217, 218
Visiting nurses, 23–24
Vital organs:
   listening to, 35
   seeing, by X-ray machine, 35–36

Vital statistics, 24–25
Vitamins, 49
   A, 63, 91
   as body regulators, 61–66
   B_1, 64
   B_2, 64
   B_{12}, 64
   B complex, 63–64
   C, 64–65
   claims concerning, checking, 66
   D, 65–66
   discovery of, 60
   K, 66
   lack of, 62–63
   naming of, 60
   protective foods, 62–63
Vitreous humor, 90
Volcanoes:
   and air pollution, 242
   beneath seas, 142
Vonnegut, Dr. Bernard, 249

W

WAC Corporal, 232
Washing soda, 167
Wasps, 73
Water:
   as body regulator, 61
   composition of, 149–150
   conserving, 160–162
   distribution of, 135
   drinking, treatment of, 159–160
   evaporation of, 136
   filtration of, 136
   impure, 159
   irrigation, 162
   lakes, 142–143
   materials suspended in, 159–160
   minerals in, 150–152
   oceans (*see* Oceans)
   rainfall, 138–139
   rainwater, 143–144
   rivers, 143–144
   sea, composition of, 150–152
   solutions, 152
   supply in cities, 157–160
   surface, 140–144
     (*see also* Water routes)
   underground, 139
   in wells, 139
Water cycle, 135–137
Waterfalls, 154–155
Water power plants, 145
Water pressure, 154–157
Water routes, 133–134
   canals, 145–147

   lakes, 144–145
   oceans, 145
   rivers, 144
   St. Lawrence Waterway, 145
Water table, 139–140
   raising, 160, 161
Water turbines, 155–156
Water vapor, 137–138
   in air, 237–240
   condensation of, 251
Water wheels, 154–155
Wax, removing from cloth, 169
Weather, 247–263
   air movement, 248, 253–256
   changes along front, 255–256, 259
   information from weather stations, 259–260
   moisture, 248, 250–253
   temperature, 248–249
   value in forecasts, 262–263
Weather balloons, 257–260
Weather Bureau, U.S., 257–258
Weather map, highs and lows on, 260–262
Weather stations, 259–260
Weather vane, 253–254
Welland Ship Canal, 145
Wells, 139
   artesian, 140
Windpipe, 114–115
Winds, 253–254
   effect on water vapor, 138
Wood, varieties of, 195
Wood pulp, 195
Wool, 197
Work, food and, 48–55
World, map of, 204–207

X

X-ray machine, 15
   chest examination, 31
X-ray photos, 105

Y

Year, 202

Z

Zones, 206–207
   time, 211–213

Skill: Reading a Warranty

A **warranty** is a manufacturer's promise to the buyer that the product is well-made. According to this written guarantee, if the product does not continue to work properly for a given period, the company must repair or replace it at no cost to the buyer.

Many products that you purchase come with warranties. The terms of a warranty may influence your decision in buying a product. Therefore, you should read a warranty carefully before you purchase a product.

Most warranties include the following information.

- **Warranty period** is the amount of time from date of purchase during which the product is guaranteed by the manufacturer.

- **Warranty coverage** is exactly what the manufacturer is responsible for in the event that something goes wrong.

Examine this warranty for a camcorder.

- **Service agreement** is what to do after the warranty period runs out to get service from the company.

- **Steps to follow** is what the buyer must do to activate the warranty.

LIMITED NINETY-DAY WARRANTY

SONIX warrants to the original consumer purchaser that your SONIX unit is free from any defects in material or workmanship for a period of **ninety days** from the date of purchase. If any such defect is discovered within the warranty period, SONIX will repair or replace the unit **free of charge** (except for a **$4.00 charge for packing, return postage, and insurance**), subject to verification of the defect or malfunction upon delivery or postage prepaid to:

SONIX
Customer Service Division
1301 Third Avenue
New York, NY 10021

IMPORTANT
Please do not return your product to the store where it was purchased. SONIX accepts the responsibility of keeping you a satisfied customer. ALL RETURNS MUST HAVE WRITTEN AUTHORIZATION FROM:

SONIX
1301 Third Avenue
New York, NY 10021

PLEASE WRITE FOR DETAILS.
This warranty does not apply to defects resulting from abuse, alteration, or unreasonable use of the unit, resulting in cracked or broken cases or units damaged by excessive heat, and it does not apply to batteries. **YOU MUST ENCLOSE PROOF OF DATE AND PLACE OF PURCHASE AND CHECK OR MONEY ORDER FOR $4.00** TO COVER HANDLING, OR WE CANNOT BE RESPONSIBLE FOR REPAIRS OR REPLACEMENT.

Any applicable implied warranties, including warranties of merchantability and fitness, are hereby limited to **ninety** days from date of purchase. Consequential or incidental damages resulting from a breach of any applicable express or implied warranties are hereby excluded. Some states do not allow limitations on how long implied warranties last and do not allow exclusion of incidental or consequential damages, so the above limitations and exclusions may not apply to you.

This warranty gives you specific legal rights, and you may also have other rights that may vary from state to state.

SERVICE AGREEMENT
If, after the ninety-day limited warranty period, your SONIX unit requires service, SONIX will service the unit upon receipt, postage prepaid, with your check or money order in **the sum of $10.00 to cover cost of repair, as well as return postage, insurance, and packing.**

This service agreement does not apply to defects from abuse, alteration, or unreasonable use of the unit and does not apply to units that require service three years after the date of purchase.

IMPORTANT STEPS TO FOLLOW
Before returning the unit, you must write to:

SONIX
1301 Third Avenue
New York, NY 10021

for a RETURN AUTHORIZATION LABEL, which must be affixed to outside of return parcel.

Before returning this unit, replace the batteries (where applicable) with fresh ones, because exhausted or defective batteries are the most common cause of problems encountered. If service is still required,

1. Remove the batteries and pack unit with all its original accessories in a well-padded, heavy, corrugated box.
2. If the warranty period has not expired, enclose your sales receipt or photocopy of it to validate the date and place of purchase.
3. Enclose a check or money order payable to the order of SONIX for the sum of $4.00 (if the product is within the warranty period) or $10.00 (if the warranty period has expired).

A. Decide if the following information can be determined from the warranty on page 150. Write *yes* or *no* on the lines.

1. where to send the product in the event of a defect _____

2. how long it will take to repair or replace a part in the event of a defect _____

3. what must accompany any products that are returned for repair or replacement _____

4. what steps to follow in the event of a problem after the warranty period is over _____

5. how long the product is under warranty _____

6. what to do with a product that becomes faulty three years after the purchase date _____

7. how to get a Return Authorization Label from the company _____

8. whether money must be enclosed with a returned product _____

9. where to telephone in case a product returned to the company is not sent back to the customer within 90 days _____

10. how frequently batteries need to be replaced in those products requiring batteries _____

B. Use the information provided on the warranty to complete each sentence.

1. The warranty period for this camcorder is _____.

2. To have a camcorder repaired or replaced, you are to send it to _____, rather than to the store where it was purchased.

3. If a one-day-old camcorder is found to be defective, repair or replacement is _____.

4. The company advises replacing the _____ with new ones before determining that the camcorder is defective.

5. If you get your brand-new camcorder home and find that it is defective, it will still cost you _____ to return it to the company. This charge covers

_____.

6. If you return a camcorder during the warranty period, you must include a sales receipt to prove _____.

7. When you send money to the company, you cannot send cash. You must send a _____ or _____.

8. To have a broken camcorder repaired when the warranty period is over, the company charges a total of _____ to fix it.

LESSON 43

Skill: Conflict and Resolution

BACKGROUND INFORMATION

"Tuned-in Telenut" is a science-fiction story about a time in the future when watching TV is illegal. Critics of television have long claimed that TV reduces creativity, fosters violence, and creates a demand for unnecessary goods. Nevertheless, two-thirds of all American homes have at least two TV sets.

SKILL FOCUS: Conflict and Resolution

The struggle to solve a problem or achieve a goal is a story's **conflict**. Three types of conflict include:

1. **Conflict With Self** A character might struggle with inner feelings. This is an **internal conflict**.

2. **Conflict With Another Character** Two story characters might disagree about an important issue, have an argument, or compete against each other. This type of struggle is an **external conflict**.

3. **Conflict With an Outside Force** A character might struggle against nature, society, or some danger over which he or she has little control.

By the end of a story, the character succeeds or fails at solving the problem or achieving the goal of the conflict. This is called the **resolution** of the story's plot.

Stories sometimes have more than one conflict. The **major**, or more important, **conflict** involves the main character. The **minor**, or less important, **conflict** involves the other characters.

▶ Think about each problem in the chart below. Describe the type of conflict each character faces and how the character might resolve the conflict.

CONTEXT CLUES: Synonyms

Sometimes a clue to an unknown word will be a **synonym**, a word with a similar meaning. What synonym in the sentences below can help you figure out the meaning of the underlined word?

*Once he fixed the computatime with a pushpin and a **smidgen** of tape. It was amazing what my brother could put together with a bit of this and a piece of that.*

If you don't know the meaning of *smidgen,* the synonym *bit* can help you. The words *smidgen* and *bit* both refer to tiny amounts of something.

▶ Read these sentences. Circle a synonym for the underlined word.

*I trudged upstairs, not knowing how to get out of my **predicament**. The more I thought about my problem, the more difficult it became.*

As you read, use synonyms to find the meanings of *mesmerized, irritable,* and *harrowing.*

> **Strategy Tip**
>
> As you read, think about the conflicts that the characters face. Predict how they will be resolved.

Character's Problem	Type of Conflict	Possible Resolution
Todd's dad wants him to play football, but Todd wants to join the drama club.		
Renee would like to sign up to sing a solo in the talent show, but she worries that her voice isn't good enough.		
A sudden cold snap threatens the trees in the Colonello family's Florida orange groves.		

Tuned-In Telenut

Of course, I should have recognized the signs. When it happens to someone close to you, though, you just refuse to believe the truth. I did notice that my brother was spending more and more time in his basement workshop. Once I even asked him, "What are you doing down there, Kamal?"

"Oh, I'm just experimenting," he said mysteriously. "Nothing to worry about, Jasmine."

I didn't worry about it then. Kamal was always doing experiments. He was a genius at constructing things. Once he fixed the computatime with a pushpin and a smidgen of tape. It was amazing what my brother could put together with a bit of this and a piece of that.

✔ On weekends, Kamal was always in his workshop before the rest of us woke up, and he was still there after we all went to bed. When he had to come up to eat, he had a faraway smile and a dazed look on his face. He seemed to have trouble answering the simplest of Dad's questions. At dinner, he often stared straight ahead, not seeing or hearing anything. He seemed <u>mesmerized</u>, hypnotized, almost in a trance. As soon as he could, he rushed back downstairs.

"What's Kamal experimenting with now?" Dad asked one day.

"I don't know," I said, but by then I had a terrible suspicion.

Later, I went downstairs and poked around. I hadn't searched very long when I found, hidden in the corner of the workshop, exactly what I had feared.

I trudged upstairs, not knowing how to get out of my predicament. The more I thought about my problem, the more difficult it became. I just couldn't decide what to do. I didn't want to tell my parents about Kamal—I'd be getting him into a lot of trouble. On the other hand, I couldn't just stand by, knowing what he was doing, without trying to help him get out of trouble.

I decided to consult my logic synthesizer, which had been a lot of help with problem-solving homework. After you enter all the information about a problem, the synthesizer analyzes the data and helps you to select the best solution. I entered this statement: "I have a problem with my brother."

"Uh-oh," the synthesizer responded, "Kamal again. Name the problem."

I did, and the synthesizer and I went back and forth for an hour. Finally I slipped downstairs to the food center. Dad was busy microwaving dinner, while Mom was planning next week's dinners on the compumenu.

"Mom, Dad," I said, "Kamal is a telenut."

"Oh, no!" Mom gasped.

I took a deep breath and said, "He has a television set and DVDs hidden downstairs."

Mom gasped again. "But that's been illegal for 20 years! Ever since the year 2030, only a few people have been allowed to watch television—and they're allowed to watch it only for research and experimental studies. How do you think Kamal got hold of a television set?"

"The same way that he got hold of the radar last year. He put it together himself. As for the DVDs, he must have found them in old, abandoned houses. The cleanup squads must have overlooked them."

"Doesn't Kamal realize what he's doing to himself?" Dad asked. "Back in 2020, it was decided that television destroys the creative powers of the mind."

"I know," I said. "To think that in the year 2000, over 95 percent of all Americans owned at least one television set."

"And the average person spent 21 hours a week in front of it," Mom added.

"Horrible!" I said with a shudder. "I'm so glad to be living in the year 2050. Thank goodness the age of television is over."

Just then Kamal wandered in. "Is it true, Kamal?" Dad asked. "Are you a telenut?"

Kamal's vacant expression and bloodshot eyes were answer enough.

"How could you?" Mom asked. "Don't you know you're letting your imagination wither and die?"

Kamal looked completely embarrassed. Sitting down at the kitchen table, he sighed and said, "Sometimes I'd like to stop being such a telenut. I know I'm breaking the law, but I can't help admiring the simplicity of the thing! You can learn a lot from watching television. No matter how complicated a problem is, it can be solved in one hour—actually in 46 minutes, leaving out commercials. Amazing, isn't it? It makes life so simple."

Mom, Dad, and I looked at each other.

"You can learn a lot from commercials, too," Kamal went on dreamily. "To get a date, all you need is the right mouthwash and deodorant; to keep a marriage together, you should use certain brands of coffee and dishwashing detergent."

At this point, we knew Kamal was in real trouble. Nobody drank coffee any more, and no one needed detergents with the new ultrasonic dishwashers. Kamal was living in the ancient past.

"Kamal," Mom said, "You can learn things from books, too. Why not try scanning one for a change?"

"Scanning?" Kamal said blankly. "Oh, that. It's too much trouble watching the words move along the display, and there aren't enough pictures."

Mom turned to Dad. "Do you think it's too late for him?" she asked. "Is there any hope?"

"I don't know," Dad said, shaking his head. "They say that once you're a telenut, it's almost impossible to change."

"We've got to do something," Mom said. "Is there no cure?"

"Some studies have shown that a telenut can be broken of the attraction slowly," I said. "We'll cut Kamal down one hour of television a day until he's down to an hour a week."

That's what we did. It wasn't easy for any of us. It was a huge struggle for Kamal, but he tried. He even made some decisions himself.

"This week, we cut out all quiz shows!" he would say bravely.

As we cut down his viewing time, Kamal grew shaky and irritable. He became so impatient that in the middle of a conversation, he would suddenly scream, "It's time for *Police Dog!*" or "I've got to know what's happening on *Rescue Squad!*" In his sleep, he muttered, "You, too, can get fast, fast, fast relief."

Kamal finally fought his way out of his telenuttery. Today, he's a normal person, a typical teenager of the twenty-first century. His powers of thinking and logic were only temporarily damaged by his harrowing encounter with television, but I know Kamal won't ever forget his terrifying experience of becoming a telenut.

Yet he'll never be quite the person he once was. Every now and then, even today, he still gets that look in his eyes, and I know he's wondering what's happening on *My Mother, the Astronaut.*

1. Where and when does this story take place?

_____

_____

2. Name three machines that give clues to the story's setting in time.

_____

_____

3. From what point of view is the story told, and who is the narrator?

_____

_____

4. Why does Jasmine consult her logic synthesizer?

_____

_____

5. Circle the correct meaning of the underlined word in each sentence.

   a. The audience was <u>mesmerized</u> by the effects of the lasers used in the light show.

       fascinated   startled

   b. Drivers who are stuck in traffic jams often get <u>irritable</u>.

       concerned   annoyed

   c. Being lost at sea for even one day can be a <u>harrowing</u> experience.

       frightening   wondering

CRITICAL THINKING

1. a. Describe Kamal's character.

_____

_____

   b. Describe Jasmine's attitude toward her brother.

_____

_____

2. Why does Kamal get hooked on television?

_____

_____

3. Do you think Kamal will be able to stay away from television in the future? Give details from the story that support your prediction.

_____

_____

4. Reread the paragraph with a ✔ next to it. Write a sentence stating its main idea.

_____

_____

5. Do you think watching television harms a person's creativity? Give reasons and examples to support your opinion.

_____

_____

SKILL FOCUS: CONFLICT AND RESOLUTION

1. a. In the story, both Jasmine and Kamal face internal conflicts. Who faces the major, or

more important, conflict? _____

b. How does this character come into conflict with himself or herself?

_____

_____

c. How is this major conflict gradually resolved?

_____

_____

2. a. There is also a minor conflict in the story. Who faces it? _____

b. Circle the statement that best describes the minor conflict. Then tell how the conflict is resolved.

Should Kamal give up television viewing?

Should Jasmine help Kamal give up television viewing?

Should Jasmine tell her parents about Kamal's attraction to television viewing?

_____

_____

3. In one or two sentences, explain how Kamal's and Jasmine's conflicts are alike or different.

_____

_____

Reading-Writing Connection

Suppose you lived in your neighborhood or community 50 years from today. On a separate sheet of paper, write a paragraph describing what you might see.

Skill: Making Generalizations

BACKGROUND INFORMATION

"A Brief History of English" traces the development of the English language. If you can read this page, you are one of the half billion people in the world who use English. You use some of its million words every day. Many events in history, including wars, invasions, explorations, and inventions, have shaped and changed the English language.

SKILL FOCUS: Making Generalizations

A **generalization** is a statement that is based on many examples or events. For example, the statement *People in many different countries learn to speak English* is a generalization. You can make a generalization after thinking about several facts that are related and what they have in common.

Read the following word histories. Think of a generalization that applies to all four examples.

> *From the words* motor *and* hotel, *we get the word* motel. Breakfast *and* lunch *were joined to form* brunch. Bionics *comes from combining the words* biology *and* electronics. Smog *is a mix of* smoke *and* fog.

Based on the four facts, you could make this generalization: *Many new English words are formed by blending parts of two older words together.*

Certain clue words signal generalizations. These words include *many, all, most, few, always, everyone,* and *generally.* When you read these clue words, you can tell that a writer is making a broad statement that applies to many examples.

When you read a generalization, think about the related facts you know and whether the facts support the generalization. A generalization must be logical and be supported by facts to be valid.

▶ Complete the chart on this page. First read the facts. Then write a generalization based on them.

CONTEXT CLUES: Using a Dictionary

When you read a new word, context clues might give you a general idea of the word's meaning. If you want an exact definition, however, you have to look up the word in a **dictionary.**

Fact 1	**Fact 2**	**Fact 3**
Old English was the language of German tribes who came to England around 500.	After 1100, the Norman conquerors added 10,000 French words to English.	During the 1500s, thousands of new English words were formed from Latin and Greek.

Generalization

Read the following sentence, and think about the meaning of the underlined words.

> *The Indo-European language was never written down. There are no* **Rosetta stones** *to help people figure it out.*

The context clues suggest that a Rosetta stone is a kind of language. A dictionary would tell you that the Rosetta stone was a stone with the same message inscribed in three different languages.

▶ Try to figure out the meaning of the underlined word in the following sentence based on context clues. Then look up the word in a dictionary. Write the definitions on the line.

These Germanic tribes invaded Britain in the fifth century, **pillaging** *village after village.*

_____

_____

As you read, use a dictionary to look up the exact meanings of *linguists, etymology,* and *subordinates.*

Strategy Tip

In "A Brief History of English," make generalizations that will help you to summarize the development of the English language.

A BRIEF HISTORY OF ENGLISH

English and many other languages of the world come from the same source. About 6,000 years ago, Indo-European, a prehistoric language, was spoken in parts of Europe and Asia. The Indo-European language was never written down. There are no Rosetta stones to help people figure it out. Nevertheless, <u>linguists</u> have been able to piece together this long-lost language. To do so, they use clues hidden in the languages of today.

By comparing modern and ancient languages, we can find similar patterns of words and sounds. On the chart below are words from four modern languages and two ancient ones. (Latin was spoken in ancient Rome, and Sanskrit was spoken in India.) Look at the variations of the word *night* in other languages. By comparing these related forms, linguists concluded that the original Indo-European word for night was probably something like *not*.

Words With Similar Patterns			
English	night	sun	three
German	Nacht	Sonne	drei
French	nuit	soleil	trois
Spanish	noche	sol	tres
Latin	nox	sol	tres
Sanskrit	nakta	surya	trayas

Old English

The flowchart below shows some of the languages that have developed from Indo-European. Notice that English belongs to the Germanic branch of the Indo-European family. The origins of English are in the Germanic **dialects** (DY ə lekts), or regional language variations, spoken by three Germanic tribes: the Angles, the Saxons, and the Jutes. These Germanic tribes invaded Britain in the fifth century, pillaging, or looting, village after village. The natives of England, called the Celts, almost disappeared in these attacks. Their language did disappear, with only a few of its words and place names surviving today.

The Angles and Saxons decided to stay. From about A.D. 450 to 1100, Anglo-Saxon, or Old English, was spoken across all of England. Most Anglo-Saxons were illiterate (il LIT ər ət). They could not read or write. Nevertheless they gave rise to English, a language that would one day have more than a million words and half a billion speakers.

If you were to hear someone speak Old English, you would recognize some of the words. <u>Etymology</u> (ET ə MAHL ə jee) reveals to us that of the 1,000 most common English words, 800 have Old English roots.

However, the order of words in Old English sentences sounds strange today. Here is an Old English sentence: *Tha sealde se cyning him sweord.*

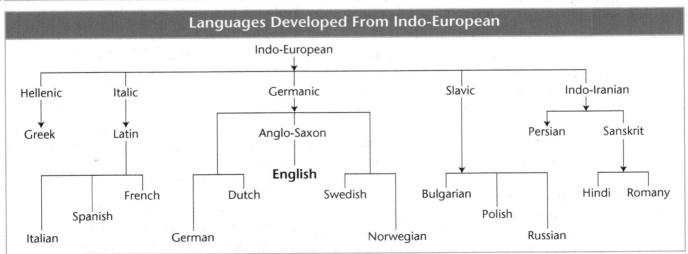

Many modern languages, including English, developed from the Indo-European language.

Translated word for word, the sentence would read "Then gave the king him a sword." Notice that the verb *gave* comes before the subject of the sentence, *king*. This is a typical Old English sentence pattern.

Old English had many special word endings, or **inflections**, that expressed meaning. One inflection that remains is the *-s* used for plurals.

Middle English

The next phase in the history of English begins with the next conquest of England. The Normans of France invaded England in the year 1066, defeating the Anglo-Saxons at the Battle of Hastings. England's best land was then divided up among Norman noblemen.

Normans were appointed to all positions in the government and the church. The French-speaking Normans became the rulers of England, and English-speaking people became their subordinates.

Although the Norman invasion was bad for the English people, it benefited the English language. After the Norman Conquest, a steady stream of French words entered the English language. On a large Norman estate, for example, a peasant would use the Old English words *cows, calf, sheep,* and *swine,* to name his animals. A servant in the manor house of the estate, however, would have to use French terms for these animals—*beef, veal, mutton,* and *pork*—when serving dinner. In courtrooms where French officials presided, the English learned new words such as *judge, jury, marry,* and *robber.* English laborers heard French builders use words such as *castle, palace, beauty,* and *art.* The Norman landlords had time for leisure activities, so the words *joy, delight, comfort, sport,* and *pleasure* entered English.

In order to rise in society, many English speakers became bilingual (by LING gwəl), speaking both English and French. Using French words was fashionable. Even today, French words such as *chef* and *maitre d'* often have more prestige than their English counterparts *cook* and *headwaiter.* In all, English speakers borrowed over 10,000 French words. We still use about 7,000 of them today.

Over time, the differences between the Normans and the English gradually diminished, or grew less. The Normans intermarried with the English. They had less and less contact with people in France.

Many Normans learned English to communicate with their servants. In 1337, war broke out between England and France, and French lost its popularity in England. By 1400, English had replaced French as the language of business and the courts.

The combination of Old English and Norman French gave rise to the language of Middle English, which was spoken from about 1100 to 1500. Geoffrey Chaucer was one of the first poets to write in Middle English. Here are the opening lines of his famous poem *The Canterbury Tales,* written in 1386.

Whan that April with his showres soote
The droughte of March hath perced to the roote,
And bathed every veine in swich licour
Of which vertu engendred is the flowr;

The lines describe April's sweet showers soaking the dry roots of flowers to make them bloom.

The Renaissance

Between the fourteenth and seventeenth centuries, educated people in Europe rediscovered the world of ancient Greece and Rome. At the same time, new discoveries burst forth in science, medicine, art, and geography. This exciting period was called the Renaissance (REN ə SAHNS), which means "rebirth."

In England, Renaissance writers used new words made from Greek and Latin roots to express ideas for which English words seemed inadequate. Thousands of new words entered English this way. Many, such as *animate, analogy, dictionary, manuscript,* and *communicate,* are still used today. William Shakespeare, who wrote at this time, probably invented almost 10 percent of the words in his plays!

The addition of new words from Latin and Greek gave English speakers more choices in expressing ideas. For every Old English word, there were now often synonyms derived from French, Latin, or Greek. This rich store of synonyms sets English apart from many other languages. The chart on page 160 shows some synonyms derived from different sources.

Each language contributed its own special strengths to English. The Old English words are short and to the point. The French synonyms add polish to speech or writing. Words derived from Latin and Greek help state formal or complex ideas.

English Synonyms From Different Languages		
Old English	French	Latin or Greek
ask	question	interrogate
end	finish	conclude
fear	terror	trepidation
help	aid	assist
rise	mount	ascend

These words are part of modern English.

English was changing in other ways, too. Most Old English inflections, or word endings, were dropped. The word order of sentences came to resemble those of today. By 1500, English looked much like it does today. Our language, modern English, dates from this time.

A Vocabulary Explosion

✔ The 1500s saw the beginning of the great age of exploration. Navigators sailed around the globe in search of new lands and wealth. English travelers and traders brought home foreign foods and fashions, exotic plants and animals, exciting new ideas—and the words that named them.

During the 1500s and 1600s, words from 50 different languages came into the English language. From the West Indies came *barbecue, hammock,* and *hurricane.* From Arabic came *alcohol, apricots,* and *algebra.* African words such as *corral, yam,* and *banana* made their way to England through Spain and Portugal. Thousands of colorful new words sailed into English during this time.

The Printing Press and Standard English

By the 1500s, printing presses had begun producing books in English. Before then, books had been copied by hand, usually in Latin. Printing gave English a new respectability. With books available in English, more people learned to read and more people began to write in English too. By 1640, more than 20,000 different books had been printed in English.

Before the development of the printing press, English had few rules. There was no such thing as **Standard English** or dictionaries, so people spelled and pronounced words in a variety of ways. Therefore, word meanings, grammar, and usage varied from place to place.

The printing press changed all that. The English used in London, where the printing was done, became Standard English. People who read books and newspapers imitated this Standard English in their own writing and speech. Soon dictionaries appeared, which helped to standardize the spelling and definitions of English words. Printing helped the English language spread. At the same time, however, by standardizing the spelling and meanings of words, printing slowed the rapid rate at which English had been changing.

COMPREHENSION

1. What was Indo-European?

   _____

   _____

   _____

2. What two invasions of England had a major impact on the English language?

   _____

   _____

   _____

3. During the Renaissance, how did an interest in ancient Rome and Greece change English?

   _____

   _____

4. Complete each sentence with the correct word.

   linguists   etymology   subordinates

   a. A word's _____ shows its history.

   b. After the Norman Conquest, English speakers were the _____ of the French.

   c. _____ study how languages grow and change.

1. Explain why the languages shown in the first chart on page 158 have similar words for *night* and *sun*.

   _____

   _____

2. After the Norman Conquest, why did people in England want to become bilingual?

   _____

   _____

3. Look at the chart on page 160. Which column of words do people use most often in their everyday conversation? Explain why.

   _____

   _____

4. Reread the paragraph with a ✔ next to it. Then write a sentence that states its main idea.

   _____

   _____

SKILL FOCUS: MAKING GENERALIZATIONS

Read each group of facts. Then write a generalization for the facts in the group.

1. Modern English has dropped most of the inflections, or word endings, that Old English used.

   Old English had a tiny vocabulary compared to the number of words in the English language today.

   The word order of Old English sentences makes them difficult for English speakers of today to understand.

   Generalization: _____

2. After the Norman Conquest, England's best land was divided among Norman noblemen.

   French-speaking Normans were appointed to all positions in the government, and French was the official language of the courts and of business.

   The French-speaking Normans ruled England, and the English-speaking people were their subordinates.

   Generalization: _____

3. *Interrogate* is a Latin-based synonym for the Old English *ask*.

   Trepidation is a Latin-based synonym for the Old English *fear*.

   Conclude is a Latin-based synonym for the Old English *end*.

   Generalization: _____

Reading-Writing Connection

On a separate sheet of paper, make a list of ten everyday words. Then check the words' etymologies in a dictionary. Write the language from which each word is derived.

Skill: Reading a Diagram

BACKGROUND INFORMATION

"How Cell Phones Work" discusses cellular telephones, or cell phones. Since the mid-1980s, more than 100 million Americans have bought cell phones. These palm-sized devices have changed how people work, play, and live.

SKILL FOCUS: Reading a Diagram

A **diagram** is a drawing that helps explain a thing by showing all its parts, how it is put together, and how it works. Read the paragraphs near a diagram first. Then study the diagram itself.

Sometimes the text might refer to a diagram by saying, "See Figure 1." When you read this kind of a reference, stop and study the diagram.

To understand a diagram, read its title, caption, and labels. The title tells what the diagram shows. The caption explains the diagram in more detail. Labels identify important parts of the diagram.

Use these steps to read diagrams.

1. Read the paragraphs that come just before and after the diagram. Then study the diagram.

2. Look back at the diagram from time to time as you continue to read.

3. Use the diagram and the text together to summarize what you read.

▶ Study this diagram. Then answer the questions at the top of the next column.

Sending and Receiving Radio Waves

Radio transmitter — Radio waves — Receiving antenna — Transmitting antenna — Radio receiver (in car)

The transmitter of a radio station sends out waves at a certain frequency. When you tune your radio to this frequency, you receive the waves.

1. What is the title of this diagram?

   _____

2. What device is used to send radio waves?

   _____

3. What device is used to receive radio waves?

   _____

CONTEXT CLUES: Diagrams

The labels on **diagrams** can often be used as context clues. In a diagram, you can clearly see what is being described in the text. Use the pictures and labels to figure out the meanings of unfamiliar terms.

Look again at the diagram on this page. What does the diagram tell you about the meaning of the word *antenna*?

By looking at the diagram, you can see that the radio station has a big antenna to send radio waves. The car has a small antenna to receive radio waves. An antenna must be a device used to send or receive radio waves.

▶ Use the diagram to figure out the meaning of the word *transmitter*. Write the meaning on the lines.

   _____

   _____

Use the diagrams in the selection to help figure out the meanings of the underlined words *frequency, nonadjacent,* and *microprocessor.*

Strategy Tip

Before you read "How Cell Phones Work," study the article's headings and preview its diagrams, noting their captions and labels.

How Cell Phones Work

There has been a big change in American life since the end of the twentieth century. Everywhere you look, more and more people are talking on cell phones. Nearly half of all Americans already own them, and the number is growing.

Cell phones are very convenient. Because your phone is always with you, you do not need to search for a public phone or fumble for change. When you're on the go, anyone can get in touch with you. In an emergency, you can always call for help. Some cell phones offer other services, too. Some let you send e-mail or connect with the Internet. Many phones also offer games, cameras, and orgnizers.

The First Mobile Phones

One important fact to remember about cell phones is that they are actually radios. They are among the most sophisticated radios ever built. When you make a cell phone call, you are like a little radio station broadcasting a message. Receiving a call is like tuning in a radio station.

Radio telephones are not new. They date back to the 1920s when police departments and taxicab companies installed them in their cars. Private individuals who needed mobile communications also installed them. The old-style mobile telephones had many drawbacks, however. Each city had only one central antenna tower serving all the car telephones in a 50- to 60-mile area. Each car phone needed a big, powerful **transmitter** (tranz MIT r) to send a radio signal across such a wide area. That equipment was expensive. A car telephone could cost thousands of dollars.

To make matters worse, each city had only 12 to 24 frequencies for mobile phones. <u>Frequency</u>, measured in hertz or megahertz, is the number of sound waves produced per second by a transmitter. (See Figure 1.) To send private phone calls, each call had to be sent in a different frequency. Because there were so few available frequencies, each antenna could handle only 12 to 24 car-phone calls at a time. A car phone user often had to wait an hour or longer

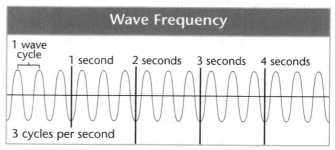

FIGURE 1. **The frequency of this wave is 3 cycles per second, or 3 hertz.**

just to get a dial tone. Many cities had ten-year waiting lists for customers who wanted car phones.

The Cellular Solution

Cellular phone technology eliminated the drawbacks of the older mobile phones. In the cellular system, every city is divided into small **cells**, or service areas. Each cell covers an area of a few square miles. A large city can have hundreds of cells.

You can think of the cells as six-sided blocks on a larger six-sided grid. (See Figure 2.) Each cell has an antenna tower. The tower is a steel structure that is several hundred feet high. At its base is telephone equipment—radio transmitters and receivers. These let the tower communicate with all the cell phones located within the cell. Different providers of cell phone service often share the same towers.

Suppose you are driving through one of the cells shown in Figure 2 and are talking on a cell phone. As

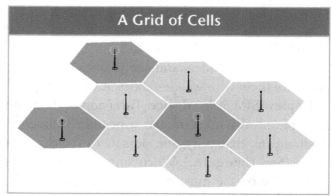

FIGURE 2. **A city is divided into many small cells. Cell phones in nonadjacent cells, such as the three dark ones, can use the same frequency.**

you near the outer boundary of one cell, computers in the base station note that your phone's signal strength is weakening. At the same time, the station in the cell you are moving toward registers an increasing signal strength.

Working together, the two base stations send a message to your phone. They tell it to change frequencies. Instantly, the frequency of your phone call automatically switches to one transmitted by the new cell. In this way, the signal of a phone call changes as a speaker moves from cell to cell. As a result, callers receive continuous, uninterrupted service as they travel from place to place.

Cellular base stations purposely use low-power transmitters to send weak signals. That allows them to reuse the same frequencies in <u>nonadjacent</u> cells, cells that are not right next to each other. The weak signals do not interfere with each other when they are used a few miles apart. Frequency reuse allows hundreds of thousands of cell phone users to make calls at the same time.

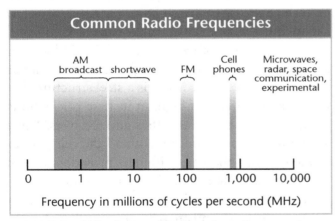

FIGURE 3. Cell phone calls travel on frequencies between 824 megahertz and 893 megahertz.

Walkie-Talkies and Cell Phones

One way to understand cell phones better is to compare them with walkie-talkies. A walkie-talkie is a **simplex** (SIM pleks) **device.** Two people talking on a simplex device must use the same radio frequency. That means that only one person can speak at a time. (See Figure 4A.) When one person finishes talking, he or she must push a button to clear the frequency for the other speaker.

A cell phone, on the other hand, is a **duplex** (DOO pleks) **device.** That means that callers use one frequency for talking and a second, separate frequency, for listening. With cell phones, both people can speak at the same time. (See Figure 4B.)

Walkie-talkies can only transmit over a small area. By contrast, cell phones have an amazing range. Switching from cell to cell, you can talk on a cell phone while driving for hundreds of miles.

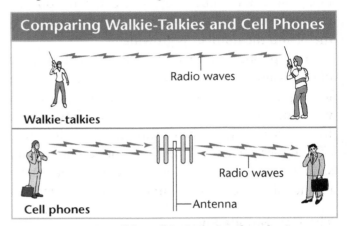

FIGURE 4A. A walkie-talkie is a simplex device. Both transmitters use the same frequency.

FIGURE 4B. A cell phone is a duplex device. The two transmitters use different frequencies.

Analog or Digital

Cellular telephone transmissions can be **analog** (AN ə lahg) or **digital** (DIJ i təl). In an analog system, your voice is transmitted from the phone to the base station as sound waves. In a digital system, your cell phone changes your voice into a signal made up of digits in a series of 1s and 0s. This numerical signal is then transmitted to the base station. The phone of the person you call converts the numerical signal back to sound. You can compare the analog system to an audiotape cassette that has sound waves recorded directly on it. The digital system is more like a CD, which stores sound in digital form.

✔ All newer phones offer digital service; some offer analog technology as well. Over the coming years, however, digital service will probably completely replace analog service. One reason is that interference and static are less of a problem with digital service. The 1s and 0s of a digital signal are not as easily distorted as sound waves. Digital service is often cheaper, too, because more calls can be compressed, or squeezed together, on each frequency. Digital calls are also more secure. That is because special digital codes make the calls harder for intruders to intercept, or listen in on.

Placing a Call

What happens once you have entered a phone number in your cell phone? First your cell phone needs to find the closest base station. To do that, it has special control channels that let it listen to the signals from a base station. The phone then chooses the strongest (closest) channel so that the phone call will have the best connection.

Next the cell phone transmits a short message to the base station. This message, which takes about a quarter of a second, gives the base station your phone number and the number you are dialing.

Once your phone number is confirmed, the base station sends a message back to your phone in another quarter second. The message tells your phone on what frequency, or channel, the conversation will take place. Your cell phone then turns to the assigned channel and begins the call.

Inside a Cell Phone

Cell phones are complicated devices. A few decades ago, you would have needed tons of equipment to do what a cell phone does. Because electronic equipment has now been miniaturized, or made much smaller, however, all of that power now fits in the palm of your hand.

The most important parts of a cell phone are the antenna, the display, the keyboard, the circuit board, the speaker, and the microphone. Use Figure 5 to locate each part as your read about its function. The *antenna* (5) sends and receives radio signals. Most cell phone antennas are only about an inch long. Not that long ago, the antennas on car phones and CB radios were often 6 to 8 feet long!

The LCD, or liquid crystal display, is usually called the *display* (2). This part of the phone has been getting larger as cell phones offer more features. Many cell phones now have built-in cameras, Web browsers, organizers, and even games.

The *keyboard* (3) or keypad is similar to that on a TV remote control. In addition to making calls, the keyboard lets you do many other things, such as program phone numbers, send e-mails or text messages, or play games.

The *circuit board* (6) is the "brain" of a cell phone. On the board are various computer chips. A microprocessor (7) on the circuit board handles signals to and from the base station. One chip on the circuit board converts the outgoing audio signal to a digital signal. Another chip on the board converts the incoming digital signal to sound waves. In addition, there are chips that remember stored phone numbers, handle recharging, and compress and decompress signals from the antenna. These chips process millions of calculations per second!

The cell phone *speaker* (1) is tiny, no bigger than a dime. The *microphone* (4) is as small as a typical watch battery. For their size, however, these two parts both do an amazing job of reproducing sound.

Cell Phone Concerns

As cell phones have become used by more and more people, new rules and laws have been passed to regulate their use. Most schools have rules about where and when cell phones can be used. So do many theaters and concert halls.

People who talk on the phone while walking on a busy city streets may be more apt to bump into others, trip, or even be hit by a car. Talking on the phone while driving is an even more serious concern. Many experts claim that using a cell phone increases the amount of time it takes a driver to respond to changing traffic conditions. As more drivers use cell phones, higher accident rates are a result. To prevent these accidents, some cities and states now ban the use of cell phones by drivers.

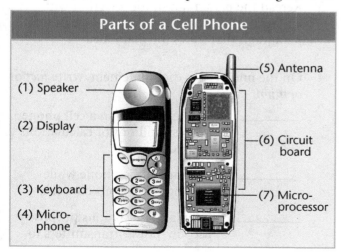

Parts of a Cell Phone

(1) Speaker
(2) Display
(3) Keyboard
(4) Microphone
(5) Antenna
(6) Circuit board
(7) Microprocessor

FIGURE 5. **A cell phone is made up of tiny, electronic parts.**

Cellular technology is developing so quickly that it is difficult to predict what the future holds. Maybe someday anyone on the planet will have the power to talk to anyone else instantly and inexpensively. How will human beings use this incredible power to communicate?

COMPREHENSION

1. What were three disadvantages of old-style mobile phones?

   _____

   _____

   _____

   _____

2. Why does dividing a city into cells make mobile phone service better?

   _____

   _____

   _____

   _____

3. Why do cell phone base systems transmit at low-power frequencies?

   _____

   _____

   _____

   _____

   _____

4. What is the difference between a simplex device and a duplex device?

   _____

   _____

   _____

   _____

5. Complete each sentence with the correct word.

   frequency   nonadjacent   microprocessor

   a. The _____ in the phone's circuit board performs millions of calculations.

   b. The _____ of a transmission is the speed at which the radio waves travel.

   c. Two _____ cells in a cellular grid can use the same frequencies.

CRITICAL THINKING

1. Reread the first paragraph of the selection. The main idea of this paragraph is not stated. Write a sentence that states the main idea.

   _____

   _____

2. Explain how cellular technology is different from the technology used in older mobile phones.

   _____

   _____

   _____

   _____

   _____

3. Reread the paragraph in the selection with a ✔ next to it. Underline the sentence in the paragraph that states the main idea.

4. On the line next to each statement, write *fact* or *opinion*.

   _____ a. The microchips in a cell phone process millions of calculations per second.

   _____ b. Talking on the phone while driving is a serious concern.

   _____ c. Cellular base stations purposely use low-power transmitters to send weak signals.

   _____ d. Cell phones are very convenient.

1. What is the frequency of the radio waves in this diagram? The time between

    each set of vertical lines is 1 second. _____

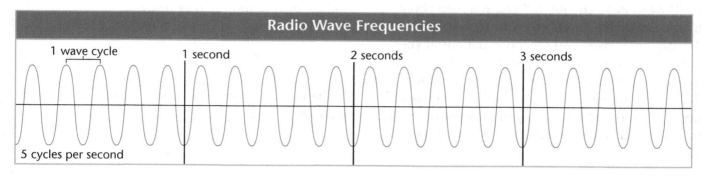

Radio Wave Frequencies

1 wave cycle

1 second

2 seconds

3 seconds

5 cycles per second

2. Look at Figure 2 on page 163. How many cells shown in the diagram could use the same frequency as the dark cell in the center?

    _____

3. Look at Figure 3 on page 164. At what frequency do shortwave radios transmit?

    _____

4. How do Figures 4A and 4B on page 164 show the difference between simplex and duplex devices?

    _____

    _____

5. Look at Figure 5 on page 165. Write the name of each part of a cell phone next to its description.

    a. used to type information into the cell

    phone _____

    b. shows the number you are calling

    _____

    c. receives the signal from the base station

    _____

    d. reproduces sound along with the

    microphone _____

    e. holds the microchips that handle the calls

    _____

Reading-Writing Connection

Interview at least three people you know who own or use cell phones. On a separate sheet of paper, write one list of the things they like about this technology. Make another list of the things they dislike about this technology.

Skill: Reading Equations

BACKGROUND INFORMATION

In "How to Read Equations," you will read about mathematical equations and how to solve them. Actually, you have been solving equations in your everyday life for years, even when you didn't realize it. Suppose, for example, you had to divide an 8-slice pizza among 4 people. Each person would get 2 slices, right? Although you may not realize it, you have just solved an equation that looks like this: $4x = 8$.

SKILL FOCUS: Reading Equations

When you solve a word problem, you state your plan for solving the problem as a mathematical sentence. If the sentence has an equal sign, it is an **equation**. An equation is a statement that says two amounts are equal.

Most equations include an unknown number, called a **variable**. A variable is usually represented by a symbol, such as x, y, or n. To solve the equation, you must find the value of the variable that makes the equation true. That value is called the **solution.**

To solve an equation, you need to undo the operation shown in the equation. That is, you use the opposite operation of the one shown in the equation. If an equation uses addition, for example, you find the answer by subtracting.

This equation, for example, uses addition.

$$x + 8 = 15$$

To solve it, undo the addition by subtracting 8 from both sides of the equation.

$$x + 8 - 8 = 15 - 8$$

Then simplify your work.

$$x + 0 = 7 \quad \text{or} \quad x = 7$$

If the equation had used subtraction, you would undo it by adding, such as the following.

$$y - 8 = 20$$
$$y - 8 + 8 = 20 + 8$$
$$y - 0 = 28 \quad \text{or} \quad y = 28$$

If the equation had used multiplication, you would undo it by dividing, such as below.

$$2x = 6$$
$$2x \div 2 = 6 \div 2$$
$$x = 3$$

If it had used division, you would solve it by multiplying, as below.

$$y \div 3 = 2$$
$$y \div 3 \times 3 = 2 \times 3$$
$$y = 6$$

Equations that have only one operation can be solved in a single step. Equations with more than one operation require more steps.

▶ Solve each equation. Find the value of x.
  1. $x + 3 = 17$

  _____

  2. $y - 11 = 42$

  _____

WORD CLUES

The words *equal* and *equation* both contain the Latin word part *equ-*, meaning "equal." In algebra, an *equation* is a statement that says two amounts on both sides of the equal sign are equal.

▶ Answer the following questions about other words used in mathematics that include *equ*.
  1. What is an *equilateral* triangle?

  _____

  2. What does it mean if two towns are *equidistant* from a third town?

  _____

> **Strategy Tip**
>
> When you read equations, pay attention to the signs of operation.

How to Read Equations

Frequently, writing a mathematical sentence is the best way of stating the plan for solving a word problem. A mathematical sentence that has an equal sign is called an **equation**. Solving equations is one of the main parts of a branch of mathematics known as **algebra**.

Read the following problem.

A telephone call from White Plains, New York, to Atlanta, Georgia, during the day costs $0.15 for the first minute and more for each additional minute. If a two-minute call costs $0.24, how much does an additional minute cost?

The following equation describes the problem.

$$x + 15 = 24$$

This is one of the simplest kinds of equations for solving problems. The letter x represents the cost of an additional minute, and all costs are given in cents. To solve such an equation, you must isolate, or set apart, the x on one side of the equal sign. You can do so by subtracting 15 from each side of the equation.

$$x + 15 - 15 = 24 - 15$$
$$x = 9$$

It costs $0.09 for each additional minute.

Similarly, to solve the following equation, isolate the x by adding 37 to each side.

$$x - 37 = 98$$
$$x - 37 + 37 = 98 + 37$$
$$x = 135$$

If you look carefully at both equations, you can see that the operation used to solve each question is the opposite of that shown in the equation.

Here is another problem.

Suppose that a phone call in your immediate area costs only $0.09, no matter how long you talk. If you spent $0.54 on local phone calls one evening, how many calls did you make?

A problem like this results in a different kind of equation.

$$9x = 54$$

In this case, the letter x represents the number of local phone calls. In algebra, $9x$ means "9 times x." To solve such an equation, isolate the x by dividing each side by the numerical factor, in this case 9. Again, you need to perform the opposite operation to solve this equation. Since multiplication is shown in the equation, you solve it by division.

$$9x \div 9 = 54 \div 9$$
$$x = 6$$

You made 6 local phone calls.

Suppose that the night and weekend rate from White Plains to Atlanta is $0.12 for the first minute and $0.07 for each additional minute. If a call from White Plains to Atlanta on a Sunday cost $1.10, how long was the call?

If you let the letter x equal the number of additional minutes, you get the following equation.

$$7x + 12 = 110$$

This is a two-step equation. First you must isolate the expression with the x in it; then you must isolate the x. To isolate the expression with x in it, use the opposite operation from that shown in the equation: subtract 12 from each side of the equation.

$$7x + 12 - 12 = 110 - 12$$
$$7x = 98$$

Then isolate the x by dividing by 7.

$$7x \div 7 = 98 \div 7$$
$$x = 14$$

The number of additional minutes is 14. *Therefore, the total time of the call is 15 minutes.*

MATHEMATICS

COMPREHENSION

1. When a mathematical sentence contains an equal sign, what is the sentence called?

   _____

2. When you solve an equation, what must you do to the variable?

   _____

3. An equation consists of a number added to a variable, and that expression is equal to another number. How do you solve the equation?

   _____

4. A number and a variable are written together with no space or operation sign between them. What does this expression mean?

   _____

5. How many steps does it take to solve an equation that involves both a product and a sum?

   _____

6. An equation consists of a variable multiplied by a number, and that expression is equal to another number. How do you solve the equation?

   _____

   _____

7. a. What is the first step in solving the equation $18x + 24 = 150$?

   _____

   b. What is the second step in solving the equation $18x + 24 = 150$?

   _____

CRITICAL THINKING

1. How would you solve the equation $x \div 4 = 3$?

   _____

2. In the equation $x = 6y$, x and y are whole numbers. How much larger is x than y?

   _____

3. In the equation $n + 16 = p$, which is larger, n or p?

   _____

4. In the equation $s - 42 = t$, which is larger, s or t?

   _____

SKILL FOCUS: READING EQUATIONS

Solve each equation. Use the space to right of each equation to work it out.

1. $x + 4 = 13$

   $x =$ _____

2. $x + 18 = 47$

   $x =$ _____

3. $x + 5 = 18$

   $x =$ _____

4. $x + 16 = 38$

   $x =$ _____

5. $x - 3 = 14$

   $x =$ _____

6. $x - 17 = 23$

   $x =$ _____

7. $x - 19 = 7$

$x =$ _____

8. $34 = x - 12$

$x =$ _____

9. $3 = x - 47$

$x =$ _____

10. $x - 5 = 9$

$x =$ _____

11. $3x = 9$

$x =$ _____

12. $13x = 117$

$x =$ _____

13. $6x = 51$

$x =$ _____

14. $2x = 10$

$x =$ _____

15. $3x = 24$

$x =$ _____

16. $10x = 150$

$x =$ _____

17. $17x = 51$

$x =$ _____

18. $0.5x = 9$

$x =$ _____

19. $2x + 3 = 11$

$x =$ _____

20. $7x + 9 = 23$

$x =$ _____

21. $13x + 11 = 50$

$x =$ _____

22. $2x - 3 = 11$

$x =$ _____

23. $9 = 2x - 7$

$x =$ _____

24. $14x - 3 = 11$

$x =$ _____

25. $14x - 11 = 3$

$x =$ _____

26. $11x + 3 = 14$

$x =$ _____

Reading-Writing Connection

On a separate sheet of paper, write the equations for three math problems based on buying food in a restaurant. Exchange problems with a partner, and solve each other's equations.

Skill: Identifying Propaganda Techniques

A **fact** is information that can be proven to be true or checked to be sure it is accurate. This is a statement of fact: *The artist Vincent van Gogh was born on March 30, 1853.*

An **opinion** is a personal belief or feeling. Here is a statement of opinion: *Vincent van Gogh is the best painter the world has ever known.*

If people believe that their opinions are very important, they may try to convince others to agree with them. When people want to convince others to believe something, do something, or buy something, they often use **propaganda**. Propaganda uses emotional language and often presents opinions as if they were facts. Most advertisements use some kind of propaganda to persuade consumers to buy a product or service. Political candidates often use propaganda to convince people to vote for them.

The following list describes six different types of propaganda techniques.

1. **Name Calling** This technique gives a bad name to someone or something in order to convince people to avoid the person or product.

   Example: The difference between our milk and the popular Alpha milk is that Alpha milk does not taste as fresh.

2. **Glad Names** This technique states positive things about the listeners or readers to convince them to agree with what they hear or see.

   Example: You're honest and hard working. Vote for the honest, hard-working candidate for senator—Ann Fong.

3. **Testimonial** This technique uses the sponsorship or support of a well-known personality. It is based on the idea that people will do something because the person they admire says that it is a good thing to do.

   Example: Raoul Hernandez, president of Hernandez Electronics, drinks A-O-K Orange Juice. Be a winner, too—with A-O-K!

4. **Transfer** This technique attempts to transfer to a product, person, or idea the good qualities belonging to something else or someone else. People then associate these qualities with the product, person, or idea.

   Example: Some of the world's most famous chefs eat at The Gold Kettle when they visit Chicago.

5. **Emotional Words** This technique uses words, particularly adjectives, that appeal to listeners' or readers' feelings or emotions.

   Example: A summer at Camp Echo makes campers active, happy, and healthy.

6. **Faulty Cause and Effect** This technique attempts to convince people that if they do something, such as buy a certain product, something good will happen as a result. However, the cause and effect are not really related.

   Example: Play tennis with a Slammo Tennis Racket, and you'll never lose another game!

A. **Fill in the circle next to the type of propaganda that each of the following statements uses.**

1. Vote for Carol Luchenski for Congress. Governor Byron is voting for her, too.
   ○ transfer   ○ emotional words   ○ glad names   ○ testimonial

2. Beautiful hair like yours deserves the best—Silk 'n' Shine shampoo.
   ○ faulty cause and effect   ○ glad names   ○ name calling   ○ transfer

3. *Monsters From the Moon* is a gory, violent, and downright frightening book.
   ○ emotional words   ○ name calling   ○ glad names   ○ testimonial

4. Snow Bunny ski jackets are made of the same material as the astronauts' suits.
○ testimonial   ○ transfer   ○ emotional words   ○ name calling

5. The Culver may cost the same as the Liberty, but repair costs will be twice as much.
○ name calling   ○ faulty cause and effect   ○ glad names   ○ transfer

6. Use a Nelson camera, and you'll never take a bad snapshot again.
○ glad names   ○ testimonial   ○ name calling   ○ faulty cause and effect

7. Many of the world's best skiers spend their winters skiing the Rocky Mountains.
○ transfer   ○ emotional words   ○ glad names   ○ testimonial

B. Read each statement below. On the line provided, write the type of propaganda technique used. Then write the words that give you a clue about the type of technique used.

1. Hockey star Greg Fleming uses Hi-Glo toothpaste every morning and evening. You, too, can be a star. Use Hi-Glo.

_____

2. Your newborn baby is one of a kind. So use Dinkies—the one-of-a-kind diaper for your special little person.

_____

3. Wear Miller jeans, and you'll be the most popular kid in your neighborhood.

_____

4. The C. C. Cycle is fast, flashy, and fun to ride.

_____

5. Haircuts by Shavers & Company make you look like you've been sheared.

_____

6. You deserve luxury. Come live at Highgate, the city's newest condominium apartments.

_____

7. The Marquis Quasi-Diamonds look as sparkling as the Crown Jewels.

_____

8. Use Pete's Plumbers the next time your kitchen sink leaks. It will never leak again.

_____

9. Chez Hamburger's home cooking is as good as the best French cuisine in Paris.

_____

Skill: Reading a Classified Ad

You don't always have to do your shopping at a store. Sometimes, what you are thinking of buying, such as a motorcycle, furniture, or camping equipment, could be less expensive if it has been previously owned. In such a case, read the **classified ad** section in a newspaper.

Study the following classified ads from a newspaper. Notice that the ads often use abbreviations to save space.

MERCHANDISE OFFERINGS
(3200)

Cellular & Telephone Equipment 3204

One-Stop Shopping for all your telephone needs. Cordless Phones, Cell Phones, Answering Machines, LOW, LOW, PRICES. PHONE FACTORY, Route 6 in Middletown, Open 10–10.

Cell phone—2 years old $45. Call 9–4 555-6365

Phone with built-in answerer. Digital recording, no tapes. 12-function remote. Asking $80. Call Ms. Ling at 555-4133.

RC-200 Telephone Ans Mac. Dual-cassette system. Auto date/time. Never been used. $10. Call Mon or Tue 555-0443

CELL PHONES & ACCESSORIES
car chargers, protective cases, & MORE.
Best prices.
Call Jack Lewis 555-1880

ATTENTION DOCTORS. Create more efficient office & save money. Call for answering service options. For info. call Sharon Amis 555-2111.

Go Wireless— Best deals on cell phones. Leading brands. Include free Voice Mail and Caller I.D. RAY'S COMMUNICATION CENTER 42 W. Borden St.

DVD Players   3207

SONIX 5-disc DVD player. MP3-CD, remote control. Just one year old. Paid $169, will sacrifice for $75. 555-6021 eves.

Soundo DVD player—older model with no fancy features, but still works great. Perfect for kids' TV. $40 or best offer. 555-2120

WHY BUY NEW? Rebuilt/reconditioned DVD players. Major brands, recent models. All with 60-day money-back guarantee. Work performed by trained technicians.
The DVD Barn
240 So. Main St. (Rte. 16), Hanover
Open Tues-Sat
9-6, Sun 12-5

General Electronics portable DVD player. Never used, still in original box. 9-in. LCD screen, built-in speakers, adjustable arm, playback time of 2.5 hrs. Sells for $299 new. A bargain at $200. 555-7297. Ask for Rosa.

SAVE $ $ $! ! !
Every in-stock DVD player now on sale. Today through Sat. RAY'S COMMUNICATION CENTER, 42 W. Borden St.

A. On the line in the left-hand column next to each advertised item, write the letter of the way you would purchase it in the right-hand column.

1. _____ older Soundo DVD player

2. _____ RC-200 answering machine

3. _____ new General Electronics DVD player

4. _____ SONIX 5-disc DVD player

5. _____ Cordless phones and cell phones

6. _____ Cell phones with free Voice Mail

7. _____ Phone with built-in answering machine

8. _____ Rebuilt/reconditioned DVD players

a. call Ms. Ling at 555-4133

b. call 555-7297, ask for Rosa

c. go to the DVD Barn any day except Monday

d. go to Ray's Communication Center

e. call 555-2120

f. call 555-0443 on Monday or Tuesday

g. go to the Phone Factory

h. call 555-6021 in the evening

B. **Answer the following questions in complete sentences.**

1. Which two types of equipment are advertised in section 3204 of these classifieds?

   _____

2. Where can you go to buy *both* a DVD player on sale *and* a cell phone?

   _____

3. How much does the cell phone that is two years old cost?

   _____

4. To buy a used DVD player with a 60-day money-back guarantee, where could you go?

   _____

5. Where could you go or call to learn about the differences between various types of cell phones and accessories?

   _____

6. a. How much money would you save by buying the General Electronics portable DVD player from the

      ad rather than buying it at a store? _____

   b. How would you go about buying this DVD player? _____

7. a. How many ads are there for answering machines? _____

   b. Explain where you would call or go if the only time you were free to discuss an answering machine was on the weekend?

      _____

8. a. Who placed a classified ad to help doctors with their phone messages?

      _____

   b. What is this person advertising?

      _____

9. How do you know that the DVD players at Ray's Communication Center are now selling for less than usual?

   _____

10. a. Which advertised DVD player is the least expensive?

       _____

    b. Why is the price so low?

       _____

CONTEXT CLUE WORDS

The following words are treated as context clue words in the lessons indicated. Each lesson provides instruction in a particular context clue type and includes an activity that requires you to use context clues to find word meanings. Context clue words appear in the literature, social studies, and science selections and are underlined or footnoted.

Word	Lesson
Aegean Sea	9
aerodynamic	11
arduous	16
bomas	10
bombardment	3
briny	35
camouflage	11
chambers	18
coalesced	3
contraction	18
crystalline	1
demographers	17
dense	28
descend	37
diminishes	37
distribution	17
efficient	36
etymology	44
exasperated	16
extraordinary	1
extraterrestrials	2
famine	27
feluccas	27
frequency	45
frigid	35
gall	26
germinating	28
harrowing	43
Helen	9
hovering	1
irritable	43
linguists	44
machetes	16
maimed	36
mandated	17
Menelaus	9
mesmerized	43
metabolism	11
microprocessor	45
mortar	2
nonadjacent	45
pulmonary	18
quarter	36
royal city	26
savannas	10
Seb	26
silt	27
simulations	3
Sparta	9
spasm	35
spiral	37
subordinates	44
transient	28
unravel	2
yogurt	10

CONCEPT WORDS

In lessons that feature social studies, science, or mathematics selections, words that are unique to the content and whose meanings are important in the selection are treated as concept words. These words appear in boldface type and are often followed by a phonetic respelling and a definition.

Word	Lesson
air mass	37
algebra	46
alliance	36
analog	45
anticyclone	37
aorta	18
area	29
arteries	18
astronomy	2
atria	18
axes	38
base number	4
blitzkrieg	36
capillaries	18
cells	45
Census	17
circle	29
circle graphs	38
circulatory system	18
civilizations	2
cold front	37
congressional districts	17
conquest	36
cyclone	37
data	38
delta	27
dialects	44
digital	45
double bar graphs	38
duplex device	45
equation	46
equilateral	29
ethnicity	17
exponent	4
exponential notation	4
factor	4
Fission hypothesis	3
formula	29
fossil	11
front	37
geologic periods	11
herders	10
hexagon	29
high	37
horizontal axis	38
hurricanes	37
hypothesis	3
inflections	44
irrigation	27
isosceles	29
isotopes	3
jerboa	28
key	38
line graph	38
line of symmetry	29
low	37
mantle	3
median	17
nomadic	10
occluded front	37
occupation	36
organisms	28
papyrus	27
parallelogram	29
pentagon	29
per	19
pericardium	18
perimeter	29
plasma	18
platelets	18
polygons	29
quadrilaterals	29
rectangle	29
red blood cells	18
rhombus	29
right triangle	29
scalene	29
sectors	38
simplex device	45
square	29
Standard English	44
stationary front	37
storms	37
succulents	28
symmetrical	29
taproot	28
technology	2
theory	3
tornadoes	37
trapezoid	29
transmitter	45
triangle	29
tributaries	27
veins	18
venae cavae	18
ventricles	18
vertical axis	38
warm front	37
white blood cells	18